**The Fred H. and Ella Mae Moore
Texas History Reprint Series**

Women
in
Early Texas

Marking a trail in a pathless wilderness, pressing forward with unswerving courage, she met each untried situation with a resourcefulness equal to the need; with a glad heart she brought to her frontier family her homeland's cultural heritage. With delicate spiritual sensitiveness she illumined the dullness of routine and the loneliness of isolation with beauty and with life abundant and withal she lived with casual unawareness of her value to civilization. Such was the pioneer woman, the unsung saint of the nation's immortals.

Women in Early Texas

Edited by
Evelyn M. Carrington

With a new introduction by
Debbie Mauldin Cottrell

Texas State Historical Association
Austin

Library of Congress Cataloging-in-Publication Data

Women in early Texas / edited by Evelyn M. Carrington ; with an introduction by Debbie Mauldin Cottrell.
p.   cm.   — (Fred H. and Ella Mae Moore Texas history reprint series)
Originally published: Austin : Jenkins Pub. Co., 1975.
"Published . . . in cooperation with the Center for Studies in Texas History at the University of Texas at Austin"—T.p. verso.
Includes bibliographical references and index.
ISBN 0-87611-142-8 (pbk.)
1. Women—Texas—Biography. 2. Women—Texas—Social conditions.
I. Carrington, Evelyn M. II. Texas State Historical Association. III. University of Texas at Austin. Center for Studies in Texas History. IV. Series.
HQ1438.T4W64   1994
920.72'09764—dc20   94-21170
                                                                              CIP

10 9 8 7 6 5 4 3 2 1   94 95 96 97 98 99

Published by the Texas State Historical Association in Cooperation with the Center for Studies in Texas History at the University of Texas at Austin

This book is number thirteen in the Fred H. and Ella Mae Moore Texas History Reprint Series

Publication of this book was made possible in part by a grant from the American Association of University Women—Austin Branch.

The Center for American History at the University of Texas at Austin provided the copy of *Women in Early Texas* used to reprint this edition.

The paper used in this book meets the minimum requirements of the American National Standard for Permanence of Paper for Printed Library Materials, Z39.48—1984

Introduction to the Second Edition

Much has happened in the study of the history of Texas women since *Women in Early Texas* was first published in 1975. When this work initially appeared, it joined a very small body of literature in what was almost a nonexistent field of Texas women's history; the burgeoning concept of women's history in national and international contexts that was well underway in the 1970s had barely reached to Texas. In 1975, most historians who considered Texas in their studies remained largely disinterested in, or perhaps unaware of, the potential richness of gender as a category of analysis. Debates about the concept of "true womanhood," the validity of the model of separate spheres, or notions of feminization reaching into politics, reform efforts, education, and other areas of vital importance in the everyday past of Texas were largely absent in the communication that scholars of the state carried out in articles, books, conference papers, and other avenues of professional exchange. Lay and amateur historians also had barely broached this area.

In 1975 accounts of Texas women's history remained limited to a small smattering of works, most of which lacked any analytical bite. Elizabeth Brooks's *Prominent Women of Texas* (1896) and Annie Doom Pickrell's *Pioneer Women in Texas*

(1929) had been among the earliest histories of Texas women in biographical form. In 1972, James M. Day and others prepared *Women of Texas*, which focused on eight Texas women and included some contributions by historians. These laudatory accounts of the past were joined by a few similarly noncritical works on individual Texas women, such as Jack C. Butterfield's *Clara Driscoll Rescued the Alamo: A Brief Biography* (1961). Virtually everything on Texas females written down to the mid-1970s focused on white women, with rare exceptions such as Ada de Blanc Simond's article entitled "The Discovery of Being Black: A Recollection," which appeared in the *Southwestern Historical Quarterly* in April 1973.

In this context, *Women in Early Texas* stands as part of the limited but established genre of its time, joining the Brooks and Pickrell books in documenting in a personal way the lives of Texas women in collective biographical form with a focus on the nineteenth century. Like them, it holds an important place as a starting point, an early piece of the history of Texas women's history, a primary documentation of the experience of females in the state before 1900. *Women in Early Texas* is also important, however, for the distinctions that mark it from other early works on Texas women. While still heavily focused on white women, *Women in Early Texas* is not an exclusive chronicle of this race, and readers will find included here, unusually, some stories of Mexican women, black women, and Indian women, as well as numerous other ethnic women. Recognizing its place in history, users of this book will also want to keep in mind what has changed in the field of Texas women's history in the almost twenty years since this book's first appearance. These changes derive, of course, from many causes and sources and are much more complex than any simple linear progression might suggest. But, a sense of the chronology of change is instructive for understanding the status of Texas women's history as well as how its evolution affects the context of this book as it is reissued in 1994.

When the Texas Foundation for Women's Resources acknowledged the importance of history as part of its work and established the Texas Women's History Project in 1978, it ensured that the decade of the 1980s would be vastly different from any previous ones in terms of direction for, outpouring of, and attention to the history of Texas women. The Project's resulting "Texas Women: A Celebration of History," which toured major museums in the state in 1981 and 1982, provided in exhibit form the first statewide attempt to tell the story of Texas women and allowed more than a million people to take a closer look at the distaff side of Texas history.

With the floodgate opened, established scholars as well as scholars-in-training took notice of the potential that the history of Texas women held in providing a more accurate picture of the state's and region's past. When the Texas State Historical Association cosponsored a conference entitled "Women and Texas" in 1985, it had the immediate purpose of addressing better coverage of women in the Association's planned revision of the *Handbook of Texas*. A larger impact from this conference, however, came in its contributions to beginning the process of seeing Texas women's history emerge as a field of true scholarship, as a part of the larger women's history movement, as something more than just throwing women into all the places from which they had been left out in decades prior. Southern women's historian Anne Firor Scott addressed participants at that gathering in 1985 in Austin and urged us to see the challenges and pitfalls that awaited those who would approach this realm and reminded us of the diversity of race, class, and region that we would have to concern ourselves with.

A mere five years later enough research and writing, enough books and articles, enough graduate work and ongoing scholarly attention, had occurred that a statewide conference on "Women and Texas History" was planned. As Nancy Baker Jones, the organizer of that event, noted, by the end of the 1980s there was a hunch "that there were enough people trained to research and write about the history of women in Texas that one might accurately state that a scholarly field of inquiry existed, and that enough research had been conducted to support an entire conference of papers devoted to the field."[1]

---

[1] Nancy Baker Jones, "Foreword," in Fane Downs and Nancy Baker Jones (eds.), *Women and Texas History: Selected Essays* (Austin: Texas State Historical Association, 1993), vii. Jones's essay, as well as Fane Downs, "Texas Women: History at the Edges" in Walter L. Buenger and Robert A.

Since that conference, the sense of community among scholars of Texas women's history has continued to develop, with networking channels and various organized groups in place. In 1994, research on Texas women benefitted further from being prominently showcased in a regional context when the Southern Association for Women Historians chose Houston as the locale for its third Southern Conference on Women's History.

With such developments in mind, *Women in Early Texas* must be considered in a different light than it was in 1975 and should be read with a different eye. Reissued in 1994, this book joins a much larger, and much more sophisticated, body of literature than it did initially. Compared to many of these more recent works, it will be readily apparent that this book does not seek to be consistently objective, does not always clarify why certain subjects were included or excluded, and, perhaps most important, does not reveal what sources were used in compiling this information. (Despite the efforts of current members of the American Association of University Women who were involved in the republication of this book to locate source documentation gathered for its original preparation, it appears, unfortunately, that these records have not survived.) *Women in Early Texas* makes no pretense of placing these Texas women into any broader context, of presenting any thematic threads to their lives, or of reaching any comprehensive conclusions about them. Yet even with these earmarks of historical writing of an earlier day and a different context, it remains a rich source of information about Texas women and its republication keeps that information readily available. When Elizabeth Fox-Genovese addressed participants at the October 1990 Women and Texas History conference in Austin, she reminded us that "the most important task that women's historians confront remains a vast increase in information about women." She also encouraged us to think, and think hard, about seeking that ground

---

Calvert (eds.), *Texas Through Time: Evolving Interpretations* (College Station: Texas A&M University Press, 1991) and Mary Beth Rogers, *Texas Women: A Celebration of History* (Austin: Texas Foundation for Women's Resources, 1981) were used in compiling this information.

between diversity and similarity in women's history, that ground between individual concerns and group efforts.[2]

Those challenges, I believe, speak to the usefulness of keeping a book such as *Women in Early Texas* available to those who seek to understand better the history of Texas by considering the lives of the women who lived here. Quite simply, it tells us more about many women, and in doing that it helps us approach a broader picture of the state's history. As another historian of Texas women has noted, "The life of every woman speaks in some way to the larger questions of Texas' past."[3]

Readers of this second publication should also keep in mind the role of the American Association of University Women (AAUW) in this book's history. The AAUW, a national organization dating to 1881, has important historical ties to changes in opportunities for higher education that women experienced in the late nineteenth century. It has consistently emphasized lifelong learning and promotion of women's concerns through its programs, publications, national office, and local affiliates. For the Austin, Texas, branch to have undertaken the original preparation of this inclusive publication in celebration of the nation's bicentennial was both consistent with AAUW's heritage and focus as well as an especially fitting way to use a historical commemoration to preserve an element of history of particular concern to this chapter—that which focused on Texas and on women. Through the direction of several women now deceased, including Evelyn M. Carrington and Barbara Likan, and with the help of numerous AAUW members, family members of the subjects in this book, and other interested writers and supporters, the Austin AAUW branch took a leadership role in contributing to the preservation of the history of Texas women and provided a foundation on which later scholars would build.

---

[2] Elizabeth Fox-Genovese, "Texas Women and the Writing of Women's History," in Downs and Jones (eds.), *Women and Texas History*, 3–8, 9 (quotation), 10–14.

[3] Elizabeth York Enstam, "Where Do We Go From Here? A (Very Personal) Response to 'Women and Texas History: A Conference,'" in Downs and Jones (eds.), *Women and Texas History*, 178.

The poignant stories related here tell of both the extraordinary and the ordinary; they are both humorous and sad, captivating and straightforward. These life stories ring with reality, and they are told in a direct yet folksy way. "She was called 'Big Mamma' by her grandchildren and their friends and everyone else who didn't call her 'Aunt Fannie,'" we are told initially of Minerva Frances Vernon Hill. The unfiltered priorities of these women are made clear to us, as when Carolyn Reeves Ericson tells us that "Sister Josephine won a place in the history of Nacogdoches by her devotion to the Church and her love for the people that she served." Some of the subjects in this book are well-known; Martha White McWhirter will be familiar to many readers as the founder of the Belton sanctificationists, and Susanna Wilkerson Dickinson is known to many as the woman who found herself viewing the battle at the Alamo from a particularly close inside view. Other names, however, are less familiar. Anna Salazar de Esparza was also inside the Alamo during its siege. Anna Hurd Palm quietly established the Palm Valley Lutheran Church. Rachel Whitfield made the transition from slavery to freedom in Williamson County.

The personal aspect of this collection cannot be overlooked; of the fifty stories recorded here, half of them were compiled by grandchildren (of various descents) of the subjects and several more were written by other relatives. That is an important point in understanding the tone and approach of these biographies, while it also reflects access to and utilization of family records, oral histories, and other personal memorabilia that are often especially critical in the reconstruction of women's past.

Scholars and students of Texas history will find *Women in Early Texas* a unique primary source document that sheds insight on nineteenth-century Texas women *and* provides clues to the evolving historiography of this field of study in the late twentieth century. It answers some questions and raises many others. It stands alone yet must be considered in a larger context. Its stories are simple yet diverse. Its implications are both clear and complex.

Whether *Women in Early Texas* is used in the classroom or for leisurely perusal, for research or for a personal glimpse of Texas's past, its readers will find it helpful in assessing the history of Texas women. Its importance and usefulness will be enhanced if it is supplemented with other works in the growing body of literature in this field. A good starting point is found in several recent works that chronicle the historiography of Texas women and provide more detailed information on further sources.

Among these are Fane Downs, "Texas Women: History at the Edges," in Walter L. Buenger and Robert A. Calvert (eds.), *Texas Through Time: Evolving Interpretations* (1991); Ann P. Malone, "Women in Texas History," in Light T. Cummins and Alvin R. Bailey Jr. (eds.), *A Guide to the History of Texas* (1988); and Ramona L. Ford, "'Why Spend Time on Women Grinding Corn?' Mainstreaming Women's History: A Texas Perspective," *Texas Journal of Ideas, History and Culture* (Spring/Summer 1990).

Archival and bibliographical information is also available in Ruthe Winegarten (ed.), *Texas Women's History Project Bibliography* (1980); Ruthe Winegarten (ed.), *Finder's Guide to the "Texas Women: A Celebration of History" Exhibit Archives* (1984); and Nancy Baker Jones and Debbie Mauldin Cottrell (comps.), *Women and Texas History: An Archival Bibliography* (1990).

Numerous local and thematic studies published since 1975 also include a focus on Texas women. See, for example, Patricia Ward Wallace, *A Spirit So Rare: A History of the Women of Waco* (1984); Julia Kirk Blackwelder, *Women of the Depression: Caste and Culture in San Antonio, 1929–1939* (1984); Mario T. García, "The Chicana in American History: The Mexican Women of El Paso, 1880–1920: A Case Study," *Pacific Historical Review* (May 1980); Jane Dysart, "Mexican Women in San Antonio, 1830–1860: The Assimilation Process," *Western Historical Quarterly* (Oct. 1976); and Vicki L. Ruiz, "By the Day or the Week: Mexicana Domestic Workers in El Paso," in Vicki L. Ruiz and Susan Tiano (eds.), *Women on the U.S.-Mexican Border: Responses to Change* (1987).

Work as a boundary of analysis for women's experiences is also considered in Richard Croxdale and Melissa Hield (eds.), *Women in the Texas Workforce: Yesterday and Today* (1979) and Fane Downs, "Texas Women at Work," in Donald Whisenhunt (ed.), *Texas: A Sesquicentennial Celebration* (1984). Work and other experiences of frontier life are chronicled in

Jo Ella Powell Exley, *Texas Tears and Texas Sunshine: Voices of Frontier Women* (1985) and Ann P. Malone, *Women on the Texas Frontier: A Cross-Cultural Perspective* (1983).

Nineteenth-century experiences are explored in Fane Downs, "'Tryels and Trubbles': Women in Early Nineteenth-Century Texas," *Southwestern Historical Quarterly* (July 1986); Harriette Andreadis, "True Womanhood Revisited: Women's Private Writing in Nineteenth-Century Texas," *Journal of the Southwest* (Summer 1989); and Margaret Henson, *Anglo-American Women in Texas, 1820–1850* (1982). A scholarly study of twentieth-century rural women is found in Mary Rebecca Sharpless, "Fertile Ground, Narrow Choices: Women on Cotton Farms of the Texas Blackland Prairie, 1900–1940" (Ph.D. diss., Emory University, 1993). Studies on Texas women's involvement in religion, law, civic work, and politics are also beginning to appear; for example, Patricia S. Martin, "Hidden Work: Baptist Women in Texas, 1880–1920" (Ph.D. diss., Rice University, 1982); Jayme A. Sokolow and Mary Ann Lamanna, "Women and Utopia: The Women's Commonwealth of Belton, Texas," *Southwestern Historical Quarterly* (Apr. 1984); Elizabeth Hayes Turner, "Women's Culture and Community: Religion and Reform in Galveston, 1880–1920" (Ph.D. diss., Rice University, 1990); Kathleen Elizabeth Lazarou, *Concealed Under Petticoats: Married Women's Property and the Laws of Texas, 1840–1913* (1986); and Megan Seaholm, "Earnest Women: The White Women's Club Movement in Progressive Era Texas, 1880–1920" (Ph.D. diss., Rice University, 1988).

Suffrage and political rights for women are covered in Janet G. Humphrey, *A Texas Suffragist: Diaries and Writings of Jane Y. McCallum* (1988); Ruthe Winegarten and Judith N. McArthur (eds.), *Citizens at Last: The Woman Suffrage Movement in Texas* (1987); Emma Louise Moyer Jackson, "Petticoat Politics: Political Activism among Texas Women in the 1920s" (Ph.D. diss., University of Texas at Austin, 1980); and Janet K. Boles, "The Texas Woman in Politics: Role Model or Mirage?" *Social Science Journal* (Jan. 1984). A comprehensive analysis of Texas women's experiences in the Progressive Era is found in Judith N. McArthur, "Motherhood and Reform in the New South: Texas Women's Political Culture in the Progressive Era" (Ph.D. diss., University of Texas at Austin, 1992).

A range of biographical works, many of which seek to place their subjects in a larger historical context, also provide helpful scholarly insights on Texas women. Among these are Jacquelyn Dowd Hall, *Revolt Against Chivalry: Jessie Daniel Ames and the Women's Campaign Against Lynching* (rev. ed., 1993); Pat Ellis Taylor, *Border Healing Woman: The Story of Jewell Babb* (1981); Virginia Bernhard, *Ima Hogg: The Governor's Daughter* (1984); Paula Mitchell Marks, *Turn Your Eyes toward Texas: Pioneers Sam and Mary Maverick* (1989); Emily Cutrer, *The Art of the Woman: The Life and Work of Elisabet Ney* (1988); Helen Sheehy, *Margo: The Life and Theatre of Margo Jones* (1989); and Debbie Mauldin Cottrell, *Pioneer Woman Educator: The Progressive Spirit of Annie Webb Blanton* (1993). Those interested in more information on Texas women and education should also consult Mary M. Scott, "Annie Webb Blanton: First Lady of Texas Education" (Ph.D. diss., Texas A&M University, 1992) and Sylvia Oates Hunt, "Challenging Patriarchy and Domesticity: Women Educators in Texas, 1840–1940" (Ph.D. diss., University of Texas at Arlington, 1992).

Collective biographies of various shapes and sizes are also increasing in number. Among these are Ann Fears Crawford and Crystal Sasse Ragsdale, *Women in Texas: Their Lives, Their Experiences, Their Accomplishments* (1982); Cynthia J. Beeman, *Women in Texas: They Made a Difference* (1989); and Mary Beth Rogers, Sherry A. Smith, and Janelle D. Scott, *We Can Fly: Stories of Katherine Stinson and Other Gutsy Texas Women* (1983). Claudia Dee Seligman's *Texas Women: Legends in Their Own Time* (1989) offers collective biography with an oral history emphasis; oral history is also utilized in Ruthe Winegarten (ed.), *I Am Annie Mae: The Personal Story of a Black Texas Woman* (1983).

Numerous other sources on the history of Texas women exist or are in the process of being prepared. A final selection of choice samplings for those interested in better understanding this growing field would have to include Mary Beth Rogers, *Texas Women: A Celebration of History* (1981); Ruthe Winegarten, *Texas Women: A Pictorial History from Indians to Astronauts* (1986); Sandra L. Myres, "Cowboys and Southern Belles," in Robert F. O'Connor (ed.), *Texas Myths* (1986); Fane

Downs and Nancy Baker Jones (eds.), *Women and Texas History: Selected Essays* (1993); and Suzanne Comer (ed.), *Common Bonds: Stories by and about Modern Texas Women* (1990). The forthcoming *New Handbook of Texas* will also incorporate a more comprehensive coverage of women and women's issues than did previous versions; it will provide further information on some of the subjects in this book. That *Women in Early Texas* is now part of such a greatly changed field—both quantitatively and qualitatively—makes the republication of this pioneering work both significant and practical. Acknowledging the important place of these earlier historical pieces, we should also be reminded that there remains much work yet to do, many more questions to ask, numerous assumptions to challenge, and countless more Texas women to seek to know as part of this state's history.

Debbie Mauldin Cottrell
August 1994

Preface

In January, 1972, with Katherine V. Weisiger, and Carolyn F. Moore, I began looking for a meaningful project of cultural interest for the Austin Branch, American Association of University Women to adopt and to relate to the American Revolution Bicentennial. We began a study of notable women from the various ethnic groups who participated in the early history of Texas in order to prepare a historical document ready for publication in 1975-76. Since history is mainly written by men about men, we felt the necessity to bring out the important role of women who contributed to the social and cultural development of Texas. We learned of rich and abundant resources in Texas which drew immigrants from many different countries during the last century to make their home.

We believed that this project fell under the American Revolution Bicentennial theme "Heritage 76, projects that are historical in nature" and also under the Bicentennial theme "Horizons 76, projects to provide for the future." It would also include the Texas Bicentennial theme "Promise of America Past, Present and Future" which deals with the evolution of woman's place in the life of the state and nation.

We realized that only if we know the past, can we understand the present and provide for the future. We felt that the American Revolution also included Woman's Revolution, her struggle for woman's rights and emancipation which led in this century to her right to vote. Since 1882 the American Association of University Women's national cultural policy included "the preservation of our historical and cultural heritage." The Association has been engaged in women's liberation since its beginning.

After several visits to the Institute of Texan Cultures in San Antonio, we realized more fully that the conditions and characteristics of a good society or community are a long time in the building—and where they exist, they are the result of hard and sacrificial work, not by ourselves, but by generations long gone.

Barbara Likan

Acknowledgements

We are deeply indebted to Barbara Likan, Katherine V. Weisiger and Carolyn F. Moore who not only proposed to the members of the Austin Branch, American Association of University Women, but also conceived, initiated and developed the idea of this publication. We also thank Kay Goodwin, Donna Johnson and Dorothy Shandera, successive Austin Branch presidents, for adopting this publication for a project and for keeping the project moving.

Special thanks are offered to Gene Brownrigg, Executive Director of the American Revolution Bicentennial Commission of Texas, for her firm belief in the historic value of the project and her subsequent support of its approval by the Commission so that it became the only single project that the Commission not only endorsed but also funded. We are grateful to the Institute of Texan Culture at San Antonio for the help its staff has rendered.

We feel extremely fortunate in securing twenty-four biographers who opened their family records and gave us stories of their own pioneer women. Also we are grateful to the other eighteen authors who prepared stories of women who came early to Texas but were not their kith and kin. Their research often involved translation from sources written in a language different from their own native one and frequently necessitated intensive search for pertinent material in faraway places.

Special thanks are due to Lois Stoneham who has been a constant and wise editorial advisor, to Mattie Lee Seymour who has helped in making photographs of pictures submitted in various states of preservation. We are also grateful to Betty Ann Korts who has helped with some of the correspondence.

We are indebted to President John A. Quinn for a picture of The Pioneer Woman, a statue erected on the campus of Texas Woman's University with an inscription written by Jessie Humphries. Permission has been secured from The University of Texas Library for the use of pictures of Anna Hurd Palm and Adina De Zavala; from the Texas State Library for the reproduction of pictures of the Alamo in 1885 and of Don Enrique Esparza; and from the Daughters of the Republic of Texas Library in San Antonio for the use of a pencil sketch of Marie Gentilz. We are grateful to Walter Maler, Editor, *Herald Tribune*, Hallettsville, for a picture of Sarah Ann McClure Braches.

The publication of WOMEN IN EARLY TEXAS was financed, in large measure, by grants from the American Revolution Bicentennial Commission of Texas and from the Texas College Bicentennial Programs. A part of the matching funds was derived from community projects sponsored by the Austin Branch, American Association of University Women. For all these funds, we are sincerely grateful.

Thanks are also due J. Holmes Jenkins for his efficient and kindly help in the publication of WOMEN IN EARLY TEXAS in this American Revolution Bicentennial Year and in the International Women's Year, in 1975.

E.M.C.
June, 1975

Contents

Nancy Millar Alley (1817-1893)

By Laura Ann Dick Rau*

Nancy Millar Alley was a typical Texas frontier wife and mother. Of Anglo-American descent, Nancy Millar was born in Tatnal County, Georgia, on September 13, 1817. Her father, Dr. John Millar, had previously lived in South Carolina where he had met and married Elizabeth Payne, daughter of a well-to-do South Carolina family. Dr. Millar was probably of French descent; however, his family had been in the United States since before the American Revolution.

Between 1817 and 1820, Dr. Millar moved with his wife and two children, Daniel and Nancy, to Morgan County, Alabama, near Decatur, where they lived until 1831 when he migrated to Texas. The Millars travelled by riverboat down the Mississippi to New Orleans, their entourage consisting of six children and a few slaves, and from that point completed the trip to Texas by ship, perhaps to the mouth of the Colorado River. Dr. Millar settled on the west bank of the Colorado at the Atascosita Crossing, located about four miles south of present Columbus. While in New Orleans, the family contracted smallpox. Shortly after arriving in Texas, two children, William and Julia, died of the disease. Dr. Millar lived only a few months after this, his death occurring on

*Great-great-great-granddaughter

Nancy Millar Alley

October 21, 1831. His widow later married Jacob Betts.

Abram Alley was one of the Alley brothers, all of whom were members of Stephen F. Austin's "Old Three Hundred" Colony. Rawson, serving as Austin's surveyor, arrived on the Colorado in 1821. Three half-brothers, Abram, Thomas and John, immigrated to Texas in the spring of 1822 from their home at St. Genevieve, Missouri, where they had been neighbors and friends of the Austin family. They travelled by boat to New Orleans and then by the schooner *James Lawrence* to Galveston Island. The remainder of the trip was by foot to the Atacosita Crossing of the Colorado River, where they joined their brother, Rawson, on his grant of land on the east side of the River. The remaining brother, William, came to Texas from Missouri in 1824. The Alley family was of French Huguenot descent, descending from three brothers named Allees who immigrated to the American colonies in 1749 and 1752.

By 1831 only William and Abram were still living. John had been killed by Indians in the winter of 1822-23 and Thomas had drowned during an Indian skirmish at the Brazos River. Rawson lived until 1833 and is buried in the Alley family cemetery.

Nancy Millar married Abram (or Abraham) Alley on April 26, 1835. The ceremony was performed by a Roman Catholic priest from San Antnio.

During the Texas Revolution Abram Alley moved his wife, Nancy, and other members of the family to the Trinity River to escape the Mexican Army, probably burning their cabin before leaving. Sam Houston gave Abram the responsibility of seeing that the women and children of the Colorado area reached the Trinity safely, thus eliminating him from fighting in the Battle of San Jacinto. Daniel Millar, Nancy's brother, was with the Texian Army during the Battle.

After the defeat of the Mexican Army at San Jacinto, Nancy and Abram Alley returned to their land and rebuilt their cabin on the same site. Nancy's mother, Elizabeth Payne Millar Betts, died on January 1, 1837, leaving two minor children, John and Elizabeth Millar, who became the wards of Abram and Nancy Alley until their maturity.

Abram was engaged in farming and the raising of cattle. According to papers in Texas Archives, he signed the petition for a new municipality to be called "Colorado" in March of 1837, registered the first cattle brand in Colorado County (Figure Brand

Book 1), and served as a juror in the first term of the District Court which met in Colorado County in April 1837, presided over by Hon. R. M. Williamson. Sam Houston appointed Abram Alley as President of the Board of Land Commissioners of Colorado County, Republic of Texas, on December 19, 1837.

The 1840 Census of Colorado County lists Abraham Alley as owning 800 acres of patented land and 4,444 acres of grant land without final title. He also declared 4 slaves, 75 cattle, 1 work horse and 1 silver watch. For his wards, Elizabeth and John Millar, he listed 6 slaves.

The Allen cabin, rebuilt in 1836 after the Runaway Scrape, is a two-room oak log square notch house of the mid-Western type, with limestone chimneys on each end. In the center is a stairway dovetailed into the wall, leading to the loft room and opening on a back porch. A well was near the house and several outbuildings surrounded it. The cabin stands on its original location about one mile east of the old Atascosita Crossing of the Colorado, approximately eight miles southeast of Columbus.

In 1849 Nancy Millar Alley received a legacy from her great-aunt Rachel Payne Leigh, a very wealthy woman of Kershaw County, South Carolina. The benefactors of Rachel Leigh's will included Elizabeth Payne Betts, daughter of Rachel Leigh's brother, Daniel. Since Elizabeth Payne Betts was dead, her share of the estate went to her children: Nancy Alley, Daniel Millar and Elizabeth Millar Bonds.

This legacy provided the Alleys with the money to remodel their cabin in 1852. Abram travelled to Bastrop, along with two slaves, purchased pine lumber from a large sawmill there and floated it on a raft down the Colorado River to his home. The cabin was enlarged to accommodate the family of seven. It was sided with pine lumber and an additional two rooms were added, making the house an L-shaped affair with another fireplace between the two new rooms and porches on the front and back. The fireplace mantels were simple pine ones in the Greek Revival style, as were the four-panel doors.

Abram Alley died on May 16, 1862, and is buried in the Alley family cemetery located six miles southeast of Columbus. Nancy continued living in the Alley homestead. Four of her surviving children married, but one son, William, remained a bachelor and lived with his mother until her death.

In later years, Mrs. Alley had a companion-servant who was with her constantly. Nancy Alley was a quiet person, not given to small talk, and dressed with simplicity. All of her dresses were made in the same manner and included a small cape over the shoulders of matching fabric. On her head was always a small cap, tied under the chin. Each afternoon, regardless of the temperature, Mrs. Alley built a small fire in the front bedsitting room of the house. The furniture was a combination of periods, some country-made walnut pieces from earlier years and some machine-made furniture of the Victorian period. Hanging in the parlor was a framed photograph of Robert E. Lee.

Nancy Alley loved flowers and always kept a small garden around the house, carefully guarded from wandering chickens by a low fence of canes tied together with strips of cloth. She knitted constantly, and when she died left a trunk of unworn socks. Since Nancy Alley was baptized a Catholic when she and Abram were married, she never affiliated with another church, but always attended whatever church services were being held in the vicinity of her home.

Nancy Millar Alley died on October 28, 1893, at the age of seventy-six in the home she had occupied since 1836. She was survived by four children and her brother, Daniel Millar, along with several grandchildren and great-grandchildren. A large number of descendants still live in the vicinity of the Alley homestead and some of them still own a portion of the original Alley grant land.

Thankful Hannah McClure Allis

Thankful Hannah McClure Allis (1842-1937)

By Anita L. Richter*

Among the important educators of the last half of the nineteenth century, the name of Thankful Hannah McClure Allis (Mrs. Melvin H. Allis) should certainly be included. Her teaching career spanned fifty or more years.

Thankful Hannah McClure was born in Monroe, Louisiana, on November 2, 1842. As a young girl she came to Gonzales, Texas; the 1860 Gonzales County Census Rolls list her as a resident of Gonzales at that time. She was graduated from the Gonzales College there in 1862; she taught in the college until 1874.

In 1866, Thankful Hannah married Professor Melvin H. Allis. After that, her life and her career were so closely bound up in her husband's life, career, hardships and pleasures that this account would be incomplete if a short biography of her husband were not included.

Professor Melvin H. Allis was born in New York on July 12, 1836. He came to Texas in 1857. He had just graduated with an M.A. from Rochester University which had been chartered in 1850 by the Baptists. He had been trained for the legal profession but accepted a position as professor of mathematics at the Gonzales College, Gonzales, Texas.

*Vice-chairman and Secretary of Lavaca County Historical Survey Committee

When the War Between the States began, Professor Allis enlisted in Hood's Brigade and followed the Southern Flag to the close of the war. He was captured and imprisoned in Rock Island Prison for eighteen months. While in prison, he wrote several books which he later used in his teaching.

After the war, he returned to Gonzales College and was made president of the institution. Here, where he had met and taught Thankful Hannah, he made her his bride.

Mrs. Allis took her place at his side and as she expressed it, "We worked together like a team and gave all our lives to our beloved work." She did truly give her life to her work, along-side that of her husband.

In 1874, Professor and Mrs. Allis established a school at Moulton, Texas (now known as *Old Moulton*), which became well-known in the state. "It was not only a day school for the several hundred children of the community, but was also a boarding school that soon became so famous that it drew pupils from all the surrounding country—from San Antonio to Houston and to the border of the state."

The school was named the *Moulton Institute*. A brochure, dated 1889, lists the faculty as Melvin H. Allis, A.M., Principal; Mrs. Thankful H. Allis, Preceptress; Mrs. Laurette F. Price, Primary Department; Sarah M. McLean, Music Department. The curriculum of the school was broad, ranking well with that of a junior college of today. The Music Department was outstanding.

The discipline of the Institute was strict—especially when compared with the kind of life the pioneer children were accustomed to which was in the freedom of the woods where they could roam with dogs and gun.

The students were prohibited from using tobacco in the school room and from smoking anywhere on the school grounds. They could not loiter about the church or leave church during the time of services. They could not bring or keep firearms or intoxicating liquor anywhere on the premises. Scuffling, wrestling, dancing in the rooms or on the galleries, and using the floors as spittoons were prohibited. The students were required to study from seven to nine, with lights out in the rooms at nine o'clock. There were no vacations at Christmas time. The emphasis was on learning!

It was truly a co-educational school. Even the girls did not escape "just" punishment when deemed necessary. An old-timer, when interviewed, laughingly recalled that one time two of the girl students engaged in a bout of hair-pulling. "Swish would go the switch," he said with a chuckle, "and then there would be a vivid flash of bright red flannel petticoat." The names of the young ladies were not disclosed, but he said that they both became leaders high in Texas society and were never heard of fighting again.

Despite the strict discipline and the demanding emphasis on the curriculum, the boys and girls learned something beside the "three R's"; they learned the art of passing notes through the holes in the sliding partition of the school building, and many of them had fond recollections of outwitting the Professor or "Aunt Thank".

Taking for an example the happiness of their patron saints, Professor Allis, the thin scholarly figure of noble example, and his sweet, beloved wife, the various clans were united into new families through marriages of students who met at the Institute.

Along with renown and success, there were hardships connected with the operation of the Institute. It was founded in 1874. In 1876, fire destroyed the school but it was rebuilt. In 1886, a storm destroyed the building, but it was again rebuilt. (In the same storm, the Old Moulton Baptist Church which was built in 1874—and is still standing (1975)—was set askew and remains so, with interior metal braces, inside front and back, to hold it up; it attests to the ferocity of the storm.)

In 1887, when the San Antonio and Aransas Pass Railroad extended its line through the area two miles east of the settlement, the town began to move gradually to the railroad station, taking with it the name, Moulton.

After the death of Professor Allis in 1892, Mrs. Allis tried bravely to keep the school going, but in 1895, she closed the school and sold the property.

She moved to San Antonio where she was employed by Col. Wesley Peacock, Sr. of the Peacock School for Boys. He "always spoke highly of her work, held her in the highest regard, valued her friendship, her services to the school, and particularly her helpfulness after his wife's death."

Mrs. Allis was the head of the Peacock's primary department for five or six years. She continued on for several more years as a sort of school hostess or "house-mother". Her total tenure at Peacock School was about fifteen years.

21

Professor and Mrs. Allis had no children of their own, but they adopted two daughters and reared several others. The adopted daughters were Mrs. E. W. Walker of Blanco County who preceded her mother in death by about five days, and Mrs. M. C. (or Otho?) Askey, 316 San Pedro Avenue, San Antonio, Texas, at whose home she passed away on Friday, January 1, 1937, at age 94.

Burial took place in Gonzales, Texas, in the Gonzales Masonic Cemetery. Her body rests beside that of her husband. The graves are marked with a double gravestone, on the base of which is carved, "Thy Will Be Done".

To those who knew her, "The remembrance of 'Aunt Thank' is as fragrant and sweet as a rose-petal jar. Even in the last years which sat heavily on her frail, little person, she was as bright and cheerful as in the days when she helped to carry on her husband's work. When asked to give some of her memoirs of the Old Moulton Institute, she modestly tried to lead us to consider Professor Allis's life instead. "You know, our success was largely due to him", she concluded softly.

Those who pause to read the inscriptions on the Texas Official Historical Markers at Old Moulton see Mrs. Allis, the remarkable educator, referred to as "Aunt Thank".

Maria Bachman Atkinson
1801-1863
Harriet Bachman Jourdan
1815-1881
By M. Jourdan Atkinson*

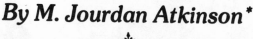

Harriet, the daughter of John Bachman and Mary Catherine Barbara Beneke Bachman, was in her twenty-first year. It was the spring of 1836. She had a tiny daughter, Harriet Emily, and an infant son, George Washington. They were safe at home with her family but in a way she was alone because her young husband, Frederic Jourdan, was across the Mississippi journeying southwest to become a Texican.

"Texican," she knew was how colonials in the Republic of the South (Mexico) were called for her sister, Maria Bachman Atkinson (eldest of eleven siblings), was now living in Austin's Colony between the Brazos and Colorado Rivers where she was neighbor to William Barrett Travis and to the early Anglo settler, Jared Groce, who had trained his own militia of thirty young Blacks and had laid out a broad Brazos bottom province.

Maria had been a young lady of fifteen summers when Harriet was born. Marrying soon after, she now had eight living children and two in the grave. Another would come in the fall.

What Harriet did not contemplate was that by the time Frederic reached the Texas-Louisiana Border, Texas would have declared independence so that Maria's forty-two-year-old husband,

---

*Granddaughter of Harriet and grandniece of Maria

Harriett Bachman Jourdan

John Atkinson, would be somewhere with Houston's army and Maria in a mad scramble getting her brook into the pinelands Frederic must leave behind.

At Bellville, Houston's order to evacuate, stating that the Alamo had fallen on March 6 and Santa Anna was coming to burn the colonists out, had thrown the Atkinsons into consternation. Their great fear was not of the Mexican army, which they believed would respect their persons whatever was done to their possessions, but of Comanches poised a hundred miles up the Colorado on the Hill Line. If they let the two armies cross the Brazos ahead of them, Tonkawa warriors (allied with Houston) would afford the only protective barrier.

Some women had Blacks to help. Maria had no Blacks, nor had she a wheeled vehicle available. But she had sixteen-year-old Sarah, fourteen-year-old Elizabeth, ten-year-old Catherine Virginia, twelve-year-old John Pinkney and seven-year-old Alexander to fetch and carry and mind the three little ones: Nancy Duraney, five; Martha Ann, three; Henry Tucker, a year and nine months. In haste, they emptied the cabin, buried all non-perishables except their most precious possession, the thigh-high Seth Thomas mantel clock, and planted the earth to mustard.

They took the barrel from the waterslide (a heavy, clumsily built sled), loaded on to it a box in which they put provisions, the clock and some balls of spun cotton, and yoked the slide to their pair of oxen. They left with the baby boy and the smaller girls riding on the sled with the box as they lumbered down to Groce's Crossing on the Brazos.

Groce, the great planter who took no part in the evacuation himself—he was middle-aged and paralyzed in both arms and had his private military to protect his property—stated that with such poor transportation the family could have no hope of staying ahead of the armies much less of evading Comanches. He lent them a high-wheeled Mexican cart in which they could all ride. He promised to keep the box with the clock and the balls of cotton until their return.

Rumbling and creaking, they drew into a *cavyyard* (Spanish corruption common to early Texans) of families in oxcarts or afoot driving cattle, children on milk cows, dogs weaving in and out scenting wild game. This was the Texas woman's movement headed for Louisiana.

The refugees traveled eastward for weeks, sleeping nights around open campfires until a rider overtook them with Houston's final order: "Turn back! The war is over! The Mexicans are leaving Texas!"

Back at Groce's Crossing, Maria found her box broken open, the clock's lead weights missing, the balls of cotton gone. Houston's army had passed that way and like all armies had taken what was needed: the lead to mold into bullets and the cotton to braid into bridles for the horses. She took the clock home some day to be repaired and there she waited for the menfolk.

Frederic, arriving after the Battle of San Jacinto, left at once to join the curious maneuver known as "seeing the Mexicans out of Texas." Santa Anna's army, except for his own contingent, had not been conquered. It was still afield but in consternation because he, as president of Mexico, had signed Texas away to save his own neck and now was out of communication where Houston had him hidden up the Brazos at Orizimbo Plantation (now Varner). John shortly joined the Mill Creek Volunteers.

She and the children retrieved the iron cookpots from under the greening mustard and set the cabin in readiness to receive a new Texas generation for whom they would often repeat an adventure story they called "The Runaway Scrape."

The reward of women like Maria and the waiting Harriet, other than dignity of family, would be landed estates. The new Republic of Texas, dubbed "the Bantam Republic" in eastern journals, with no money but a surplus of land was generous with men who had starved and chilled and furnished their own horses and equipment in the strange upheaval that tore Texas from Mexico. To Frederic it gave a section of land (640 acres)—he would settle over on the Yegua—and to John much more, some of it adjoining that which he and Maria already held as colonists.

Maria would never again leave the hill above Bellville where she had three more children and there, during the Civil War, John would bury her.

* * * *

Before 1840, Frederic brought his family out from the States, Harriet cradling their newest infant, Mary Catherine, to rocking of the oxcart. Now, at last, they were all together—and all Texicans.

* * * *

A decade found Texas joined (not totally to Frederic's liking) with the burgeoning Republic of the North. Four years later he took Harriet westward and upward into the Indian country because a doctor said she could not last longer in the malarial low country. The family story is that they traded their land for a blooded stallion, intending to go into the horse-raising business near Austin, the new state capital. The next day the horse died. It left its brand burned deep in family psychology. Try selling any of them a fine expensive animal! The answer would always be, "Oh, no; it might just lie down and die!"

Driving their other cattle, they went from the Yegua, an arm of the Brazos (yegua, meaing *mare*), across to the Bastrop area of the Colorado. In two years the Colorado rose and flooded them out. Soon after this, they bought a simple though well-built house on Walnut Creek where the Tonkawa had a favorite camp. It was seven miles from the capitol building that was also serving as church, opera house and general community hall. Comanches were still keeping watch from limestone balconies along the Hill Line and proving deadly to travelers sighted alone on the prairies below.

Only once did anything happen to mar the Anglo new-comer's pleasure in their Indian neighbors' presence. A Tonkawa woman, falling from a pecan tree, broke her arm. She let the doctor the Anglos brought set the bone. When they left the camp, she pulled away bandage and splint and died of gangrene.

Tragedy never really took a holiday. Over on Gilliland's Creek, Elizabeth Boyce and her children must every morning fill in the rocks and dirt wolves scratched from the graves at night, trying to get at the bodies of her husband and her son, the one killed by a fall from his horse, the other found by friends, scalped and muti-lated on the Austin trail. "Texas," some were saying, "is heaven for men and dogs, but it's hell for women and oxen!"

The Jourdans thought otherwise. Fascinated by the depth of black humus and the lure of cotton, they bought more and more land at fifty cents an acre. Frederic, a North Carolinian, was, like other French anglicised along the Atlantic seaboard, interested in commerce. Harriet, a South Carolinian said to be of Alsatian descent, knew how to organize and manage a plantation. The place on Walnut was right for both.

There were Blacks in field and kitchen but Harriet taught her children how to do whatever had to be done, though, like Maria, she never let her offspring forget they were scions of nobility. The story they told their families was that their own mother, Mary Catherine Barbara Beneke, had been one of two children, the elder a duchess. When the duchess came on a visit to the Caro-linas, she was thrown from a horse and killed, leaving the younger to inherit. The new heiress said she had crossed the Atlantic Ocean once and would not cross it again for all the lands and titles in Europe. So the fine estate had gone a-begging.

Two of the Jourdan daughters who had herded cattle upriver on horseback had been of courting age. They lost nothing in popularity by the move. However, there were other problems. They set tucks in their under petticoats and ran in mustang grapevines to make their skirts bell fashionably. Unaware of performing an ancient animistic rite, they set gourd bowls under the drip of the cut vines and washed their hair in the sap they caught, hoping it would grow luxuriantly long.

The two main rooms of the new house were, like Mexican houses, ceiled with canopies of homespun. The girls, bringing in wild flowers for the mantels, scolded to find both always cluttered with corncob dolls, cocklebur furniture, split cane animals; but Harriet, a stickler for everyone's rights, took the children's part, the playthings stayed where they were.

When she said evening callers could stay only until the back-log burned to ash, she did not watch to see if the girls damped the log from the rain barrel. Unlike her younglings in their quick attachment to Walnut's grapevine swings and swimming holes, Harriet's teenagers had formed emotional ties with Bastrop. Courting went on apace.

Custom required a bride's parents to give the wedding feast, the groom's parents the "infare dinner" for which their new daughter would don her "second day's dress" in which, more than likely, her wedding picture would be made. Following the marriages of Harriet Emily and Mary Catherine to the Alfords, Baldy and William Thomas, and of their brother George (after the death of his first wife Zuelima C. Kuykendall, and two children) to Lucy Payton, there was room for all the couples, if they chose, to settle to housekeeping in "The Field" as the spreading plantation was always called. The girls' children would be double cousins.

Harriet's eleventh and last child, later than some of her grandchildren, was stillborn. Except for George's troubles, it was the family's only fatality until the sorrows of the approaching Civil War. Frederic, of French revolutionary lineage, stood fast as an anti-secessionist, saying he had seen what was coming and that was why they left the South. However, their elder sons: George W. and William A., the latter unmarried, and their son-in-law, Baldy Alford, held different views. All three would die in Confederate uniform and six grandchildren would be orphaned.

*   *   *   *

Reconstruction, when it came, was not appalling to the Jourdans. The Blacks moved to places of their own, some buying right in The Field and settling down like the newlyweds. Baby daughter Julia would, even through all her years as Mrs. Ocie

Cato in Montana, continue addressing her sisters in the manner picked up from Black familiars as "Miss Em'ly," "Miss Mary," "Miss Sallie," "Miss Jennie." Perhaps because she could not at first twist her tongue to say "Amanda," or perhaps because she heard so much about Comanche Indians, she reduced it to "Manch" and omitted the title.

Amanda married her widowed sister-in-law's brother, Daniel Rufus Payton, a month after Appomattox, thus doubling the possibility of double cousins in the future, and went to live with her husband's mother in the Bastrop area.

"Miss Sallie" and "Miss Jennie," soon to marry Confederate lieutenants-turned-farmers, William Leroy Giles and James C. Maxwell, would remain on Walnut, but with a difference in their accustomed life styles. They would ever be handling Dutch ovens and yams in the hot ashes for themselves, but they would take over the hearths specially built for them without a doubt that in any domestic crisis the Blacks-turned-neighbors would come to their rescue.

Banditry was rife during and after the war. Word got about that Frederic kept money in the house. On the day he sold his cotton crop in the fall of 1875, masked men came after nightfall.

While they stood, guns clicking at his head as his hands trembled on the combination of his safe, Harriet, never before a demonstrably religious woman, fell to her knees to call down the of Almightly God on those "who would rob an old man of his hard-earned gains!" Beside her, a frantic pre-teen grandson, Baldy Alford, pleaded, "Hush, please hush, grandmother, they may kill you, too!"

He failed to interrupt her plea to her Maker which was chorused by the bandit's urging, "Hurry, hurry, old man, we have to get to every other house around here!" (A purely mischievous assertion for they went to no other place.)

Further dialogue of the hold-up is interesting. When Julia, by then a teenager, slipped from a window intending to go to the nearest Blacks, the guard outside marched her back in with the compliment: "Why, I wouldn't hurt a hair of your pretty head!" When a thump in the room across the hall brought two of the masked men with cocked guns, visiting daughter Sallie, sitting straight among the pillows, reassured them: "Don't be alarmed, gentlemen, it was just my little child, falling out of bed."

The cotton money was not in the safe. Frederic had banked it in town. Part of the $500 there belonged to his widowed daughter, Mary, who lived a half mile away; and part to young Zackie, who was out with friends, perhaps the Daughertys. (He later married Margaret Isabelle Daugherty.) Son John, two years married to Judge Seaborn Sneed's niece and ward, Jody Butler, had but recently moved with her into a house of their own farther over in The Field.

The robbers knew all the family's whereabouts. They had "cased" the place well. The lone womenfolk had glimpsed strange men lounging about the Crossing during the day and remembered it as they told how, when some of the loot fell to the floor in the bandits' get-away, Harriet's skirt covered the bills.

Julia and her young nephew, when they dared venture into the dark on foot, went to wake William Shanks, the nearby Black, who so sped the alarm that by daybreak the house was filled with excited people, all sure the highwaymen had been the gang from over by Manor.

But nobody made a move toward Manor. They hoped to become a law-abiding people and could wait for Austin courts to handle frontier crime.

A series of country store robberies followed the Jourdan robbery and the courts went into action. By and by the gang leader was called to account in Austin. When a whisper spread that he was about "to turn state's evidence to save his own hide," his confederates "took matters into their own hands."

*   *   *   *

Five years after the robberies ceased, Harriet, sound in health, prosperous and keen of mind was stricken. Mary's eldest son, Thomas, coming home from down the country, brought the measles. The family, so long cut off from the general stream of human traffic, had no built-in immunity; for them the disease was virulent. He recovered but his mother and his grandmother died. It was the spring of 1881.

Those who loved them brought wild flowers into the room where they lay. In sight of the house, Frederic, seventy, marked out a cemetery plot. He put them in the earth where the wild flowers grew. He had never known where strangers put his first two sons.

Unlike John Atkinson, he would not re-marry.

*   *   *   *

Sallie inherited the homeplace. Her children, Laura Lewis Giles and Eugene Victor Giles, gave the property as a public memorial to Frederic and Harriet and their pioneer neighbors. It is now known as The Jourdan Bachman Park.

Elizabeth Thomas Davis Bagley (1826-1911)

By Jean Lockwood Williams*

Elizabeth Thomas Davis, my grandmother, was born in Alabama, May 16, 1826, the eldest daughter of Nathaniel Davis and Rhoda Craig Davis. Because Mrs. Davis was asthmatic, had to stay with the younger children, and manage the farm, Elizabeth served as hostess for her father when he was a State Senator in Montgomery, Alabama, during the legislative sessions.

In Montgomery, Elizabeth bought all household supplies, linens, and dress materials including silks and work clothes for the coming year. At home in Tuscaloosa, Alabama, (now the site of the Red Stone Arsenal) she oversaw the sewing, cooking, and medical care of the family and servants.

Elizabeth became a school teacher and fell in love with a fellow teacher, William Henry Bagley, two years her senior. Because he needed her, her father opposed the marriage. Nevertheless, Elizabeth was married on November 25, 1849, in the home of a friend, William Cameron. A year later a son, Nicholas Josiah Bagley, was born.

In 1851 the Bagleys decided to move to Texas, a wide-open State desiring new residents. Elizabeth's father helped the young couple get ready for the trip, made by wagon. A young servant girl

* Granddaughter

Elizabeth Thomas Davis Bagley

was provided to help with the baby. They stopped at Caldwell, Texas, and built a substantial house, still occupied in the late 1930's.

Farming was the business of most settlers and the Bagleys tried it for many years, raising chickens, pigs, cows, and horses as well as corn, vegetables, and fruit. William decided to go into cattle raising in West Texas. He kept his cattle ranging from Lampasas to Sweetwater. He rode horseback and came home for frequent visits. During the decade four more children were born: Mattie, Franklin, Nannie, and William, Jr.

Texas was slow to mobilize. William joined the Texas Brigade but he never left Texas because the Union Army at the Battle of Vicksburg cut the South off from Texas. Elizabeth ran the farm, raised chickens, made clothes for her boys from her husband's clothes, and sewed dresses, coats, and underwear for the girls from what fabrics she could get, even feed sacks. All manufactured articles were very scarce and there was little money. Elizabeth told me of relatives dropping their silver coins in the bottom of lard cans so the coins would not be stolen.

Elizabeth spent the War years teaching her children, working, and holding the family together. The girls learned to sew, knit, crochet, and make lace as the Belgians do with bobbins attached to pins which plot the design. As the bobbins are thrown the design grows in wondrous patterns. My grandmother had all the tools of the art when she lived with us when I was a child. She had yards of lace she and her daughters had made, and her granddaughters put it on their panties, corset covers, and petticoats.

After the Civil War, William came home. He did not care for farming and went back to cattle raising. By now his eldest son, Nicholas, was old enough to help on the range. As late as 1938 the people in Caldwell remembered the fine figure Nicholas cut on his beautiful horse with a fancy saddle.

When she was forty-one, Elizabeth believed she was too old to have a child and did not know she was pregnant. However, on July 18, 1867, she gave birth to a premature baby girl weighing about 1½ pounds. She was named Emma Johnson Bagley and became my mother.

In spite of the July heat, Elizabeth sat very near the fireplace with the infant cradled in her arms in warm blankets. The infant would be placed on a pillow on warm bricks and covered first with cotton batting because of her sensitive skin and then with blankets.

The baby wore no clothes for months. She was first fed with an eye-dropper. Her brother, who was seventeen years old at her birth, said Emma could have been put in a coffee pot and covered up. She thrived. Her first dress was a large circle of very fine cotton batiste with a circle cut out for the neck and sleeves inserted in slits below the neck. The dress was ripped at the cuffs as she became older. It was her Christening dress and is still carefully preserved in a delicate pink and white round straw basket.

I was twelve years old when my grandmother died in November, 1911. I had become a sort of handmaiden to her as she became less active, filling her bedside waterpitcher and turning on and off her small Emerson fan. Sometimes Grandmother would take me by the hand and tell me long stories of her childhood, her father, her strenuous days when her husband was away at war or on the range. She told me with sadness how several of Sherman's men knocked the top off sister's grand piano, put it on the lawn, filled it with hay for their horses, and commandeered her home for their men.

In the early 1870's Rockdale, Texas, became a growing town with two railroads for shipping cattle: the International and Great Northern and the San Antonio and Aransas Pass. They were nick-named the I and GN and the SAAP. When my mother, Emma, the youngest child, was about seven, the family decided to move to Rockdale. They built a good-sized house with land enough for a garden, barn, horse and cattle lot, and an area for raising chickens and pigeons. My grandfather loved squabs, and my grandmother said when sudden company arrived they could go out and get squabs just the size for cooking. No one knew about allergies then, so when my grandmother developed asthma, the chickens and pigeons at the backdoor were not suspected.

Nicholas, the eldest son, managed the cattle when his father became too old to ride the range. Sometime in the 1880's there was a terrible freeze and all the cattle were lost. Grandfather then went into sheep raising with headquarters around Lampasas.

Nicholas had not married until he was about forty, in 1890. A daughter was born April 7, 1892, named Mattie. The wife and baby went to live in the Lampasas area. When their second child was due, Nicholas started out in the wagon for his wife's home for the delivery. She had kept notches on a stick for each period of her pregnancy, but she did not reach her home in time. The boy was born out in the open country with no medical care or even water. The wife died in childbirth. After her burial on the prairie, Nicholas took his four-year-old daughter, Mattie, and the new baby to his mother-in-law. He went horseback in order to travel faster. At first the baby thrived but about one year of age, he died of diarrhea. Nicholas took Mattie to his mother, Elizabeth, in Rockdale. Mrs. Bagley was then seventy years old.

Elizabeth was stricter with her grandchildren than she had been with her own children. Caring for a small child and an aging husband was too taxing for grandmother. When she became ill, my mother brought her to our house. She and her granddaughter became permanent members of our household which had four children then and was to have two more.

Grandmother helped with the sewing, made all the button holes and smocking, and entertained the children with stories and poems both classical and "elocution" style. She could quote endlessly from the Bible and English poets. Her Spencerian handwriting was exquisite.

She was always afraid of automobiles and would not ride in one. Elizabeth loved to sit on the porch and count the cars that turned the corner on the way to the fair grounds in the summer.

Her daughter, Mattie, became an excellent dressmaker and milliner. She had many suitors but did not get married when she was young. Elizabeth said that she would be like the girl who went through the woods hunting for a straight stick and the farther she went, the more crooked they became. In her 30's Mattie married an old beau, who was a widower with six daughters. She was a loving and indulgent stepmother. On a visit to her mother, Mattie died suddenly of jaundice—probably hepatitis.

Elizabeth's daughter, Nannie, died when she was four of a strange fever never diagnosed.

For several years William Henry Bagley lived in his home with his second son, Franklin, and Franklin's family. Nearly every Sunday we took grandmother in the surrey to see grandfather. He seldom came to see us. Nicholas and William, fine horsemen, came often to see their mother. The whole Bagley family celebrated Thanksgiving together, alternating homes.

Grandmother was in her last decade when I knew her: a quiet woman, to me a learned woman, strict on good manners, and deferential to my father who was very good to her.

We had an elaborately illustrated book on Queen Victoria I used to read and pore over. Queen Victoria was a real person to me. She was born five years before my grandmother, but I considered them of the same generation. Victoria, who became queen at age sixteen, and my grandmother as a young woman were in sharp contrast.

Grandmother, who started her early adulthood as hostess and housekeeper for her family in the capitol at Montgomery, Alabama, as the buyer for a large family, and as a schoolteacher, had little opportunity to exercise her skills in any career or in a public way after she became a pioneer in a rugged country and bearing five children. Her deep devotion to her family and the training and nurture she gave her children and their children make her a great woman in my eyes. For sixty years Elizabeth Bagley was a pioneer in Texas.

Sarah Ann McClure
Braches
(1811-1894)
By Elsie Turk Smothers*

The eldest of twelve children, Sarah Ann Ashby was born in Shelby County, Kentucky, on March 12, 1811. Her father was John Miller Ashby, a descendant of a family in England in whose veins flowed the blood of Chickahominy Indians. One of John Miller Ashby's ancestors was the son of Pocahontos and John Rolfe.

Sarah Ann's mother, Mary, was the daughter of Benjamin Garnet and Mary Wolfolk, both members of the fine Kentucky families.

In 1828 Sarah Ann married Bartlett D. McClure. Their son, Alex, was born in 1829. In 1831 the McClure and Ashby families migrated to Texas. The trip was a perilous one, for near Rockport on the Texas coast, they were caught in a storm. Losing his bearing, the pilot steered the ship into unfamiliar waters. The ship was thrown time and time again against a bar. However, the ship was sturdy and withstood the storm.

Bartlett McClure and a few shipmates went inland to secure permission from the Mexican Government to land. Permission was granted. This trip consumed five days and it took another

---

* Author and historian

Sarah Ann McClure Braches

Sarah Ann McClure Braches' House and the Sam Houston Oak

week for the Mexican carts to arrive. These Mexicans took the passengers and cargo only as far as the Guadalupe River. Then other carters were hired to take them to their destinations.

Although the Ashbys settled five miles south of Hallettsville, the McClures settled on Peach Creek in Gonzales County. Here Bartlett McClure built a house patterned after their home in Kentucky, with wide porches across the two story structure and large, wide columns from the roof to the bottom floor. In this house in 1833 John McClure was born and in 1839, Joel McClure.

In order to win the goodwill of the Indians, the few white families residing in or around the town of Gonzales gave a dinner for one hundred Comanche braves. The Indians seemed to enjoy the hospitality and rode away without an unpleasant incident. However, a year later when itinerant French traders fed poisoned bread to the Comanches, the Indians declared their hatred of all white men.

After Sarah Ann's mother died in 1835, the McClures made many trips to the home of Sarah Ann's father to help with the chores and see after the family. According to Army Records, John Ashby was blind and therefore excused from military service during the Revolution.

It was while returning from one of these trips that Bartlett and Sarah Ann ran into a band of twenty-seven Comanche warriors. The McClures were on horseback and the Indians tried to outwit them by cutting them off from their regular crossing at Boggy Creek.

The McClures separated: Sarah Ann going toward a point on Boggy Creek and Bartlett riding to an upper crossing. Sarah Ann arrived at Boggy Creek where the banks were almost upright and a chasm about twelve feet wide lay in her path.

Sarah Ann fastened her reins in the horse's mane, wrapped her arms around his neck, and buried her spurs in his flanks. The horse vaulted into the air, landing with his forefeet on the opposite side. His hind legs bogged in the sand but, with a huge lunge, he scrambled up the bank. In a clipping from the *Hallettsville Herald*, Sarah Ann tells of the incident:

I didn't expect him to jump clear across but I thought he would strike his feet on the opposite bank and I would be able to jump over his head, but when he landed, he managed to scramble up the bank and we galloped away safe and sound. The Indians rode up to the place and whooped and whistled, and shook their spears at me. Mr. McClure took the opposite direction, when we became separated, and I thought all along that he was killed, but he succeeded in reaching the crossing above, and joined me several miles further on. The Indians had spears which they had fastened to their wrists. These they threw at us several times during the early part of the pursuit, their object being to cripple our horses.

Sarah Ann McClure had many other encounters with the Indians. In 1834, starting on a business trip to Bastrop, Bartlett left with Sarah Ann a carpenter to build an addition to his house. The carpenter, a Down-East Yankee, knew little of Indians or guns. A morning or so later, Sarah Ann saw Indians skulking in the brush and two of the band chasing the cattle. She at once armed herself and told the carpenter to do likewise. Turning deathly pale and trembling, he declared that he had never shot a gun and could not fight. He suggested that they go to the bottoms and hide until the Indians left. To this suggestion Sarah Ann replied: "No sir, you can go to the bottoms if you want, but I am going to fight."

The Indians killed a few calves and moved on. The following morning, Sarah Ann told the man to go to the lake back of the house for a bucket of water, so she could prepare breakfast. When he said that he was afraid to go, Sarah Ann, strapping a brace of pistols around her waist, took the bucket and started for the lake. The carpenter followed behind her a few steps, holding a gun in his hands.

Angered, Sarah Ann told him that if he dared to follow her another foot, she would shoot him dead in his tracks. He beat a hasty retreat to the house. Several days later, he left without finishing his job.

When her father died on board a ship as he was returning to Texas from Kentucky, Bartlett and Sarah Ann reared Mary, Isabella, Fannie, Euphremia, William, and Travis Ashby as if they were their own children.

Sarah Ann was at her home on Peach Creek when the Alamo fell. Her husband had been sent to East Texas by General Sam Houston to round up some of the "Redlanders" to help fight the Mexicans. In Sarah Ann's home were twenty-seven women whose husbands were in the Alamo. It was here they heard the sad news.

On his second day's retreat, General Houston stopped at Sarah Ann's house. Sitting on his horse in her yard under a big liveoak tree (later referred to as the Sam Houston oak), he ordered a retreat, saying that those who saw fit to remain must suffer the consequences. Thus, began the incident known as "The Runaway Scrape."

Sam Houston helped many to get started, sending the women and children on ahead. When they had gone about four miles, they heard the explosion at Gonzales of the magazine blown up by Colonel Patten who later overtook them at the Navidad.

Santa Anna camped at Peach Creek for five weeks and made his headquarters in the McClure home during a part of the time. The Mexicans drove off or killed all the stock on the farm, filled the well with bricks torn from the kitchen's floor, and burned everything except the dwelling house. The house still stands and is still being occupied.

Jim Bowie was also a friend of the McClures. When Bowie and his party started on their San Saba Expedition, Sarah Ann had beeves killed and dressed, food cooked, and a general supply of provisions prepared for the men on their march. Although Bowie insisted on paying her, Sarah Ann refused to accept any payment.

Judge Bartlett McClure died in 1842 and lies buried at Gonzales. He and Sarah Ann had been married only fourteen years. These were action-filled years, covering the Texas Revolution and the establishment of the Republic of Texas. Bartlett McClure had organized the first County in DeWitt's Colony and was its first County Judge. He had been a member of the 1833 Texas Convention.

On March 2, 1843, Sarah Ann married Charles Braches of Gonzales County, a native of Gaulhausen, Kruznach, Rheim, Prussia. Prior to his coming to Texas, Charles Braches conducted a Music School in Mississippi. In 1842 he had been elected to represent his district in the Texas Congress. He had participated in battles of the Hondo, Plum Creek, and the Medina and in numerous other expeditions against the Indians. He and Sarah Ann were members of the Cumberland Presbyterian Church which they generously supported so long as they lived.

During her second marriage Sarah Ann lived a peaceful life, financially independent and among good friends and neighbors. Charles Braches died July 7, 1889, at his home in Gonzales. Five years later on October 17, 1894, Sarah Ann died at her home.

Confined to her bed in her later years, Sarah Ann was optimistic and cheerful. She enjoyed recounting her early hardships and perils and continuing her gracious hospitality.

John Henry Brown, noted Texas historian of the 1800's, who knew Sarah Ann personally, had this to say of his friend:

Mrs. Braches was the soul of patriotism—a lady of rare refinement and intelligence, and her deeds of kindness and charities were innumerable. Her grave will be watered by the tears of widows and orphans. Her life is a part of, and interwoven with, the most stirring period of Texas History. Peace be to her ashes and lasting honor to her memory!

Angela Salvaggio Cangelosi (1855-1925)

By Frank E. Tritico*

On September 5, 1855, in Poggioreale, Province of Trapani, Sicily, Angela Salvaggio was born. Her parents, Antonio and Francesca Palasotta Salvaggio, lived and died in Sicily.

Angela married Giovanne (John) Cangelosi, a man ten years her senior and of a well-to-do family. A story is told in the family that the Baron of Palermo after seeing the Cangelosi farms, vineyards, and buildings said to Calogero Cangelosi (John's father): *"Me chimate Barone, ma voi siete baronetto"* (You call me Baron, but you are a baronet). His descendants in Sicily are still called *Baronetto.*

The young couple were happy and in time had three sons (Carlo, Francesco, and Antonio) and two daughters (Maria and Francesca) to share their large comfortable stone house. However, the climate of the mountain region of Sicily adversely affected John's health and he was unable to recover from recurring spells of pneumonia. In the 1880's his doctors advised him to seek a drier, warmer climate. John thought immediately of Texas where his brother Joseph already lived in the Brazos County area. It was his intention to go alone, to stay with his brother, and when a cure hopefully was effected to return to Sicily.

---

*Great-grandson

Angela Salvaggio Cangelosi

This plan was rejected by Angela who insisted that the children and she would go with him. Quickly they put their house, furniture, silver, vineyards, orchards, and farms into the care of relatives and sailed for New Orleans arriving after a month or six weeks journey.

In Texas the family settled in the area known as Mudville between Mumford, Steele Store and Stone City, near Bryan and purchased about 260 acres of Brazos River bottom land which had been scorned by the American planters. This proved a fruitful choice.

With the building of a wooden house, Angela's life became that of a typical pioneer woman of the day: preparing meals, sewing, washing, cleaning, educating her children and rearing them in the knowledge of their Savior.

Up at dawn, Angela prepared the day's meals and sent breakfast and lunch to the men and boys in the fields by their younger sisters and brothers. The staple Italian meal of *pasta* (spaghetti) had to be rolled by hand and placed in the sun to dry. Later when John had sent to Italy for a spaghetti maker, the girls were given the chore to hand feed the machine on the back porch. The first time they used the maker, they did not notice that the family's dog was busily eating the *pasta* as they ground it out. When Angela noticed, it was too late and a sparse supper was placed on the table that night.

Bread was made by hand and baked in outdoor ovens of brick heated by coals. The first year the cooking was done in the fireplace which served as the house's heating unit also. Special grills and cooking pots which sat in coals and had coals heaped above served as cooking utensils. Later an iron wood-burning stove was purchased and used, but bread continued to be baked in the outdoor ovens.

Large iron wash pots were placed over fires outdoors. The family's clothes, washed by hand, went into the pot where they were stirred with a stick, rinsed, and hung in the sun to dry. The soap used had been made by Angela from lye and grease renderings. Later the clothes were ironed by Angela and the girls with flat irons heated in the fireplace or stove.

There were now two more children: Domenico born in Louisiana and Giuseppe born in Brazos County. Although help was hired for work in the fields, housework was always done by Angela and her daughters (Mary and Frances).

The main crop was cotton but a garden of nearly everything needed was maintained: tomatoes, beans, okra, onions, garlic, sweet potatoes, squash, gourds, egg plants, turnips, carrots, cabbages, lettuce, mustard greens, spinach, corn, artichokes, fennel and other herbs used in Italian cooking. The orchard of fourteen acres, consisting mainly of peaches, plums, pears, grapes and figs, was also maintained. Most of the fruit was eaten fresh as the dessert in the Italian tradition, and not canned. Chicken, turkeys, goats, cows and domestic animals were also raised.

Angela and the girls churned butter, made clabber and prepared various kinds of Italian cheeses. Corn was taken to a nearby miller to be ground and such staples as sugar, white flour, coffee beans (which were roasted and ground at home) were purchased each six months on a trip to town, as were shoes, the men's suits and clothing material. Most of the clothes, however, were made at home: dresses, boys' and men's shirts, and even everyday trousers. Lace was crocheted and tatted by the women in the evenings by firelight or lamplight to be used as trimmings on the girls' and ladies' dresses.

Angela and John were very religious and since there was no church near, they gathered the family and relatives on Sunday mornings and read the Mass and Gospel from a missal brought from Sicily. Evening devotions were led by Angela after supper in front of the fireplace; the rosary, litanies, and other prayers, which she had taught the children, were said. Angela also instructed her sons and daughters in their religious studies. Later when an Italian priest was sent to Bryan, he came to the Cangelosi household one Sunday morning each month and said Mass for the people in the area. Angela, with some help, the day before prepared enough *pasta* to feed the weekly crowd and served *biscoti* for dessert.

Each year on March 19, the feast of St. Joseph, Patron Saint of Italy, an altar of sweets, bread, fig newtons made into the shape of fish and crosses, eggs with dough around them shaped like chicks, etc. and other fancy foods were prepared weeks ahead. Neighbors, friends, and relatives were invited to participate. The night before, the rosary of St. Joseph was chanted and the following morning a statue of the saint, prepared and clothed by Angela, was carried in a procession by the men in the neighborhood. The procession ended with a feast at the Cangelosi home.

Angela was a woman of medium height, fair complexion, dark hair, and stout in her later years. Her home was a frame house with a front porch, three bedrooms (one for the parents, one for the girls, and one for the boys), a parlor, a dining room, a kitchen, and a back porch. A cistern in front held the water and later a pump was installed. Behind the house was "the Convenience" and the large orchard. The house is still standing in 1975 and lived in by my Aunt Lena La Barbera Cangelosi, widow of Giuseppe (Joe).

Life on the Texas "frontier" was not easy for immigrants. One of the Cangelosi boys almost drowned in the Brazos. Mosquitoes, unknown to the Cangelosi in Sicily, had to be coped with in the Brazos "bottom". Small smoke fires were lighted in the warm evenings so that the family could sit on the porch and listen to stories told by their parents.

Although earthquakes had been familiar to them in Sicily, Texas floods were not. The floods of 1899, 1913 and 1915 were particularly bad. In 1913 when the flood came, the family rushed to the nearby cotton gin, taking little with them. The water rose to the second floor and the Cangelosi dipped water into buckets out of the window and then boiled it over grills with coals in order to have drinking water. There was little food to cook so their fare consisted mainly of flour-water cakes dried in the sun. The house fortunately was not carried away but the women scrubbed for weeks to clean the mud out, and boiled their white crocheted bedspreads, etc.

The hardships of pioneering were alleviated in part by the regular Sunday evening dances Angela arranged in her home where one of her sons played the accordion and friends and neighbors brought their adolescents to dance and visit. The younger children played in the yard while the older folk visited and exchanged reminiscences.

There were no doctors in the area and Angela was much sought after as a midwife and *doctoressa*. She made home-remedies and used folk-medicine and herbs in treating her family and those who came to her for help. It was said that she had "healing hands" and a massage by her often helped.

When John finally was cured of his pulmonary difficulties and broached the subject of returning to Sicily to Angela, she refused to go. She said that their sons were then of conscriptable age and might be sent off to die in an Italian war (there was no draft in the American army at that time) and that now Texas was their home. So the family stayed.

All the Cangelosi children except Dominic married, set up their own homes and had their own families. On April 24, 1912, John, riding the small railroad called the "Jack" to see Mary Tritico's newborn son (my father) at Stone City, a few miles from Mudville, had a heart attack. He died at a neighbor's house. He was buried from St. Anthony's Church in Bryan (which Mary Tritico's husband, Frank, with his father-in-law had help found) in Sacred Heart Cemetery with an Italian priest saying the service.

Francesca Falsone preceded her father in death at childbirth, leaving a daughter bearing her name. Frances Falsone II married Joe Restino of Hearne, a well-to-do farmer. Charles was a merchant, owner of a cotton gin, and farmer in Stafford along with his brother Frank who was the first Italian millionaire in Texas. Anthony lived in Houston and owned property, a store, and land throughout Texas. Mary and her husband, Frank Tritico, owned a store and rent property. Dominic lived with them. Joe lived on and worked the Cangelosi farm until he retired. After his death his widow continues to live on the place and leases the land to farmers. Mary's son, Leonard Tritico, is administrator of the estate.

In 1916 or 1917 Angela moved to Stafford to make her home. Her house, similar to the one near Mudville was between Charles' and Frank's houses with Mary Tritico's house only a mile or two away. In 1924 when she became ill, Angela went to Houston where Anthony lived. Here she died. She was buried from Blessed Sacrament Church in Houston in Holy Family Cemetery.

Today all of John's and Angela's children are dead. The third and fourth generations of Cangelosi are men and women of character like their forebears. They love Texas and are patriots in the best meaning of the word. They are successful business men and homeowners, farmers, attorneys and educators. One of them headed a committee which called upon Governor Price Daniel to ask the Legislature for a Texas Archives and Library Building and was honored on the day the Building was dedicated April 10, 1962.

Maria Gertrudis Perez Cordero Cassiano (1790-1832)

By Edith Olbrich Parker*

The life-span of Maria Gertrudis Cordero Cassiano included the last years of Texas' peaceful acceptance of Spanish rule, the eleven years of turbulence preceding Mexico's independence from Spain, and almost the whole duration of Mexico's sovereignty over Texas.

Her baptismal record reads: "Maria Gertrudis Perez, legitimate daughter of D. Juan Ignacio Perez and Da. Clemencia Hernandez, was baptized on the parish church of the Villa of San Fernando, Royal Presidio of San Antonio de Bexar, January 12, 1790, being ten days old. Spanish. Her godparents were Francisco Javier Galan and Herlinda Bustillos, who take the responsibility of teaching her Christian Doctrine if she loses her parents, and who become her spiritual parents." (Translated from the Spanish.)

She was born in the old Perez homestead south of the church property, facing east on the main Plaza. This property remained in the hands of the descendants until recent time when the house was destroyed by fire; it was rebuilt in 1852.

Her father was a Lieutenant Colonel in the Royal Spanish Army of Texas Province, great-grandson of Maria Robaina de Bethencourt, called the Widow Granado. Her mother was descended from the Spanish settlers of 1715. Gertrudis' generation was almost the last that could trace pure Spanish

* Linguist and librarian

Diagram of the arrangement of
numbered homesites granted to
the Canary Island Settlers.
Sixteen families drew lots and
were given the homesite cor-
responding to the number drawn.

The buildings are an artist's
concept.

SAN FERNANDO DE BEXAR
Original Plan

50

ethnic background; for after 1823, settlers from the United States, with many different nationality backgrounds, poured into San Antonio and married the "beautiful Spanish maidens."

Gertrudis' childhood was happy. Her brother, Jose Ignacio, was four years older, and her sister, Concepcion, five years younger. There was also a foster brother, Jose Antonio Perez, mentioned in her mother's will. Families were large. Gertrudis had twelve uncles and aunts on her father's side alone, and innumerable cousins.

From an early age the children were carefully trained: in the meticulous practice of their Catholic faith; in love, respect and implicit obedience to their parents; in the knowledge of, and strict adherence to, family background and traditions; and in the elegant courtesy and social graces of the times. Girls were carefully sheltered, never leaving the home without a chaperone "duenna" or older companion. The Perez girls were well educated for women could own, inherit, administer, buy and sell property.

The most vital force in the lives of these Spaniards was their religion. The church of San Fernando was in the very center of the Villa, built in the form of a cross, the front door facing Main Plaza and the back door opening on Military Plaza, then called Plaza of the Presidio. A "presidio" was a military post or fortified settlement in areas under Spanish control. As the Perez children sat decorously in the family pew, near the front of the church, they gazed with awe at the scene painted above the main altar. According to legend, it depicted the gentle St. Anthony, "astride a mustang, and in the war paint of a bold Comanche—halo floating above—and buffalo scuttling before his arrow!"

Whenever the Indians were not on the warpath and their father was at home, Gertrudis never tired of hearing him tell how their great-great-grandmother Maria, after having sailed from the Canary Islands via Havana, Cuba, to Vera Cruz, Mexico (where her husband, a potter, died) walked with her six small children, the forty-seven other Canary Islanders and an armed guard, from Vera Cruz to Mexico City, to Saltillo, where the young Perez brothers joined them, and then on to San Antonio. The Viceroy had orders from the King of Spain to grant them land and help them build homes. But it was March 9, 1731, planting time. Everything had to be postponed until the seed was in, or there would be no food the next winter. All fifty-six of them were housed in the presidio temporarily. Paula, their great-grandmother was nine years old, with black hair and eyes like her mother. Later she married Jose Perez. In their days, the narrow streets leading into the Plazas were closed at night-fall by curtains of tightly stretched rawhide, impervious to Indian arrows. In the patio of their home, the children "play-acted" these adventures, keeping them ever fresh in their imaginations.

In 1804, when Gertrudis was fourteen years old and considered an adult, socially, though still closely sheltered, her father bought for eight hundred pesos, the Commandancia of the Presidio, now known as the Spanish Governors' Palace. It was built of "rubble or stone, a very strong edifice." It remained in the family's possession for one hundred twenty-five years, and was sold in 1929 to the City of San Antonio for fifty-five thousand dollars.

The next year Don Antonio Cordero y Bustamente was appointed Military and Political Governor of Texas *(ad interim)*. He had been sent from Spain to Mexico in 1772 as an officer, to discipline the Mexican troops and to carry out certain reforms. He was a cultured gentleman of considerable learning, spoke French, read Latin and was adept in the social graces.

Zebulon Pike, who was entertained by Governor Cordero in 1807, attributed the prosperity of San Antonio to "the examples and encouragement given to industry, politeness and civilization by the excellent Governor Cordero and his colleague, Herrera." Herrera was Governor of Nuevo Leon. "The population of the city was about two thousand, most of whom resided in . . . mud-daubed grass-roofed houses. To the east, across the river was the station of the troops" (the Alamo).

Cordero had known Gertrudis since her childhood, for even the old Perez homestead had been the center of military and social activity. Now the Commandancia offered wider scope. Pike says, "Enough jingling spurs and clanking swords and rustling silks have been heard in these old rooms to satisfy the most avid romantic fancy."

Even in this late day, one's heart goes out to Gertrudis, when her father solemnly told her that a marriage had been arranged between her and the esteemed Governor, older than her father! The implicit obedience instilled since birth stood her in good stead. Gracefully (if sadly) she accepted his dictum, then fled to the small chapel-room of Our Lady, to pray for strength to give up forever her dreams of the dashing young officers with whom she had exchanged "come-hither" glances over the tip of her feathered fan.

The bridal couple would have graced a fairy tale. Cordero was considered "a strikingly handsome man." He was five feet ten inches tall, of fair complexion, with blue eyes, and wore his hair turned back, in keeping with his military bearing. Gertrudis was unequaled in poise and beauty.

A wedding procession to and from the church, in those days, was an imposing affair. Bride and bridegroom, beautifully mounted on fine horses, were followed by elaborately costumed bridesmaids, groomsmen, parents of the bride and groom (Cordero had none here), relatives and guests, all mounted and in cavalcade, with flowers and the music of guitars and violins. According to Pike, there was a coach in San Antonio, so we can picture the coach, carrying, perhaps, elderly aunts.

After the solemn marriage ceremony in San Fernando Church, "a Baile and Boda Cena (dance and wedding feast) continued for one or two nights in succession."

Her marriage brought to Gertrudis immediate release from the strict conventions of her girlhood. For this phase of her life, we have the report of an eye-witness. Madame Candelaria says she, when quite young, was brought into the Cordero home as a trusted companion and assumed the role of "chocolate-maker," chocolate being the Cordero's favorite beverage, "morning, noon, or merienda (snack time)."

She says, too, that the elderly Cordero so cherished his lovely, eighteen-year-old bride, that when he was absent, he authorized her to take his place, and she "conducted affairs of state in grand style and reviewed the Troops as expertly as Queen Isabella."

Gertrudis was affectionately called "La Brigaviella" (Mrs. Brigadier-General) by officers and soldiers. The Military Review, on Military Plaza, in front of the Palace, was an historical tableau. Picture Gertrudis, mounted on a spirited horse, side saddle beautifully tooled, in her riding habit of dark green velvet with long skirt, her military jacket heavily embroidered in gold thread, wearing a plumed hat, facing the Troop formation. The Royalist Spanish Troops' military uniforms consisted of short blue coat, blue velvet small-clothes open at the knee, red velvet capes and cuffs, spurred boots and broad-brimmed hats decorated with ribbons and plumes, the latter often the gift of some fair senorita. From this admiring assemblage, Gertrudis accepted military salutes and honors in the Governor's absences.

From her high estate, one wonders if Gertrudis looked with compassion upon another beautiful woman some twenty years her senior among the on-lookers, mounted on a large white horse, cherished by no one, ostracized by all women, but aided on occasion by their husbands, active manager of the Ranch de las Cabras. Maria del Carmen Calvillo Delgado had left her husband in her youth, and never returned to him, though she lived until she was sixty years old. She lived, it is said, to be one hundred and twenty years old, and is buried in an unmarked grave. Did Gertrudis wonder what made it impossible for Maria del Carmen to accept the lot of women of her era, inexorable wifehood and motherhood, and whether all she had sacrificed was compensated by her being "free"?

Gertrudis was truly modern for her times. Her clothes were of the latest mode of her day, imported from Spain. Her jewels were priceless: diamond earrings, pearl necklaces, bracelets, a Rosary filled with gold; and her household effects included solid silver plates, cutlery and a salt cellar.

She was a grand hostess at the levees and balls celebrated in the Palace. Here visitors from many nations were feted, wined and dined. Here Governors, alcaldes, impresarios, diplomats and ecclesiastics met, shaped the destinies of city and province, and made history.

In this medium Gertrudis moved, "kind, lovable and distinguished." Other old-timers who knew her personally reported that "She was loved by all, and, being rich in her own right, she was exceedingly generous to the poor, and on one set day of the week —Saturday—she regularly dispensed alms and favors to them." Add her deep piety and selfless dedication to duty. In any age, she would have been a great lady.

Gertrudis' marriage was a brief interlude, barely outlasting the honeymoon. In 1810, when Father Miguel Hidalgo y Costilla began the Mexican Revolution against Spain, Governor Cordero went to Mexico. He died in Durango and was buried there.

The news of his death reached San Antonio by horseback. Gertrudis, twenty years old, prayed for the strength to accept and observe the strictures of Spanish mourning and widowhood. She had not even a grave to tend!

Soon the Revolution spread to Texas, and Gertrudis sitting alone and lonely at her window, thinking of the gay serenaders of other years, heard from out of the distant darkness the "grito," battle-cry of the Revolution:

Viva la Virgen de Guadalupe!
Viva la Independencia!
Muera al mal gobierno! (Down with the bad government!)

Gertrudis and her mother were grateful for the strength of the Palace in 1813, when the Revolutionists briefly held San Antonio. Her father must have been away on campaign, for the Mexicans, under pretext of safe-conduct to New Orleans, took the fourteen leading Royalists a mile and a half out of town and "slit their throats." Herrera, a family friend was among them. One by one the mainstays of Gertrudis' life were vanishing.

In 1814 San Antonio had become a desolate place, surrounded by hostile Indians. Prices were prohibitive and food scarce. Gertrudis had many opportunities to dispense benevolence, almost the only joy left to her.

From mid-1815 to March, 1817, Ignacio Perez was acting Governor of Texas Province. Now Gertrudis' mother was First Lady and Gertrudis her able assistant. But where was all the gaiety? Ignacio was "the hard riding militant Don who made upholding allegiance to Spain his life's work."

Gertrudis watched in sorrow when the 1819 serious flood drove many families to La Villita, and filled in her time aiding these refugees. And in 1820 Moses Austin petitioned the Governor for a permit to settle families in Texas. The population of the whole Province, not including Indians, was about four thousand.

Came 1821. The Royalists had to accept the heart-crushing fact of Spain's defeat and Mexico's sovereignty over Texas. Ignacio had done his best. His reason for living was gone.

His burial record reads: "On the 7th of October, 1823, I . . . gave ecclesiastic burial in the Chapel of the Immaculate Conception of the parish church of this city, to the corpse of the Lieutenant Colonel Don Ignacio Perez. He left his widow, Donna Clemencia Hernandez . . . three grown children . . . two women and a man. He made a last Will. He received the Holy Sacraments and died of diarrhea. His funeral was large, with Mass, and the Office of the Dead and Responsory in his home, with an attendance of five corps" Signed: Br. Francisco Maynes.

Gertrudis' mother found life most difficult without her husband of forty-two years, and in 1825, at age sixty, she died of dropsy, and was buried near Ignacio. Her death record, signed by Refugio de la Garza, contains a revealing statement, "She made a Will. She left no other pious legacy than the required donation."

By her father's will, Gertrudis inherited the old Perez homestead, where she now made her home. Here she had first met Antonio Cordero, and here a second romance began when she met the widower Jose Cassiano, three years her senior. He was openly sympathetic with, and very generous to, the movement for independence from Mexico.

Gertrudis had been a widow for sixteen years, was thirty-six years old. Her mother had been dead less than ten months when she married Cassiano.

Their marriage record reads, in part: ". . . on April 12, 1826, after the publication of the banns of marriage, and the celebration in this Cathedral (San Fernando) of the usual Religious Ceremonies: were married . . . Don Jose Cassiano, native of Genoa (Italy), with Donna Gertrudis Perez, widow from her first marriage, of the Governor Don Antonio Cordero y Bustamenta, native of this city. . . ."

The Cassianos lived in the Perez homestead (though Jose had a home in another part of San Antonio) and there in a "west room" their only child, a son, was born. His baptismal certificate says, "In the city of San Fernando de Bejar on November 23, 1828, Br. D. Francisco Maynes . . . solemnly baptized" (and confirmed?) "Jose Ignacio Clemente, eight days old, legitimate son of D. Jose Cassiano and of Da. Gertrudis Perez. His godparents were D. Francisco Flores and Da. Maria Josefa Montes, whom he advised about their responsibilities and spiritual relationship. . . ."

Signed, Refugio de la Garza

Life began anew for Gertrudis with a devoted husband and a little Ignacio to care for, in her beloved home. With her inheritance from her father and the great wealth of Cordero, added to Cassiano's vast possessions, they were easily the richest couple in the city.

Outside events no longer touched her so keenly, though she was aware when Veramendi was elected vice-governor and was favorable to the Americans, and when the Department of Texas was divided into two districts, San Antonio remaining the capital of Bexar, and Nacogdoches becoming the seat of the political chief of the eastern district.

One more joyous social event occurred in her lifetime, the 1831 marriage of Veramendi's daughter to James Bowie, brother of Resin Bowie, inventor of the "Bowie Knife." This was also the centennial year of the arrival of the Canary Islanders. On March 9, each year, a Requiem Mass was said for them.

The next year Gertrudis died. "In the city of San Fernando de Bexar, on the 29th of September, 1832, I . . . D. Refugio de la Garza, Pastor of this city, gave ecclesiastical burial, in a large opening (crack or breach) in one of the chapels of this parish church, to the corpse of Da. Maria Gertrudis Perez, who left as widower, D. Jose Cassiano. She made a Will. She left nothing for pious works; she received the holy sacraments and died of dropsy at forty-two years of age.—And in order that this may be official, I sign it.

Refugio de la Garza"

A handsome tablet erected to her memory gave evidence that she was buried "near the altar."

ADDENDA

RE: The curious statement in Gertrudis' and her mother's burial record about "no legacies for pious works" ought not be passed over without comment. These were religiously oriented women, both of considerable wealth. It seems to be the only way left to them to show their distaste for the political regime without bringing penalties on their survivors, to make sure that none of their assets ever, however indirectly, reached the coffers of the Mexican government.

Gertrudis' son, not yet four years old, acquired a stepmother the next year, and when she died at age thirty and he was thirteen, acquired, briefly, a second stepmother. He grew to honorable manhood, married, had nine children, and as late as 1936, his and Gertrudis' descendants were still living in San Antonio—no longer "pure Spanish," but splendid examples of the American melting pot.

Fannie Baker Darden

Fannie Baker Darden
(1829-1890)

By Jeanette Hastedt Flachmeier*

Fannie Baker was born on September 13, 1829, at the plantation home of her parents, Mosley and Elisa Baker, at Montgomery, Alabama. In 1832 Mosley Baker, an attorney, came to Texas, participated in the independence movement, and served as a general at the Battle of San Jacinto. In the spring of 1837, he brought his family to Texas. To seven-year-old Fannie, Texas was

> then an almost unknown country, a far away foreign land. The Stars and Stripes did not wave there, but a strange insignia, an isolated star twinkled in feeble light above it.

The Bakers came from New Orleans on the brig *Eldora* through two severe storms. After a voyage of eleven days, they landed on Galveston Island, the water being too shallow for the ship to reach the mainland. In a letter to a friend, Fannie who had been very seasick wrote

> How beautiful Galveston looked lying amid the blue waves as we approached it in the yawl!

According to Fannie, a house on the east end of the island served as headquarters for the officers in charge. There were a number of tents nearby filled with Mexican prisoners of war about to be returned to Mexico. When Fannie showed her fear of the large number of Mexicans, Colonel Morehead tried to reassure

---

* Former Staff Writer, *Handbook of Texas*

her by saying they had no arms. However, Fannie had seen a statue of an armless woman and could not be deceived. She told the Colonel he must be mistaken; for she could plainly see their arms. He took her away then to the beach where she could run "to and fro . . . gathering shells or chasing the retiring waves" in this fairy land of her dreams, Texas.

The Bakers journeyed in a small boat toward Houston. Fannie spoke of the joy of sailing in a small craft, "the dancing waves, the dim gray outline of the mainland as we approached." They spent the first night at Spillman's Island in a one room house curtained off into apartments. Early the next morning they continued their journey "alternately sailing and rowing." Night found them at Patterson's, a few miles from Harrisburg. The next morning the passengers continued on their way.

They landed at San Jacinto battlefield where her father had distinguished himself by his courage and daring. Fannie described it as a field

> where so lately had been done such valorous deeds with such glorious results. . . . My mother led me to the seven graves of the Texans killed in that memorable conflict. The earth was still fresh above them. They seemed so peacefully lying there in the soft mist of the spring morning, with the grass gently waving around them, interspersed with innumerable flowers, while the gleaming waters swept in hushed silence at their feet. It seemed hard to realize that one year before this silence had been broken by the turmoil of battle: by the shouts of victory and the groans of agony and despair.

After a few days in Harrisburg, the family continued their journey to Houston on the steamboat *Laura*. Although the boat was small, it had a hard time getting through the narrow and winding waters of the bayou underneath overhanging branches. One of these would have brushed Fannie overboard had her father not quickly pulled her out of the way. Arriving at Houston at night, they were given shelter in General Houston's log cabin. A large number of people lived in the area of Houston at that time. Many lived in tents, in shanties, and in the shade of the strong oak trees.

Fannie's first home in Texas was on the east shore of Galveston Bay where her father had a league of land. The Bakers lived in Galveston in the summer and in Houston the rest of the year. According to Fannie's description, the house in Houston had "five rooms, built of poles and clapboards . . . comfortably

furnished and carpeted plus a limb-covered shed for a kitchen."
Describing life in the house, she said:

> The four grown servants whom we had were kept busy waiting upon
> and providing *cuisine* for the numerous guests with which it was always
> filled, for in those days Texas hospitality was a proverb. . . . The table
> glistened with cut glass, china, and silverware.

Fannie especially recalled the beautiful cut glass pitcher that General Houston lent her mother to use until he married.

In the summer of 1838 her sister, Eliza, was born and reported to be the first white child born on Galveston Island. As a girl Fannie enjoyed singing and listening to her mother play the piano (the only piano in Houston then). One evening in 1837 while her mother played with Fannie at her side, Indian men, women and children appeared in the doorway and at the windows. Fannie uttered a cry of alarm at the sight but her mother calmly arose and went toward the visitors. They gestured for her to continue playing, saying, *"Baba Sheelah!"* Mrs. Baker played as the Indians stood entranced by the music, giving every sign of delight until they departed.

Since Mr. Baker was both a lawyer and a planter, his family enjoyed the many advantages of the growing city of Houston. There were church services conducted on Sundays in the Hall of the House of Representatives by the Presbyterian Chaplain McCullough for a large number of people of all classes. The same hall was used for dances, such as the San Jacinto Ball.

Fannie described one of these balls:

> I shall ever take a pardonable pride in my first escort to a ball. This was
> Gen. Houston. . . . Taking me by the hand, we proceeded to the ball
> room in company with my parents. . . . The ladies were handsomely
> attired in satins and lace, while Gen. Houston wore a magnificent suit of
> black silk velvet, and a black beaver hat surmounted by long black
> plumes of ostrich feathers . . . I was elated . . . and in my childish delight
> cried out: "I've got the finest dressed man in the crowd!"

When her opportunity came to dance, she did so with all the energy of her being and wondered how proud and happy her black childhood teachers, Betsy and Rhody, would have been at seeing her.

Since Houston did not have adequate schools, in 1842 the Bakers returned to Alabama by way of Houston and New Orleans. Fannie remained there in school until the spring of 1846 when she came back to Texas. The Lone Star flag had been replaced by the Stars and Stripes of the United States.

On January 26, 1847, Fannie married William J. Darden, an attorney, who had come to Texas from Norfolk, Virginia. In the summer of 1852 or 1853, the couple moved to Columbus, Texas, where he practiced law. In 1857 when the Colorado College, the first Lutheran college in Texas, opened, Fannie taught art there. During the War Between the States, William served as a Captain in Hood's Texas Brigade. He died in 1881 and was buried in Columbus Cemetery.

One of Fannie Darden's sons lost his life in the Galveston flood of 1900 and somewhat later the other one died in Columbus of typhoid fever. As family duties lightened, Fannie devoted more time to painting and writing both stories and poetry. She continued to live in Columbus until her death in October, 1890.

Fannie Baker Darden was an artist well known in Columbus, Houston, Fort Worth, Dallas, and other Texas towns. She not only taught painting but also painted for her own enjoyment. Many of her pictures had religious themes. One of her oil paintings, "The Good Shepherd" is in St. John's Episcopal Church in Columbus.

In the diary which she kept for many years, Fannie wrote that for $1,000 and a Negro man she had acquired a whole block of land across the street from the present Oaks Theatre on Walnut Street on which the present home of the E. R. Irwin family is located. She also told about "the hire" of slaves for a year for the Columbus property, valued at $2,800.

In the diary she complained that wages were very high, such as:

> $2.85 to a man for cutting wood and trimming trees; $1.00 for her washing; $1.50 for stove wood; 5 cents for work in helping around the place; 25 cents for a chicken to bake; and 5 cents for Episcopal Aid dues.

She thought grocery prices also were high, for she wrote that a month's grocery bill at the Wagner Grocery Store was $5.75. The reason for the high bill was that she had bought sugar for preserving and vinegar for making pickles. In her opinion, taxes were high for she had to pay

> $3.00 in taxes for lots in Allen survey in Houston; $7.00 on 320 acres in Parker Co. and $9 on property in Columbus on January 19, 1885.

Fannie wrote interesting news items about persons in Columbus.

Mrs. Fannie Mahon (Mrs. Felix Mahon) had a son born March 1, 1885; a hailstorm May 21 tore down part of Mrs. West's concrete wall and killed Mrs. Mahon's cow; Willie Mathis married on January 26 in the Methodist Church; India Green married Mar. 12, 1885 (Miss Green's husband was John Duncan).

Among her writings were novelettes, series of stories and poems as well as articles for the local paper, *The Colorado Citizen*, *The Houston Telegraph*, *Texas Siftings* of Austin, *Texas Prairie Flower* of Corsicana and northern periodicals. The subjects of some of her extant articles suggest their variety: "Only a Trip to Houston" and "Over the Sunset Route" dealt with her personal experiences; "Dillard Cooper" gave an account of Cooper's escape with three companions from the Goliad Massacre; and "Extracts from the Manuscript of Mosley Baker" edited from father's papers. Her best prose writings were *Reminiscences of Childhood* and *Romances of the Texas Revolution*.

Fannie's poems were published in Samuel H. Dixon's *Poets and Poetry of Texas*, in David W. Eagleton's *Writers and Writing of Texas*, and in Ella H. Steuart's *Gems from a Texas Quarry*. The esteem in which her work was held by the editors of the time is indicated by their comments. Ida Raymond in *Living Female Writers of the South* puts Mrs. Darden the "first of our Texas authors," and Die Rivers in *Views of Southern Literature* wrote:

> As a Southern author, Mrs. Darden deserves special mention. Her productions are of the highest type of art, and compare in beauty of conception and design with the Southern *literati* in general.

Fannie Baker Darden was called the poet laureate of Columbus as she wrote many of her poems from her Columbus home. She wrote a poem for the newsboy who delivered the *Colorado Citizen*. He used the poem each New Year's Day in hopes of a monetary reward for his services.

An example of her writing is a short poem about her birthplace, "Cedar Grove" in Alabama:

CEDAR GROVE

Under the cedars a babe was born,
Just at the break of a Sunday morn,
Out of the struggling dark and gloom,
The light, and the babe to the world had come,
Under the waving cedars.

Under the cedars the infant grew,
Waked with the morn, and slept with the dew,

Grew with the flowers in the trembling light
That streamed through boughs from skies ever bright,
Gleaming through the shadowy cedars.

But a dark day came when the years had sped,
When the summer bright with the South wind fled,
And the wintry winds through the branches wild,
Bitterly swept 'round the weeping child,
Weeping beneath the cedars.

'Twas the hour of parting, the hour of tears,
Typing the unborn, sorrowing years
That came to her in a distant land,
Where the ocean swept 'round a sunny strand,
Afar from the waving cedars.

Hannah Elizabeth Denny (1807-1903)

By Evelyn M. Carrington *

Hannah Elizabeth lived almost a century, experiencing life in the South and the Southwest, living through the Texas Revolution and three wars, and seeing raw country develop into small, thriving communities. Her life was a happy one although filled with adversities that tried her strength.

Hannah Elizabeth Hall was born on the high seas a week before Christmas in 1807. Her widowed mother was on her way across the Atlantic Ocean to make her home with her sister in Charleston, South Carolina. This aunt and an Indian nurse, Ma-Katy, reared Hannah Elizabeth after her mother's early death.

Charleston had been settled in 1670 by the English under William Sayle. Surviving Spanish and Indian threats and fighting during the American Revolution, Charleston became a seaport and cultural center. In lovely Charleston, young Hannah Elizabeth grew into a young woman, married a Captain Robinson, and by him had two children: Charlotte Elizabeth and Eleanor Zepherina. On August 6, 1828, Hannah Elizabeth married William Gowdey Denny, her first husband having died. They had four children: Charles William who died in infancy; William Charles who died unmarried; Charles Adolphus who married twice; and Mary Ellen who was born when Hannah Elizabeth was forty years old.

In May, 1834, the Denny family and the two Robinson

---

* Great-granddaughter

Top: Mr. and Mrs. W. L. Carrington (grandson and wife).

Bottom: Hannah Elizabeth Denny, 93 years old, Evelyn and Gladys Carrington (great-granddaughters), Ellen Denny Carrington (daughter)

daughters went by ship to New Orleans. They took their Waterford glass, etched hurricane globes, plantation-made furniture, fine linens and silver with them as well as their other belongings. The family stayed in New Orleans briefly. During the Texas Revolution, William G. Denny became Colonel Thomas Toby's agent and assisted in furnishing the Texas Army with war supplies.

The Dennys received a land grant of 640 acres by virtue of Certificate No. 856, dated December 21, 1839, and given by the Land Commissioners of Galveston County. This grant stated that William G. Denny and his family had resided in the Republic and State of Texas over three years and had performed all the duties required of him as a citizen. The grant was filed May 7, 1847, at the City of Galveston.

The family took up residence on the west end of Galveston Island. They owned a large dairy and knew the Bordens. The west end of the Island was undeveloped and alligators were said not to be uncommon. Tales are told about tying ropes to Negro children who sat on the banks of the bayous. When the presence of the child attracted an alligator, the child was pulled out of danger by the ropes, the alligator was killed, and certain portions of the reptile was used for food.

Fastidious Hannah Elizabeth, wearing her long skirt, fitted basque, and high heeled shoes, disliked sandy Galveston with its few trees and the houses built on stilts. In 1837 a tropical storm had turned the frame houses to mere shells or washed them away. It was not until 1838 that a real foundation for Galveston was laid. Progress was slow until steam connections were made with New Orleans.

The isolation of the Island, the lack of gracious living, and the death of Eleanor Robinson in adolescence added to the family's unhappiness. A bright spot was the marriage of Charlotte Robinson to James Powell Sherwood, a descendant from an old Maryland family and himself a shipbuilder. After meeting General Sam Houston in New Orleans, James Sherwood had come to Texas to outfit the Texas Navy.

During these difficult years, Hannah Elizabeth "ate not the bread of idleness." She rose early and worked late to supply food and clothing for her family and household. She saw that a flower garden was planted, shared her wisdom and religion with her children, gave prestige to her husband, and helped the poor and needy. Some way or other, she found time even to do fine handwork.

On January 30, 1841, President David G. Burnet authorized the establishment of the Galveston Artillery Company, a Volunteer Company in the City of Galveston, to consist of not more than a hundred or less than thirty-two men. The duty of the Company was to protect the Harbor and City of Galveston subject to the order of the Mayor, to suppress riots, and enforce the administration of the laws. The Company was not liable to any draft of the Republic by which it could be called from the Island except in an emergency and was exempt from military duty except such as mentioned in the Charter. Of this Company, John Howe was Captain; A. C. Crawford, 1st Lieutenant; L. E. Nordmai, 2nd Lieutenant; and William G. Denny, one of the Sergeants and the Secretary of the Company.

William G. Denny was a fine looking man, warm in friendship, and strong in affection for his family. He was methodical in his business habits and his courteous bearing and kindly disposition won him the respect and esteem of those with whom he was thrown in contact.

Neither William nor Hannah Elizabeth Denny wished to stay longer in Galveston and in 1849, the Denny family moved to Bastrop. As early as 1824 Bastrop had a permanent settlement. The town was named in honor of Felipe Enrique Neri, Baron de Bastrop, who saw that Austin's petition to the Mexican Government, asking permission to colonize three hundred families in Texas, was forwarded to the proper authorities.

Bastrop, located picturesquely on the Colorado River, had trees, good soil, and attractive houses built by such citizens as Marcelle Triplett, Mayor A. M. Brooks, and Colonel Washington Jones. East of the city were pine forests known as the "Lost Pines" because they are about ninety miles away from the main pine belt in Texas. Bastrop had a drugstore, established in 1847. There was talk also of establishing a Bastrop Academy.

The years in Bastrop went quickly. Mary Ellen, the little daughter born in 1848 in Houston, added much pleasure to the life of the family. In September, 1853, under the preaching of the Reverend I. G. John, William G. Denny was converted and joined the Methodist Church at Bastrop in which he was a consistent worker and a faithful steward. The eldest son of the family, William Charles Denny, went to California during the gold rush and, after prospecting unsuccessfully for several years, returned to Texas.

In 1851 William G. Denny became secretary for Risher,

Sawyer, and Hall, owners of one of the largest stage lines in the great Southwest. He remained with the company until it disbanded about 1880. During the Civil War, William G. Denny was named postmaster at Bastrop by Postmaster General John H. Reagan, Confederate States of America.

When Galveston was bombarded by Union gunboats during the Civil War, Mr. Sherwood sent his wife, the former Charlotte Robinson, and their children by stage coach to Bastrop. Mrs. Sherwood and her children stayed with the Dennys in Bastrop and Austin for the duration of the War.

During the Civil War, there were many deprivations. One fall when her grandsons needed new suits, Hannah Elizabeth had only a bolt of bed ticking from which to fashion these. She sent the boys to gather huckleberries. Using the berries, she dyed the material. Then she cut and sewed the suits.

Confederate money gradually lost all of its value. At the close of the War, for several months Texas was without any real civil government. General Gordon Granger came to Galveston on June 19, 1865, declared martial law, and emancipated the slaves. This was followed by Carpetbag Rule which continued until January 15, 1874, when a new era under Governor Richard Coke arrived.

The Dennys moved from Bastrop to Austin in 1865. Their Waterford glasses and compotes, etched hurricane globes, plantation-made furniture, fine linens and silver as well as their other belongings that had been moved to Bastrop from Galveston in oxcarts again were packed and again carried in oxcarts this time to Austin.

Austin was designated the capital of Texas in 1840. Formerly known as Waterloo and then named for the Father of Texas, Austin was located on the north bank of the Colorado River. The city had bright blue skies flecked with cumulus clouds, green hills to the northwest, groups of trees, many wild flowers and shrubs, and much native charm. In spite of the pressure of the times, citizens had erected private mansions and business houses.

The Dennys lived at Lavaca and Eighth Streets. Their home was a favorite meeting place of the legislators and there many political issues were discussed. Among the Dennys' closest friends were Colonel R. S. Shipley and his wife, Fannie. Colonel Shipley was stationed at the Headquarters of the United States Army Fifth Military District located at East Fifth and Red River Streets from 1868 until 1870 when Headquarters were moved to San Antonio.

The Dennys were among the first people in Austin to receive northerners in their home as guests.

On the evening of March 23, 1867, Mr. and Mrs. Denny gave a formal announcement party for Mary Ellen's approaching marriage to Robert Emmett Carrington who had served as a Lieutenant in Baylor's Regiment, C.S.A. R. E. Carrington, at the time of his marriage, was associated with his father, Captain Leonidas Davis Carrington, in a flourishing mercantile establishment. The large cut rock house of L. D. Carrington, located at 1501 Colorado Street, still stands and is marked as a historic monument.

Until 1880 William G. Denny was a familiar figure in Austin and to miss him from the stage office was enough to provoke comment. When he was seventy-four years old, William and Hannah Elizabeth Denny went to live with R. E. and Ellen Denny Carrington at 1108 Neches Street. In 1888 the State Capitol was dedicated. The following year William G. Denny became blind and his health failed rapidly. On January 10, 1891, he died and was buried in Oakwood Cemetery in Austin.

Hannah Elizabeth met the death of her husband of more than sixty-two years and the death of her elder son, William Charles Denny, on January 14, 1895, with fortitude. On September 9, 1900, nine of her grandchildren and great-grandchildren, descendants of Charlotte and James Sherwood, were drowned in Galveston during a hurricane and flood. This storm produced one of the greatest disasters in history.

Hannah Elizabeth suddenly was old. Toward the end of her ninety-fifth year, her mind reverted to her childhood in Charleston, her Indian nurse called Ma-Katy, the panthers and the other wild creatures that once preyed upon the people of Charleston, and friends of her youth. Even up to the time of her death, Hannah Elizabeth Denny was fastidious in her dress, observant of the social amenities of the early parts of the 19th Century, and devoted to her daughter, Ellen Carrington, and Ellen's children and grandchildren.

Hannah Elizabeth died December 16, 1903, two days before her ninety-sixth birthday and was buried beside her husband in Oakwood Cemetery in Austin, Texas.

Although a small woman, Hannah Elizabeth Denny was never bewildered nor uncertain in a crisis. Her husband knew well her wisdom and strength and her integrity. Her family never doubted her concern and love.

Susanna Wilkerson Dickinson (1814-1883)

By Willard Griffith Nitschke*

Deep in the Blue Grass country of Hardeman County, at Bolivar, Tennessee, Susanna Wilkerson was born in 1814. When Susanna was fifteen years old, she married Almeron Dickinson whose family had good standing in the County as shown by tax records for land, slaves, and other properties.

The Dickinson family had come into Tennessee from Pennsylvania where Almeron was born in 1810. Almeron had joined the U.S. Army and served for a time. After his enlistment ended, he came to Hardeman County, Tennessee, where he farmed a few years before his marriage and subsequent migration to Texas.

The marriage license was issued by Thomas J. Hardeman, Clerk of Hardeman County, Tennessee, on May 24, 1829. On the same day the wedding took place with Joseph W. McKean, Justice of Peace, officiating.

It is said that when Susanna and Almeron had a lover's quarrel, Almeron began courting one of Susanna's friends. The two planned marriage with Susanna as a bridesmaid. Shortly before the wedding took place, Susanna and Almeron ran away, were married, and made plans to migrate to Texas.

Almeron and Susanna may have arrived in Texas earlier than 1831, but there is absolute proof of residence in Gonzales as early as February 20, 1831. A petition for a Mexican headright is

---

*Great-granddaughter

Susanna Wilkerson Dickinson

on file in the State Land Office, which translated from the Spanish, stated in part that Almeron Dickinson, a citizen of the United States, had appeared in person and swore that he was one of those admitted by Empresario Green DeWitt to settle in his colony, that he was married, and entitled to petition for a grant of a headright of land. The document locates the land to the northeast of the San Marcos River and the old Bexar Road. It was signed clearly and distinctly "Almeron Dickinson . . . Villa de Gonzales on the 4th of May, 1831." He received one league of land in DeWitt's Colony in what is now Caldwell County, May 4, 1831.

Perhaps the newly-wedded couple had come the favorite route into Texas, from Memphis by boat down the Mississippi to New Orleans and from there to a coastal station at the mouth of the Lavaca River. From the Lavaca station the early settlers usually traveled on foot up the Lavaca to Gonzales.

In 1827 Gonzales had started to flourish and the townspeople together with new settlers erected blockhouses and a small fort for refuge in case there were an Indian attack. The pioneers of DeWitt's Colony were the only settlers west of the Colorado. Their nearest neighbors were one hundred miles away. The 1828 Census listed seventy-five men, women, and children.

According to Noah Smithwick, in 1827 the settlers had meager supplies (honey, dried venison, and other game). Great were their hardships, privations, and dangers. The dull monotony of the lives of the people was even greater. Their mode of travel made it impossible for the early immigrants to bring spinning wheels, looms, domestic animals, books, or any of the refinements of home and community. Newcomers were always welcomed and given the best that DeWitt could offer: venison, hot bread, and coffee.

Being born of second generations of pioneers, Almeron and Susanna settled down to frontier life. Almeron set up a gunsmith shop and Susanna planned for a new arrival in the family. From a family Bible record, little Angelina came as an early Christmas gift, being born in Gonzales on December 15, 1834.

During this same year, 1834, forces were moving Texas closer to Revolution. Santa Anna had become dictator of Mexico, the Mexican Congress dissolved the states' legislatures, Texas fell under military rule, militias were ordered to be reduced, and the Zacatecas had been slaughtered for failure to follow Santa Anna's commands.

Ugartecha, Mexican commander at Bexar, demanded that the people of Gonzales surrender the small brass cannon given the Texans for protection against the Indians. They refused and challenged the Mexicans "to come and take it." The cannon was fired and thus Gonzales became the Lexington of Texas, having fired the first shots of the Texas Revolution.

Almeron Dickinson was one of the Gonzales men who fired the little brass cannon. While he was in the U.S. Army, Almeron had gained knowledge of firearms and artillery. Later the knowledge gained him the attention of Colonel Travis and caused Almeron to be elected First Lieutenant of Artillery by the General Council of the Provisional Government of Texas.

Santa Anna with a large force crossed the Rio Grande on his way to capture San Antonio. The Mexican population of San Antonio became very excited and many families began to move to rural areas. On February 21, 1836, an advance regiment attacked San Antonio and drove the Texans into the Alamo. Almeron Dickinson went to the home of the Don Ramon Musquiz family and took Susanna and Angelina into the Alamo.

Shortly afterward, the siege of the Alamo started. The heroic defense is so well known it need not be retold.

Morphis in his *History of Texas* recounts Susanna's story of the Fall of the Alamo.

> The struggle had lasted more than two hours when my husband rushed into the church where I was with my child, and exclaimed: 'Great God, Sue, the Mexicans are inside our walls! All is lost! If they spare you, save my child!'
> Then, with a parting kiss, he drew his sword and plunged into the strife then raging in different portions of the fortifications.

She added that three unarmed gunners who had abandoned their then useless guns came where she was. She saw them shot down. One was tossed in the air by the Mexicans with their bayonets and then shot. A Mexican officer, General Alamonte, came into the room and asked Susanna whether she was Mrs. Dickinson. When she answered in the affirmative, he added: "If you wish to save your life, follow me." She, carrying Angelina, went and, although shot at, was spared. She spoke of the dead and dying lying about the Alamo, and the horror of the battle that she wished to forget as much as possible.

Released by General Santa Anna, Susanna was sent to Gonzales on a pony to deliver a letter written by General Santa Anna to citizens of that town.

John Bruno and his wife, Sarah Nash Bruno, had moved near to Gonzales where they were living in 1836 on some 1280 acres of land. About 9 o'clock one night in March they were awakened by Mrs. Dickinson, her baby in her arms, and a Negro servant of the late Colonel Travis. Mr. Bruno was surprised to see a lone woman with a baby. The Negro had not followed her to the house but kept in the woods for protection.

The first words that Mrs. Dickinson spoke were those bringing news of the fall of the Alamo. She told how the defenders had died to the last man and how General Alamonte had taken her and her baby to the Musquiz home. Santa Anna ordered three Mexican guards to take her and the child to the third picket line. She was told to proceed along that same "beef" trail until she came to the first house. This house was the home of John and Sarah Bruno.

In a few days Mrs. Dickinson continued her journey to Gonzales. The letter she had carried suggested that the adventurous Texans who had caused the rebellion were to be punished but Texans who obeyed the laws had nothing to fear and should return to their homes.

A few days later Colonel J. W. Fannin's command was executed after surrender, at Goliad by order of Santa Anna. This massacre along with Mrs. Dickinson's story, General Houston's retreat, the removal of the seat of government from Washington to Harrisburg, and the onward march of the Mexicans under General Sesma left the people terror-stricken. Men and boys joined the army. Women and children were left alone. It seemed safer for all to go eastward. The roads were thronged with wagons, oxcarts, horses, and even cows loaded with women, children, and household goods. Many colonists were on foot. Mrs. Bruno said that Mrs. Dickinson with Angelina went with them in an oxcart that took them to East Texas. The Brunos went to Mrs. Bruno's old home at Nash Creek but no one recalled whether Mrs. Dickinson went with them or not.

After Santa Anna was defeated at the Battle of San Jacinto and the Mexican armies withdrew from Texas, most of the settlers returned to their homes. Some five weeks later Susanna and Angelina went to Houston where they had help from Pamela Mann. Mrs. Mann ran a rooming house known as Mansion House. She had a bad reputation as did her Mansion House.

Susanna was penniless. She could scarcely read or write, and there were no jobs for a woman except to keep roomers and take in washing. So utterly alone except for Angelina, she soon entered into a series of marriages to get the security that all human beings desire.

In 1838 she married Francis P. Herring in Houston. They were divorced within a few years and she was again married. This time she married Peter Bellis. Evidently he did not support her for she continued to run a boarding house and do washing for the boarders. Being high-spirited and determined, she parted company with Peter Bellis. He later accused her of leaving him to run a disreputable rooming house.

Susanna had joined the congregation of Rufus Burleson who had a large following in Houston where he was holding a revival during the summer of 1849. Burleson says in his *Memoirs* that Susanna was converted during this revival and aided him in his every good work. But still the gossipers were at work and some of the congregation objected to having Susanna attend as a member of the church. Burleson defended Susanna, but she withdrew from the church of her own accord in consideration of her "preacher."

Susanna was having trouble other than marital ones. Angelina had grown up in an environment where she had received much attention and apparently little discipline. She was a pretty, black-haired, blue-eyed young lady with a will of her own that was bent on the pleasures of life.

Susanna selected John Maynard Griffith as a husband for Angelina. He was a farmer and steamboat captain from Montgomery County, East Texas, about sixty-five miles from Houston. John M. Griffith stayed at Susanna's boarding house while in Houston. He was older than Angelina and was strict in his ideas of morality and religion.

The Reverend Rufus Burleson performed the marriage ceremony of John and Angelina on June 8, 1851, in Houston. He is said to have remarked afterwards, "When people marry where they do not love, they are apt to love where they have not married." Angelina made a prophet out of the preacher.

Angelina lived five years as a farmer's wife. She mothered a girl and two boys, slighting her plodding husband by naming them all after her kin. Her children were Almeron Dickinson Griffith (1853), Susanna Griffith (1855), and Joseph Griffith (1857). The last child named for J. W. Hannig was born shortly before the grandmother, Susanna Dickinson, was married to Mr. Hannig in Lockhart, Texas.

At the Cypress "blow out," John Maynard Griffith lost his patience with Angelina and the homeward trip was a nightmare for Angelina. With aching head and sore feet, she listened to her husband pound at the evils of drinking and dancing. They were divorced soon afterwards. Of the three children who were left in Montgomery County, the oldest (Almeron Dickinson) was taken by his uncle, Joshua Griffith, until he was old enough to make his own way. The two younger children were taken by Grandmother, Susanna Dickinson Herring Bellis Hannig.

Angelina had placed the two children in a convent in New Orleans where they stayed until taken by Susanna. With her, they stayed in Austin until Susie was old enough to marry and Joseph was old enough to make his way. The brightest lights nearby in those days belonged to New Orleans. Angelina felt she belonged with them. Her mother finally found her and pleaded with Angelina to return. Angelina found herself a husband, too, an individual known only as Mr. Holmes. From this marriage, one child, Sallie, was born.

Because of litigation, Susanna Dickinson sold the large tract of land near Lockhart for $2,500 or 50 cents an acres, which at the time was a large sum, and by frugal living she managed. City lots were sold to Frank Hannig whose descendants still own them. The small, unpretentious home of Mrs. Dickinson stood in Lockhart until a few years ago when it was moved off of the original location to another. Business had encroached on the land.

In 1857 Susanna was married to Joseph W. Hannig in Lockhart. They moved to Austin and Mr. Hannig opened a furniture and cabinet shop at 205 East Pecan. The first City Directory listed their residence as Pine Street (5th Street) between what is now Neches and Red River. This home is still standing and though occupied by Randy's Barbecue, the main part of the cottage is still there.

Charles W. Evers, a journalist of northern Ohio, reported to his newspaper that Susanna Dickinson Hannig was living in the 70's in comfortable circumstances at the corner of Duval and East 32nd Street. Although not far from sixty years of age, she readily spoke of that dark episode in her history which robbed her of her husband and partially of her reason for a time. She stated that through all those eventful thirteen days preceding the final, bloody culmination, she helped care for the sick and the wounded.

In 1870 my father, Almeron Dickinson Griffith, visited Susanna and found her enjoying the luxuries that wealth can provide. Her house at the corner of Duval and 32nd Streets, faced toward Waller Creek. The house was large, comfortable, and well furnished. It had a wide veranda on the east side. Susanna had many servants some of whom were German girls who became her friends and cared for her in her last illnesses.

Mr. Hannig was one of the wealthiest men in Austin, friendly, concerned in civic improvements, and a good husband. Susanna was an excellent cook, reared her grandchildren and helped to educate them in Catholic schools and convents, enjoyed concerts at Presslar's Gardens in the evenings, attended church functions, participated in social affairs such as inaugural balls, and made a good home for her husband and his friends.

In 1872, Susanna gave her husband complete control of all property and signed papers giving Eugene Bremond the power of attorney in case of Hannig's death. All property was to belong to J. W. Hannig to dispose of by will as he pleased.

On Sunday, October 8, 1883, Susanna died. A memorial in the paper recited her place in Texas history and expressed the hope that she would be buried in the State Cemetery. However, she was buried in Oakwood Cemetery and later her husband was laid to rest by her side.

Annie Dunlavy Dorbandt (1831-1907)

By Willie Mae Smith Price[*]

Annie (Dunlavy, Dunlevy, Dunlathy) Dorbandt was best known as the mother to a noted family of fourteen children. She quite naturally filled the place of leadership, courage, and love that was required of the pioneer woman.

Annie Dunlavy, a native of Lathman, County Cork, Ireland, was born February 6, 1831. We do not know the circumstance of her coming to the United States but in the early 1850's she was in New Orleans, Louisiana, visiting her uncle who was a cotton buyer. On this visit she met a young man, Christian Dorbandt, a native of Husdslub, Denmark, who was in the United States Army.

Christian Dorbandt came to the United States in 1834 when he was sixteen years old. He fought in the Mexican War (1846-1847) under General Winfield Scott and received a Certificate of Merit from President James K. Polk November 25, 1848, for his courage in the Battle of Cerro Gordo.

Christian wooed and courted lovely Annie and she became his bride. The young couple lived first at Ft. Sill, Indian Territory, but were soon transferred to Ft. Croghan at Hamilton Valley (Burnet) where Christian filled the post as quartermaster sergeant.

Ft. Croghan was abandoned in 1853 and the Dorbandts, having retired from the army, moved to the rock home that they built in Blackbone Valley. The house still stands on Highway 281

---

[*]Director, Burnet County Free Library

79

Christian and Annie Dunlavy Dorbandt

between Burnet and Marble Falls. It was here on December 27, 1853, that their first child, Henrietta, was born.

When the war between the States broke out in 1861, Christian Dorbandt became a Captain in the Confederate Army. Annie was left with the responsibility of caring for their family of five children and facing undue hardships. With so many of the men folks away in the war, the Indians became a great menace in Burnet County as they did elsewhere along the frontier.

One day Annie sent her oldest son, Newton, to the mill with a sack of corn to be ground for bread. On his way home a raiding party of Indians took after him. With the help of his good horse, the boy made it to the safety of the rock house. Annie bolted the doors, quieted her frightened children and hustled them to the safest part of the house. She then kept guard with a gun while the Indians dashed around the house giving out hair-raising yells. However, they soon gave up and marched off to better hunting. It was Annie's Catholic faith that sustained her in hours like these.

The war was over and Christian returned home. The family moved to Dorbandt Gap near Smithwick. We do not know how long they lived here. However, in the early part of the 1870's Captain Dorbandt and Annie bought some land about a mile from what is now Bertram. It was on this land that a beautiful semi-colonial home was built for Annie.

The Dorbandts were instrumental in building South Gabriel, a town that sprang up a mile from their home. It was located on the Austin-Burnet road between Liberty Hill and Burnet. Three times a week a hack line from Liberty Hill to Burnet passed through the village. In 1880 South Gabriel had a population of thirty-nine.

The South Gabriel Creek, from which the village was named, had water for the settlers and their livestock and hunting along its bottoms. There were many trees, plenty of good grass, and good soil for farming.

The settlement was first called Lewiston in honor of Thomas Lewiston who was postmaster and kept the store. After he moved away, the village was called South Gabriel. Annie and Christian, along with Lewiston, bought three and a quarter acres of land on September 5, 1872, on which they built a gin. In 1872 Annie and Christian also bought one and one-quarter acres from James G. Connell and built a saloon, which was closed in 1878 because the villagers in an election voted South Gabriel dry.

Annie bore and reared fourteen children: Henrietta (1853), Newton G. (1855), Christian, Jr. (1857), Rose Ellen (1858), Louis W. (1860), Jefferson Davis (1862), Robert Lee, known as Andy (1865), Nannie Jane (1867), Emma (1869), Thomas C. Moor (1871), Charles Henry (1872), William Edward (1874), who died less than a year old, James R. (1876), and Seth Shepard (1878).

After seeing thirteen of her children reach adulthood, she reared three of her grandchildren and kept still others and sent them to school at Bertram. Judge Dorbandt recalls the year that he spent with his grandparents and went to school as well as the disciplinary measures that his grandfather used in making sure that each night shoes were cleaned, polished, and lined up in rows ready for the next day's rush to school. He assumed this was a carry-over from Christian's army days.

The village of South Gabriel was moved to a new location on the tracks of the Austin and Northwestern Railroad in 1882. The new town was called Bertram in honor of Mr. Rudolph Bertram, a merchant of Austin.

Although many of the homes of South Gabriel were moved to the new town of Bertram, the house that was built for Annie still stands on the same ground and is well preserved. It is now known as the Edith Heusser place.

When the Dorbandts sold their property to the Heussers, they moved to Burnet where they had a successful business for several years.

Of their thirteen children who lived to adulthood, married and set up their own homes in the area, one daughter, Rose, lived to be 102 years old. Annie had many grandchildren and was proud that several of her sons and their sons served the community as tax collector, sheriff, judge, etc. One son went to California and one son and one daughter never married.

Annie died in 1907 at the age of 76 and was buried in the picturesque South Gabriel Cemetery near Bertram. The cemetery is all that remains of the once flourishing community of South Gabriel. Christian died several years later and is buried on Annie's left, an unusual arrangement. Four of their children are buried near them.

Marie Fargeix Gentilz (1830-1898)

By Catherine Meranda Goodwin*

Marie Fargeix was nineteen in that year, 1849, when she left her native Paris to go with her bridegroom, Theodore Gentilz, to his home in San Antonio, Texas. A Parisian, Theodore was an artist who had been educated at the Ecole Imperiale de Mathematiques et de Dessin. Soon after leaving school he joined Henri Castro, an empresario of the Texas Republic to work as a surveyor, artist and journalist, and in 1843 went with other French colonists, mostly Alsatians, to colonize Castro's grant of land west of San Antonio.

Henri Castro was a Frenchman born in St. Esprit to a Jewish family of Portuguese-Spanish background. They were people of wealth, prominence and distinction. In 1786 Henri Castro accompanied Napoleon I to Spain in his Guard of Honor. He helped defend Paris against invasion in 1814. In 1818 he was an officer in the Legion of Honor. In the 1820's he was appointed Consul for the Kingdom of Naples at Providence, Rhode Island.

Charmed by America or weary of French politics, Castro became a naturalized American citizen in 1827. In 1838 he returned to France as a partner of Lafitte and Company. In that capacity he met General James Hamilton with whom he tried to negotiate a loan of $5,000,000 for the young Republic of Texas. The loan was not negotiated, but Castro became interested in

---

* President of the Austin Branch, AAUW, 1971-73 when Bicentennial Book Project was begun.

Marie Fargeix Gentilz at the piano

Hamilton's immigration-promotion activities and returned with him to Texas in 1842.

Texas had recently become independent of Mexico. The emerging nation had much land but few inhabitants—40,000 persons. To attract more people, the Texas government evolved colonization projects.

Castro contracted to bring 600 families or single persons seventeen years old or over to Texas over a two-year period, later extended to three years. Each family was to receive 640 acres and each single man 320 acres. Colonists received full title only after they had built a "comfortable" cabin and kept under cultivation and fenced at least fifteen acres. Castro was to receive half the land to compensate him for bringing the families from Europe.

In addition, Castro was to receive ten sections of land for every 100 families and the same ratio for every 100 single men. Only persons of high moral character were considered. The lands granted were on the frontier west of San Antonio and on the Rio Grande in the Laredo area, claimed by Mexico and held by the Mexican Army at that time.

Castro returned to France to recruit his colonists. Officially France was uncooperative because France was trying to colonize Algiers and thought too many Frenchmen were coming to Texas. Castro's enthusiasm for his project and high hopes for a better life in Texas appealed particularly to the people of Alsace who had suffered greatly in the Franco-German Wars.

Each family, or single person, was required to have $32.00 for the voyage plus $10.00 deposit for good faith, necessary clothing, farming and other implements of labor, and money for the first year.

On November 2, 1842, the first group of 114 immigrants sailed on the *Ebro* with Captain Perry from Harve. The trip lasted 66 days ending at Galveston on New Year's Day 1843. By the end of Castro's contract, 27 ships carrying 485 families and 457 single men left the northern ports of Europe for Galveston and Port Lavaca in Texas.

Marie Fargeix Gentilz had a clear picture of Texas before she left Paris. Her husband's paintings which he had brought to sell in France showed the environment, the people and their activities. Her husband's good friend, Auguste Fretelliere, had written an entertaining description of his arrival at Galveston on the *Jean Key De Teau* December 30, 1843, after a 72-day trip from

Antwerp. He fluently described the 200-mile trip inland to San Antonio, his first view of an Indian, the Mexicans and their way of life, the gathering of the colonists at San Antonio, the trip west to the Medina River where the community was established in September, 1844, and named Castroville in honor of Henri Castro, and the first months of the colony. Many paintings and words remain today giving us the same clear view of early Texas.

Theodore Gentilz and Auguste Fretelliere had been friends since the day in 1844 when Theodore arrived in San Antonio. Auguste invited him to share his living quarters *(jacal)* on Soledad Street while they waited for Castro colonists to gather. Their similar backgrounds, ages and interests resulted in an enjoyable association for the remainder of their lives. After the first crop matured, Auguste was so discouraged with his inability to create a fortune by farming that he returned to his home in Montpellier, France.

Theodore Gentilz continued to survey Castro's land grants, laying out towns and writing for Castro's promotional work in France. In 1847 a fire burned Gentilz' Castroville home and destroyed all his papers, valuable drawings and sketches, maps, surveying instruments, books and souvenirs.

In that same year Henri Castro sent Gentilz to Europe to conduct a group of farmers to the Texas colony. Twenty-nine families came to settle a new community which was named D'Hanis honoring the Belgian merchant who provided financial support for the venture. Gentilz is credited with founding D'Hanis.

By 1848 Theodore Gentilz had finished his surveying work for Castro and moved permanently to San Antonio. He was joined there by his old friend, Auguste Fretelliere, who returned to San Antonio to establish a business. Theodore was occupied with painting a visual record of the Spanish and Mexican influences on the area. A major project was his notebook, "Missions of the Province of Texas." Included were the eight Texas missions, five of which were in San Antonio. He painted at least one picture of each mission and painted the San Antonio missions in at least three sizes and several media.

In 1849 Theodore Gentilz was thirty years old. He returned to Paris to visit his family and friends, particularly his friend and teacher, Ramon Quesada Monvoisin. While there he retrieved a sketch of the Monvoisin studio and left his Texas paintings with his relatives to be sold.

The primary reason for the trip was to marry. He married Marie Fargeix, a young woman of nineteen. When the couple returned to San Antonio, they were accompanied by Theodore's sixteen-year-old sister, Henriette. The two well-educated young women were warmly welcomed by the French community in San Antonio.

Marie and Theodore established their first studio-home at 127 North Flores Street. Later, they moved to 318 North Flores Street permanently. Marie was happy and quite at home in San Antonio. She was an accomplished musician and gave lessons in piano and voice at their home. She loved flowers and gardening which kept their dooryard a blaze of color.

In 1852 Auguste Fretelliere and Henriette Gentilz were married, drawing Theodore and Auguste even closer. The ceremony was performed at the San Fernando Church on February 7, 1852, by their Castroville pastor, Abbe Claude Dubuis, who was now Bishop Dubuis in San Antonio. Witnesses at the wedding were Messers. Guilbeau, LaCoste and Gentilz as recorded on record #701. Marie and Theodore had no children of their own and especially enjoyed the Fretelliere children: Mathilde, (b. 1853), Louise (b. 1857), Auguste (b. 1861), and Henri (b. 1864).

As the girls grew they were taught by their Uncle Theodore to draw and paint. Louise, particularly, had the Gentilz bent for painting and as an adult taught painting.

Marie Gentilz joined in these painting sessions and became a skilled painter herself. She was particularly adept at painting butterflies and other insects and flowers. Marie and Theodore produced a series of exquisite parallel flower paintings. They are now owned by the Daughters of the Republic of Texas Library at the Alamo. In addition, the DRT Library owns approximately forty flower paintings by Marie and twenty flower paintings by Theodore also unpublished.

In 1859 Bishop Claude Dubuis retired to return to France. The French community gathered for a last farewell to their beloved friend. Climaxing the evening, Marie sang a song, "Au depart de Monsieur Dubuis," which she had written for the occasion. The score and lyrics, handsomely decorated with motifs drawn from nature by Erhard Penterides, is extant.

During the War Between the States, Theodore Gentilz began teaching studio arts at St. Mary's College. He was on the faculty for thirty years until the school was relocated at the west edge of

San Antonio in 1894. In a letter written in 1958 Jack Butterfield, who was a student at St. Mary's from 1889-1894, said that he had studied oil painting with Theodore Gentilz. Several times he had the privilege of visiting in the Gentilz home. He commented that Marie Gentilz was a

> delightful little French lady, lively and vivacious. She taught music and could play wonderfully even then. Their yard was a profusion of bloom all the time.

In 1877 Marie and Theodore made a trip to Europe. In existence are a number of watercolors of European landscapes made by each of them dated 1878.

Marie was among the students in the Drawing and Painting School opened by Theodore in their studio-home in 1879. Instruction was offered in all kinds of drawing, painting, principles, of geometry followed by linear and aerial perspective especially for artists.

Marie Fargeix Gentilz died on October 20, 1898, the first of the Gentilz-Fretelliere foursome to depart. She was buried in the San Antonio City Cemetery A-1. She had made a great impact on the cultural life of San Antonio and left as gifts her music and her paintings.

Harriet Newell Gray
(1818-1889)

By Evelyn M. Carrington

Mary Winifred Grace was born in Georgia on September 29, 1818, the eldest child and only daughter of James Grace and his second wife, Mrs. Mary Richardson Bollinger, formerly of High Hills of Santee in South Carolina. Mary Richardson's family were interested in fine horses and indigo and had been of great assistance to General Francis Marion during the American Revolution.

James Grace, the son of Thomas Grace and Mrs. Mary Willoughby Williams, was born in North Carolina in 1770. James first married Leacy Mobley and by her had nine children. Later, he married Fred Bollinger's widow, Mary Richardson Bollinger, and added her four children to his nine. It was a large family into which Mary Winifred was born.

During a yellow fever epidemic in Savannah when she was quite young, Mary Winifred was separated from her parents. She was found and cared for by Mr. and Mrs. Nathaniel Williams and their daughter. The little girl wore a small locket with "Grace" engraved upon it. All efforts made to discover her identity were of no avail.

The James Graces, after the quarantine had been lifted, were told that their little girl and her nurse had died during the epidemic. Grieving, they went back to their home in Milledgeville, Georgia.

* Great-granddaughter

Harriet Newell Gray

Harriet Gray's granddaughters: Mabel, Bertha and Edith Gray

The Williams, devout Presbyterians, decided to give the child a name of her own choosing. They put the names of several Presbyterian missionaries in a hat and asked the little girl to draw one. The name thus chosen was Harriet Newell.

The Williams were people of substantial means. In their home Harriet was happy and had many educational and musical advantages. Mrs. Williams died when Harriet was fourteen years old and Mr. Williams married soon afterwards. This brought many changes into the home and Harriet no longer felt wanted. When Stephen Alfred Gray asked her to marry him, although she was only fifteen years old, she consented.

On January 2, 1834, they were married and went to Clinton, Jones County, Georgia, to live. After the birth of Stephen Alexander Gray on December 5, 1834, the Grays moved to Girard, Russell County, Alabama. Here their second son, James Byrd Gray, was born on August 26, 1836.

During the Creek Indian uprising, Harriet heard that Captain Byrd Grace had rescued women and children from the sections under attack. She wrote Captain Grace asking if his family had ever lost a little girl. He came to call and she learned that he was her half-brother and that her name had been Mary Winifred Grace.

Captain Grace also told her that he and his brother, Martin, had used their steamboats in the Indian War rescues. A third brother, John W. Grace, called Tuttaloosa Micco, meaning "King Cheekin" by the Creek Indians, had done much before his death on December 14, 1834, to placate the Indians.

Captain Byrd Grace reported his visit with Harriet to the James Graces, now of Hightown, Alabama. They immediately invited their long lost daughter, her husband, and her two little boys to visit them. There was great rejoicing. At the boat landing on the Chattahoochie River, the Grays were met with a great concourse. The slaves were given a half holiday by the overseer, Mr. Grimsley. Dressed in their best clothing, the Negroes formed a line from the landing to the house. It was as if Death himself had returned a daughter to the family. For the first time Mary Winifred, or Harriet as she preferred to be called, met her own brothers, Henry Bartlett and Willoughby Williams Grace.

After a pleasant visit, Stephen Alfred Gray took his family to Kosciusko, Mississippi, where their third son, George Edwin Gray, was born on August 23, 1837. On October 31, 1843, in Augusta,

Georgia, a daughter, Laura Gray, was born. Stephen Alfred Gray was working on an invention that would improve the cotton gin. His experimentation caused his removal from place to place.

Byrd Gray died in early childhood. A few years later Stephen Alfred Gray, on a business trip to New Orleans relative to his invention, died of cholera on a riverboat.

Life was difficult for the young widow, but her sturdy faith helped her to face her problems. Her cultural background helped her to secure the position of matron or hostess in several girls' schools such as Judson Female Institute in Marion, Alabama. Her husband's invention was patented and his friends, who had financed the carrying of the work to completeion after his death, secured fifty percent of the profits for the widow.

On January 24, 1842, James Grace died. Although he owned many slaves and an extensive farm with a large fine dwelling, outhouses, a gin house, etc., Harriet received no patrimony. By her own efforts and with money derived from her husband's invention, Harriet Gray supported herself and her three surviving children. To the latter she gave better than an average education and some musical advantages.

When George E. Gray became Commissary Sergeant of Libby Prison in Richmond and Dr. Willoughby Grace joined the Confederate Army as a surgeon, Harriet served as a nurse in the several hospitals to which her brother was assigned. During these troublesome times, Harriet carried her silver and other valuables in a featherbed.

Stephen Alexander Gray, Harriet's eldest son, moved his family to Austin, Texas, in 1864 because of his delicate lungs. He was foreman on the "Statesman" news office. He died four years later of tuberculosis, leaving three children and his widow, the pampered daughter of the Swedish Consul in New Orleans. Louise Gray expected her own family and her mother-in-law to support her and her three children in luxury. As Harriet once wrote: "Lou's family has ever been a cause of sadness that I could not overcome. May God help me to do something for them!"

Laura Gray, after a divorce from W. C. Griffin, went to Austin, Texas, with her daughter, Emily. Laura was an accomplished pianist. In 1870 Harriet came to Texas, kept Emily, and managed the house while Laura taught music in Austin. Later Laura married William D. Moore, who proved to be a good husband and a considerate son-in-law as well as good father to Emily and his own children: Harriet, Elizabeth, and George Moore.

In July, 1876, George E. Gray made his first visit to Texas, going by ship from New Orleans to Galveston and hence by train to Houston, Brenham, and Austin. The trip from Galveston to Austin consumed sixteen consecutive hours. George's trip to Texas was occasioned by his desire to see his mother and sister, Laura Moore, who were living in Austin on East Sixteenth Street; to visit the grave of his brother, Alexander, in Oakwood Cemetery; and to see Alexander's children: Alex, Louise, and Dan Gray.

In a letter dated July 23, 1876, George described the Moore home as "a real nice cottage, painted green with brown trimmings." He found Austin a beautiful little place.

> There are some magnificent white stone buildings 4 or 5 storys high on the principle streets and several being erected among which is the Court house, a building that I think will surpass anything we have in N.O. both in material and architecture. The Capitol, however, is a very tame looking affair not half as inviting as the county Jail which by the way is a very handsome structure and the Jailor's house is a perfect pallice.

George Gray's wife, Victoria, in 1878 died in New Orleans of tuberculosis, leaving three little girls: Bertha, Edith, and Mabel. Harriet loved Victoria deeply and her love was reciprocated. Earlier Harrit had written Victoria not to be troubled about her children. As long as she lived, she promised to care for them.

> My heart is grieved for you all, I love the dear wife of my Son for her devotion to you and her children. I know her peace is made with God. She was allways gentle and kind to me, and for that reason I was anxious to have her near me but God wills it outher-wise.
>
> My Dear Son, try to bear up with your tryals. God will bless you and yours. You have ever done the best you could for your fellow-Mortals and taken care of all he made it your duty to care for.
>
> Love your neighbor as your self is next to love my God and I do not think they are seperate commandments but one grate and holey commandment. You have allways kept them and so has your Dear patient wife.

Harriet took charge of three granddaughters, the eldest of whom was eight years old. In them she engrafted her own robustness of spirit and fineness of character.

After his wife's death, George on the advice of his doctors in New Orleans went to San Antonio, Texas, to see whether a drier climate would benefit him. While he was taking the warm spring water in San Antonio, Harriet rented a house next door to her daughter's home in Austin and established a home for Bertha, Edith, and Mabel.

The doctor in San Antonio heard of the waters at Lampasas and recommended that George try these. Willing to try anything that might alleviate his rheumatism, George moved his family to Lampasas. His health was much improved and in 1884 he moved back to New Orleans. His mother went with him and remained in charge of his household until she was recalled to Austin by the serious illness of her grandson, George Moore. Miss Lizzie Seymour chaperoned the Gray girls until their maternal aunt, Mrs. Adele Rothhaas Gribble from Palm Grove, Louisiana, came to care for them.

Unfortunately the humid air of New Orleans caused George Gray's rheumatism to become more painful. Again he moved his family to Texas. This time he settled at 306 East Sixteenth Street in Austin. Harriet, now that George Moore had recovered, resumed the training of George's daughters and the management of his house. His health restored, George became city drummer for John Orr, Wholesale Grocer, who had been his companion during the Civil War.

On March 10, 1889, Harriet died from a stroke suffered in Austin. She was buried from the home that she had made for George and his daughters. She was buried beside her first born, Alexander, in Oakwood Cemetery in Austin.

Harriet Gray lived to be seventy years old. Her life was saddened by her separation from her parents and by the deaths of many she loved: her young husband, her two older sons, her beloved Victoria, two grandsons, and her foster-mother. Her life was made harder because she received no part of her father's estate and because she was plagued by the unreasonable demands of Alexander's widow.

Harriet worked hard all her life. She was too busy to find time to feel sorry for herself. She expended her boundless energy in caring for her fatherless children and her motherless grandchildren. She was forced to reconcile herself to existing situations. Although she had few to give her sympathy and support, she was ever a reassuring tower of strength to others. Wherever she was needed, she went.

Margaret Hallett
(1787-1863)

By Elsie Turk Smothers*

The town of Hallettsville in South Central Texas and the County seat of Lavaca County was named for Margaret Hallett, an early pioneer. Because of her bravery, strength of character, insight, and willingness to help her neighbors, Margaret was acclaimed leader of the settlement and soon became a legendary figure in the area.

Mrs. Hallett was born Margaret Leatherberry on Christmas Day, 1787, in Stafford County, Virginia. Of Scotch-Irish ancestry, Margaret was the youngest child of a prominent and well-to-do family which took great pride in its heritage and social position.

In 1805 Margaret met and fell in love with John Hallett, who was somewhat older than she and a merchant seaman. Her family opposed the marriage. Actually, John was the youngest son of an English gentleman of Worcester, England. He had joined the Royal Navy at an early age but, because of threats against him by an officer, John had jumped overboard one night and swam to an American ship anchored nearby. He was allowed to stay aboard, brought to the United States, and adopted by a merchant seaman.

Despite her parents' pleadings, Margaret declared: "I would rather marry John Hallett and be the beginning of a new family, than remain single and be the tail-end of an old one." In 1808 she

---

* Author and historian

Margaret Hallett's marker at her grave in Hallettsville named for her

joined John where he was working on a merchant vessel in the Chesapeake area. After their marriage by a chaplain, the Halletts lived in Baltimore for several years. In 1812 John fought with distinction against his former countrymen in the Chesapeake Bay area.

Hearing that lands west of the Mississippi River were being opened to homesteaders, the Halletts began to build a wagon for the trip. With only the barest necessities, they joined a wagon train moving westward. People from all walks of life were their companions on the journey.

Before settling in Texas, the Halletts spent several years in Matamoros, Mexico, where they had a mercantile business. Their first two children were born in Matamoros: John, Jr., in 1813 and William Henry in 1815. Their other two children were born in Goliad, Texas: Benjamin in 1818 and Mary Jane in 1822.

The Halletts' home was in Goliad, but John built a log cabin on the Lavaca River on a tract of land granted him from the Stephen F. Austin Colony. He dug a well nearby and made a moat five feet wide and three feet deep around the cabin to protect it from unwelcom visitors. He made trips back and forth between his home in Goliad and his cabin on the Lavaca until his death probably in 1836.

Two Hallett sons served Texas in her fight for freedom from Mexican tyranny. Both John, Jr. and William served under Sam Houston. John, Jr. was in William J. E. Head's Company at San Jacinto. Benjamin died when he was ten years old. Some say he was captured by Indians and never seen again, but no records have been found to substantiate this.

After the War, William Henry was sent to Matamoros to buy land. He was captured there and, as an alleged spy, sent to prison where he met his death in 1836. John, Jr. returned home after San Jacinto and was killed by Indians in 1836. Only Margaret and Mary Jane were left.

During the time of "The Runaway Scrape" when settlers were forced to flee to East Texas to avoid Santa Anna's armies, Margaret Hallett was among those who fled for their lives. When they returned home, they found desolation and destruction on every side. Life had to go on, so the settlers went about the task of repairing their homes, planting their crops, and wherever possible replacing that which had been destroyed or stolen.

Sometime after her husband's death, a young rider brought Margaret news one night that settlers were making their homesteads on her land near the Lavaca. Margaret immediately decided to move to the cabin. She and Mary Jane packed up their belongings, saddled their best mounts, and made their way to the cabin on the Lavaca. They found other settlers moving into the area. Here, too, were two friendly Tonkawa Indians: Morning Star and Rising Sun.

The white settlers told Margaret of the constant threat of raids by the Comanches living nearby. The men were afraid of leaving their women and children to go in search of food. Margaret decided that something must be done immediately to relieve the situation.

She called all the men and the two Tonkawas together to make some plan for action. It was decided that several white men and the two Tonkawas would go to Bexar to seek the help of the Texas Rangers in ridding the Hallett League of the wild Comanches. Margaret prepared meat and cornmeal cakes for the trip and suggested the safest routes. In two weeks the "tall men with long rifles" came from Bexar and quickly cleared the area of the dreaded Comanches.

Since the Hallett League of land was one of the largest and most desirable, Margaret realized that was her responsibility to help develop the settlement as far as possible. She stocked her cabin with essential supplies and it became a thriving trading post. Acting as trader, seller, and clerk, Margaret bartered coffee, sugar, and other necessities for hides, pelts, and corn which the settlers and Indians brought in. In time she planted large crops of corn and stocked her land with cattle and a few horses.

The Tonkawas proved to be good friends. When there was a threatened Comanche raid, the Tonkawas would warn her, giving her and the other settlers ample time to hide until danger of an attack passed.

Although generally friendly, a few Tonkawas were lazy, untrustworthy, and treacherous. Though known to be brave and able to stand her ground, on one occasion Margaret's bravery was tested. Several braves came into her store and asked for whiskey. Their request was denied but the Indians would not leave.

One brave bent over the barrel, planning to help himself. Margaret picked up a hatchet and hit the intruder on the head, raising a noticeable knot. Lolo, the Chief, heard of the incident and was so intrigued with Margaret's display of bravery that he made a special trip into town to get details from her. He was so impressed with her bravery that he made her an honorary member of his tribe.

Margaret never wore black, always bright colored clothing, and carried a chatelaine bag. Two of her neighbors were curious about what she carried in the bag. They surmised that she carried powder but not the kind used on a powder puff. Neither one of them volunteered to ask her.

Mary Jane was sent to school at St. Mary's Convent, located three miles west of Hallettsville to study under the Reverend Edward Clark. Interested in the education of all the children in the community, Margaret helped organize a school. Through her efforts and gift of a piece of land, the Alma Male and Female Institute was organized in 1852. This was the first public school in the settlement.

Mary Jane married Colatinus Ballard, the young man who had ridden years before into Goliad to tell Margaret that settlers were moving onto her property. A native of Virginia but long a Texan, Colatinus was a first cousin of Mary Todd Lincoln.

When the Congress of the Republic of Texas created Lavaca County from a part of several surrounding Counties, Margaret's cabin was used for County and District Court sessions. It was also used for community gatherings as when a minister might come through the area and hold Church services in the cabin.

There was a controversy about whether the Zumwalt Settlement (Petersburg) or Hallettsville would be the County seat. An election declared Hallettsville the winner. The Petersburg citizens burned the election returns. A second election showed Hallettsville again was the winner but Petersburg would not give up the records. Margaret saw that the records were loaded on an oxcart and brought to her cabin. This settled the dispute.

Left a widow at forty-nine years of age, Margaret had been forced to make her own way and to protect that which was hers. She died in 1863 at the age of seventy-six. She was laid to rest near her original home on the Hallett League, a spot she loved and had selected for her resting place. The Indians who had been her friends assisted in her burial. Her remains were moved years

later to a favorite place in the City Memorial Park with the Hallett
Marker placed at her grave.

Hallettsville
founded 1838
County seat, Lavaca County
since 1852
Named for Mrs. Margaret Hallett
Widow of John Hallett
A member of Austin's Colony
A veteran of San Jacinto
who donated the town site.

Dilue Rose Harris
(1825-1914)

By Jeanette Hastedt Flachmeier*

Dilue Rose, daughter of Dr. and Mrs. Pleasant W. Rose, was born February 28, 1825, in St. Louis, Missouri. In 1833, eight-year-old Dilue came from New Orleans to Texas with her parents, a brother and a sister on a schooner that had spent two weeks en route before being driven ashore on Galveston Island by a heavy storm on April 28.

Captain Denmore and Pilot James Spillman had planned to take the family to Harrisburg, but following the calm a storm washed the schooner ashore at Clopper's Point (now Morgan's Point). Here, on a makeshift table of planks, in a log house without a floor but with a fireplace the passengers ate their first meal in Texas. After a night in wet clothes, the next day Dilue and her family traveled in a boat up Buffalo Bayou to Harrisburg where they arrived at night.

Dilue's first home in Texas was a new frame house about half a mile from Harrisburg to which a friend took the family and their luggage the next morning in an ox cart. The Roses found meal, butter, eggs, milk and honey and supper ready. Mrs. Rose later remarked that she would be willing to live in a camp the rest of her life rather than cross the Gulf of Mexico again.

Dilue recalled that Harrisburg had two dry-goods stores but no church, preacher, schoolhouse nor court house. Twice a year a

* Former Staff Writer, *Handbook of Texas*

Dilue Rose Harris

schooner brought groceries and other necessities for the people and took their cotton and hides to sell. Dr. Rose bought a horse and began his medical practice.

In December, 1833, with the help of neighbors, the Rose family moved to a house on the Cartwright farm on the Brazos River about fifteen miles from Harrisburg. Night fell before the travelers reached their destination. A fire was built to keep the wolves away, the horses were tied, and the cattle guarded. Mrs. Rose and the girls slept in a cart and her son and the dogs beneath. According to Dilue, it was a night of horror for "the owls were singing a funeral dirge and wolves and buzzards were waiting to bury us."

Next morning things looked brighter and the Roses reached their new home and began a new life. Dilue's father and her uncle, James Wells, began their field work and her mother (a farm girl) after getting things settled, doing household chores and keeping children busy, began spinning and weaving. Dilue watched and helped in the making of ropes and plow lines from hides and hair from the manes and tails of horses.

Time passed. Immigrants from many lands stopped and visited the Roses. A neighbor was scalped and killed by Indians, a small boy was run over by a wagon wheel, a schooner failed to arrive from New Orleans with food, medicine, and clothing.

Ben Fort Small and two other men arrived with a gang of Negro slaves. The men and slaves stayed at the Rose's farm waiting for help to arrive to move them to the Smith plantation. One of the slaves escaped and, after nightfall, came to the Rose's house. Dr. Rose was away and the Negro tried unsuccessfully to break into the sturdy two-storied house. When morning came Mrs. Rose discovered that the slave had carried off her chickens, been captured and was again under guard.

Dilue remembered how happy the Rose family was over their good crops which were hauled to Harrisburg on a home-made sleigh and traded for household necessities and medicine. In December, 1835, her father took a cart of "pelfrey"—skins of otters, deer, bears, panthers, wildcats, wolves, and 'coons—to Columbia and Brazoria to be traded for a supply of medicine, powder and lead.

Her mother was Dilue's Texas teacher until her father employed David Hensen of New Orleans to conduct a school for the neighboring children from May until the end of August, 1834.

Thirteen pupils with their school books and multiplication tables on pasteboards attended the school in a log house (formerly used as a blacksmith shop with rough-hewn log floor but without windows) until interrupted by the Anahuac affair. The school was reopened on July 10 and continued until September 1 when it was closed because war excitement hindered study.

While the men of the neighborhood were away on a trip to Brazoria, a tribe of Indians—two or three hundred men, women, and children—with many ponies came to the Rose home for corn and camped in the area. They traded bead-embroidered moccasins, and planned to sell buffalo hides and bear skins at Harrisburg. On March 1 the Indians left—the men with guns first, then the squaws with their papooses tied to their backs leading the ponies loaded with buffalo hides, blankets, bear skins, pot, kettles and other utensils and children suspended in baskets across their backs.

The farmers were busy planting their crops in February, 1836, when neighbors who had come from New Orleans reported that Generals Santa Anna and Cos with a large army were marching into Texas. A courier brought news that the Convention had set up a provisional government with David G. Burnet as president and Sam Houston as commander-in-chief of the Texas Army. The men returned to work because they thought General Houston could whip the Mexicans before they reached the Colorado River.

However, when the Mexican Army entered San Antonio the Provisional Government moved to Washington-on-the-Brazos. When a courier brought a message from Colonel Travis asking for help in defending the Alamo, almost all the men in the neighborhood joined General Houston's army except Dr. Rose and Mike Shipman, two old men; a cripple; Granville Rose; and two other boys of 13 and 15 years who remained behind to do the essential work.

Dilue worked hard all day "melting lead in a pot, dipping it with a spoon and moulding bullets." All the families including small boys and Negroes were busy gathering their belongings, cattle, wagons and other vehicles for the overland trip to the United States. Dilue's father hauled some household furniture, a chest of bedding and clothing and farm implements to a hiding place in the bottom. Personal belongings were packed and ready to leave on a moment's notice.

When news of the fall of the Alamo and the retreat of General Houston's army reached the Roses, they joined in the Runaway Scrape. The Rose family with a very ill child were finally put on a boat that needed eight men to steer it across the swollen river. On landing the family found the lowlands flooded and in darkness. The bridge they had to cross to reach the campsite was under water. The Roses spent the night with a friend (Mrs. Foster) who gave them food, dry clothing and a bed.

Next day a raft was built to take the refugees and their belongings across the flooding river. The Roses were the last to leave because of the death of their little girl. A few days later, a messenger crossed the Trinity River in a skiff and brought news that the Mexican Army had crossed the Brazos and was between the Texas Army and Harrisburg; that Fannin and his men had been massacred at Goliad; and that President Burnet and his Cabinet had moved to Washington-on-the-Bay on their way to Galveston.

Courier McDermot on horseback brought news of Houston's victory at San Jacinto. Although everyone shouted, the Rose family could hardly believe their ears. McDermot, an Irishman and former actor, spent that night enacting incidents from the retreat.

The return trip homeward was slow, joyful, difficult, dangerous and sad for the Roses had to recross the Trinity River and the bayou where there was no bridge but quicksand and alligators. The trip took them across the San Jacinto Battlefield where they saw the graves of the fallen Texans and glimpsed the bodies of the unburied Mexicans. Thence they moved across the boggy prairie where friends and families met and recounted many of the hardships they had endured. They heard of the burning of the "sugar-mill, cotton-gin, blacksmith shop, grist-mill, dwelling houses, Negro houses, and farming implements." The saving of the corncrib with a thousand bushels of corn was a great help to the families returning.

Because Vince's Bridge had been burned the Rose family, traveling a round-about-way home, spent two days and two nights with a hundred families at Sims Bayou before reaching their home. They arrived home on June 1, 1836.

The scene at home was heartbreaking. The floor had been torn up, broken bookcases lay on the ground, books and other things were scattered, and hogs were sleeping indoors and in the yard. After breakfast, Dr. Rose went to the field to begin plowing and Mrs. Rose started to wash dirty clothes. Dilue and her sister rode to Staddord's Point to get their brother, Granville. He was dirty, ragged, barefoot, and with shoulder-length hair.

A Mexican man helped the Roses for a while. Before he left, the Mexican revealed that he was a Colonel in the Mexican Army and a wealthy gentleman from Mexico. The chest recovered from the river bottom proved valuable because of its contents: bedding, clothes and even a bonnet. The men went to the Brazos River near Brazoria to make a flat boat to ship their stored cotton and hides to New Orleans. Trustworthy Uncle Ned brought a big wagon to carry supplies for the families in the neighborhood.

Dilue continued her education in a school held in a shed of the log cabin when Mr. Bennet opened the school with eight pupils. In August six young men enrolled and stayed until December. Dilue used to tell of an exciting adventure when two bulls had a fight under the shed while the girls and the teacher sat on the roof, very frightened until the boys drove the cattle away amid much laughter.

The neighborhood families seized every occasion to celebrate and to have fun. There were barbecues, quilting parties and all-night dances on such occasions as a wedding, completion of a roof, introduction of new neighbors, end of a trial, elections and special days such as July 4th and April 21st.

In February, 1836, the Texas Congress divided the State into judicial districts and appointed judges. In March, 1837, the first court of the Republic of Texas was held in Houston. Dilue's father was a member of the grand jury that sat on logs under the pine bushes. In September, 1837, the Rose family moved to their log cabin on Bray's Bayou, five miles from the new town of Houston.

Dilue continued her education with the children of more than thirteen families in a two-room school house. The "desks were made from rough planks put on barrels and nail kegs." There were several teachers: Mrs. Sawyer, Mr. Hambleton and Mrs. Robertson. Dilue also enjoyed the advantages of the growing city such as church services, theatre parties and meeting important people at social functions. Something was always happening in town: steamers arriving from time to time, a court house and jail being erected, as well as the building of many fine homes.

At a theatre party the seats had been reserved for President Houston, his staff, the Milam Guards and school children. Regardless of the sign, gamblers occupied the seats. Houston persuaded the gamblers to leave peaceably and get their money back. Then he gave fatherly advice to the children.

In 1839 snow and sleet covered the ground, a rare event in Texas. The capital was moved to Austin. Mexicans and Indians harrassed the Texans in many ways. Times were hard; Texas money was down to twenty-five cents to the dollar. Immigration had almost stopped.

On February 20, 1839, fourteen-year-old Dilue married Ira A. Harris, the handsome young man whom she had met and enjoyed as her escort at the wedding of Flournoy Hunt and Mary Henry. The service was read by Judge Andrew Briscoe (the hero of Anahuac). Dilue's bridesmaid was Mrs. Mary McCrory, later Mrs. Anson Jones and Ira's groomsman was a Mr. Allen of New York. Among the wedding guests were General Thomas J. Rusk, Dr. Ashbel Smith and other important persons of early Texas government.

The young couple made their home near Houston in a house the groom had remodeled. In the year Texas was annexed to the United States, they moved to Columbus, Colorado County. Ira was a Texas Ranger, Company E. In 1860 Dilue and Ira built a new house of "tabby" construction on Washington Street. Today this is known as the Dilue Rose Harris House and bears a marker placed by the Texas Historical Survey Commission.

In the course of time Dilue and Ira had nine children. During the Civil War, the older sons served in the Confederate Army. The family lived in their Columbus home until Ira died in 1869. He was buried in the Columbus Cemetery. In her later years Dilue lived with her children and grandchildren in the Houston area, in the Indian Territory and for a few years before her death on April 13, 1914, with her daughter, Mrs. George Zeigler of Eagle Lake.

A great and valuable contribution that Dilue Rose Harris left Texans is the written account of early life in Texas based on her father's diary and her own vivid recollections. She wrote in an interesting, historically sound and sometimes humorous fashion that has made her writings a primary source of information about early Texas happenings. Her observations and thoughts as a child show her to have been a person of mature judgment. Dilue said of herself: "I do not remember a time when I did not regard myself as fully grown and willing to share responsibility."

Her written record, "The Reminiscences of Mrs. Dilue Rose Harris," was published in *The Quarterly of the Texas State Historical Association*, volumes IV and VII.

Magdalena Hornberger Henninger

Magdalena Hornberger Henninger (1825-1906)

By Pansy Luedecke*

Magdalena Hornberger was born on April 26, 1825, in Rohrbach, Bavaria, near Landau. Her father was George Peter Hornberger, manager of a flour mill in Rohrbach. Her mother, Katherine Schaurer Hornberger, was born on September 8, 1800, in Rohrbach.

Magdalena married John Henninger, a native of Karlstadt, Rheinfaltz, Bavaria, where his family owned large vineyards and extensive real estate. Because of the many wars between France and Germany, the taxes on their property became so excessive that John and Magdalena decided to migrate to America.

In 1853 the Henningers sailed from Germany to New Orleans. It took them seventy-three days to cross the Atlantic. On the way their sailboat was rammed, and the passengers had to bail water until repairs could be made. It was also a sad trip, for they had left their infant son, Jacob, in Bavaria with Magdalena's sister, Katherine Hornberger Krumeich.

Magdalena's brother, Adam Hornberger, had preceded the Henningers to America and was the owner of a candy manufacturing plant in New Orleans, Louisiana. John's and his pregnant wife's plan to land in New Orleans had to be changed because a yellow fever epidemic was raging and their boat was diverted to Galveston, Texas. Adam died of the fever.

---

* A granddaughter

Since Magdalena's other two brothers, Jacob and Christian, were established as merchant-tailors in Austin, the Henningers decided to go to Austin. They went to Houston by rail and then on to Austin by oxcart. They arrived in Austin May 10, 1853. After greeting Jacob and Christian and exploring the area, they bought a farm on the north side of the Colorado River. Their home on the west side of Congress Avenue at Third Street was a two-story rock house. Later the house became the first location of the International and Great Northern Railroad Station until much later when a new station was built just off Lamar Boulevard and West Third Street.

Magdalena and John later sold their farm to the former owner and bought two lots on San Antonio at Seventh Street. This home-place had only "Deeds of Love" for over a hundred years. They also bought a tract of land extending from Airport Boulevard at 19th Street (the present location of the Ambassador Apartments) to Govalle. This land John farmed until his death on June 18, 1881.

The Henningers had four children born in Austin: Katherine, Philipena, Emma Dorothy, and Henry. Jacob, the son born in Bavaria, joined the family after the Civil War when he was sixteen years old. During the war years, John hauled supplies for the Confederate Army. Magdalena's nephew, Fred Hornberger, died of wounds received during the Civil War.

Magdalena saw that their children received an education.

She even sent Emma Dorothy to the German-American Ladies College run by Matile von Schench and Alice Nohl although there was a West Austin School. At the College there was a large house where boarding students lived and smaller cottages on the property where classes were held. The school not only taught the academic subjects but also manners and fine handwork. Emma Dorothy rode to school on her pony and returned home each evening.

According to a granddaughter, Magdalena was short in stature and had pretty dark eyes and hair. She and her husband had considered settling in California shortly after the first gold rush but the Agent whom they consulted said that she did not think Magdalena could stand the hardships of such a trip. However, she was a sturdy housekeeper, an excellent cook, and did fine handwork. She was good to her neighbors and was loved by all who knew her.

Magdalena Henninger's teacher: Miss Alice Nohl, at German-American Ladies College at Austin

Magdalena was a charter member of St. Martin's Lutheran Church located for many years on Thirteenth Street east of the North Gates to the Capitol Grounds. When St. Martin's congregation was moved to a new and larger building on Congress Avenue at Fourteenth, a pew was dedicated in her memory and a name plate attached.

After her husband's death, Magdalena lived on the farm with her mother who had migrated to Austin and with her son, Henry. Jacob was involved in a vegetable business. When her mother and Henry died on June 30, 1886, she again moved. This time, she was to spend the rest of her life with her youngest daughter; her son-in-law, William Luedecke; and their children at Manor, Travis County, Texas. Her grandchildren adored her and profited by her presence.

Magdalena died January 13, 1906, at Manor and is buried next to her husband in Oakwood Cemetery in Austin.

Minerva Frances Vernon Hill (1832-1896)

By Fannie Ellen Crockett*

She was called "Big Mamma" by her grandchildren and their friends and everyone else who didn't call her "Aunt Fannie"; Big Papa called her "Fan," and her name in the Bible was Minerva Frances Vernon.

Her husband was "Big Papa" to his grandchildren, "Major" to his friends and "Major Hill" to the general public; Big Mamma called him "Mr. Hill" and his name in the Bible was William Hickman Hill, Jr.

Big Mamma met him in the summer of 1846 at a Masonic picnic in the vicinity of Murfreesboro, Tennessee. The only comment she was ever known to make concerning that event was, "He was the ugliest man I had ever seen, but the politest, and still is." Picture him a man six feet, two, ungainly yet distinguished in his Knights-Templar regalia, showing deferential attention to the trying-to-act-grown-up little girl with jet black curls, flashing brown eyes, dressed in a voluminous white muslin dress, adorned with a blue sash.

An ardent courtship followed, and he came to the point at once. Her family's only objection to an immediate marriage was her youth. She was fourteen while he was twenty-four. However, Great Aunt Rowena Pease solved the problem by casting her

---

* Granddaughter

113

ballot for the "good catch," saying Fannie would soon get over being too young.

The young couple was married on November 5, 1846, in Murfreesboro, Tennessee, at the home of her grandfather, Dr. Vernon. They went to live at Garden Hill, his father's planation near Franklin, Tennessee. Although William was the third son of five, nevertheless he was his father's manager and right hand man.

The "living happily ever afterwards" was soon interrupted, for Big Papa developed consumption, as tuberculosis was then called. The only treatment doctors of that day knew for the deadly disease was frequent toddies and to go to Texas. So to Texas went William, Minerva Frances and their three little daughters, along with William Hickman Hill, Sr., his wife Sarah Brown Hill and their youngest son, Alexander Campbell, age eighteen.

They reached Austin in the fall of 1852. There they were welcomed by Big Papa's favorite sister Martha, called Pattie, and her husband L. D. Carrington, who a few years previously had caught the Texas fever and with their young son, Robert Emmett, had migrated from Columbus, Mississippi. The older folks stayed with the Carringtons, but the rest of the party and their slaves camped at the present site of the Driskill Hotel.

After looking around for several months, Big Papa and his father bought adjoining farm lands on Gilliland Creek, twelve miles northeast of Austin. They were disappointed when Mr. Carrington decided not to join them, but to stay in the city and expand his mercantile business, an enterprise in which he had been quite successful in Mississippi. He became one of the most outstanding pioneer merchants of Austin.

Before leaving Austin, however, William Hickman Hill, Sr. and his wife united with the Christian Church which, with a membership of only ten, had been organized in the year 1847.

Life was not easy for twenty-year-old Minerva Frances Hill with a sick husband, three little stairstep daughters and a tract of bald prairie which had to be made into a home and from which a living must be made. Yet the only complaint that anyone ever heard her voice was: "Texas is hard on women and oxen."

That she was equal to the task is attested by the fact that although the doctors had given Big Papa only five more years to live, he lived forty-seven. He outlived all the fourteen people who came with him, except his second daughter, Sallie, and a little slave girl named "Miss" for Old Miss.

Big Mamma was kind to every living creature, man or beast. Her sympathy for their slaves was a vexation to the overseer. He complained to Big Papa that he couldn't do nothing with them lazy niggers on account of Miss Fannie. He explained that he wasn't even techin' Jess, only poppin' his whip on the ground, but Jess yelled and here come Miss Fannie and tuck him to the kitchen and giv' him a cup of coffee, when what he needed was a whippin'.

Big Papa's reply was that nothing could stop Miss Fannie's interferring when anyone was in trouble. Furthermore, he had noticed that his farm was one of the best kept in Travis County, and that he had never had any run-away Negroes.

Big Papa's health did not permit him to volunteer for service in the Confederate Army. However, he did his full duty as a civilian, for he was a member of a committee in Travis County that looked after the welfare of the families of Confederate soldiers. Then to each of the neighbor boys who enlisted he gave a horse and to each Big Mamma gave a pocket Testament. When their first son William Hickman was born, Big Mamma told "Mr. Hill" that he had just as well get rid of his cattle for she wasn't raising any son to be a cowboy (you see she was from the gentle mannered society of Tennessee) so Big Papa did and invested in sheep and horses, and that's why he had horses to give away when they were a scarce commodity.

During the last years of the War Between The States, each community selected a patrolman whose duty was to see that no slave was away from his home base without a pass from his master. The only man in the Hill Community who would accept that office was a Mr. Brewer (this name is fictitious). He was noted for being very harsh toward his slaves. Now, Dan, from an adjoining plantation had married Bet, one of the Hill's house servants, but so trustworthy were both of them that Dan came and went without a pass. One night when Big Papa was away from home, Dan was caught. When Big Mamma heard the commotion, she arrived on the scene doublequick. She first ordered Mr. Brewer to stop the beating, saying that she could explain. When he paid no attention, she told him in very vivid language how the Lord was going to punish him for beating a poor, helpless negro. Still the beating continued, but when he paused for breath, Big Mamma threw her arm around poor, trembling, bleeding Dan. That stopped all action on Mr. Brewer's part. I do not know how the matter was smoothed over, but I do know that to this day, none of the Hills are on friendly terms with any of the Brewer connection.

The most thrilling story I have to tell was of her bout with robbers. This happened during Carpet Bag Rule, when neither life nor property was secure in the South. To add to the general tension, there were reported activities of a band of highwaymen from a hideout in the Cedar brakes near Austin. Again, Big Papa was away from home. He felt no uneasiness about his family, for his former slaves had either remained with him or by then had tired of the responsibility of freedom and had returned to home base and security, especially trustworthy were Aunt Emily and Uncle Jess.

Late one evening a lone horseman drew rein and asked to spend the night. Big Mamma welcomed him not only with frontier but Biblical hospitality as well, for she was an ardent believer in the injunction: "Forget not to entertain strangers."

It was later recalled that the stranger objected to turning his horse over to Uncle Jess, but just then Aunt Emily called to supper. In spite of Big Mamma's friendly overtures, the guest gobbled his food in silence. After hastily finishing his supper, he asked to be directed to the stables, explaining that he was very particular about the care of his horse.

On the heels of his departure, Aunt Emily grabbed up a basket, murmuring that she had "clean forgot to bring in Mrs. Willum's chips." She shortly stumbled back wild eyed and trembling, minus the chip basket, and ejaculating, "Jes ez I got to de woodpile, I seed his hat bobbin down de holler what goes ter de creek, whar he's gwine ter meet de udder robbers. I knowed he was one caze he wouldn't look me in de eye, doe I passed him de biskets three times a purpose. Lord hep us! dey's gwine ter murder we alls in our beds." She suddenly stopped her wailing, when Big Mamma gave her a candle and told her to put clean sheets on the far room bed. She first made a detour to the tool chest to put a hammer and nails in her apron pocket.

The Hill home was of the typical Texas frontier style, a story and a half with two rooms in the half story. One was furnished to be used for company that stayed several days or more. The other one was the plunder room, piled high with extra comforts and feather beds and furnished with only one chair and a decrepit bedstead. It was used only when there was no pallet space left in the entire house, for the bed creaked loud and long whenever the occupant so much as wiggled a toe.

Just as the stranger re-entered the back door, sounds of vigorous hammering came from above. He seemed not to notice however, only asked to be shown his room, explaining that he was very tired, for he had been traveling since daybreak. As soon as he was out of sight up the stairway, Aunt Emily disappeared. She soon returned, dragging a pallet in one hand, while holding the ax from the wood-pile in the other. She spread her quilt alongside the baby's cradle, explaining that he was teething and might need her. At the same time, she tucked the ax out of sight.

Soon a loud creak came from the direction of the far room. Big Mamma listened intently then asked, "Did you hear his boots drop?" "No, Mam," replied Aunt Emily, "He jes flung his sef down hard on de bed with all his clothes on so ez to fool we alls. He sho aint up to no good."

Then Big Mamma and Aunt Emily, working silently as a team, stacked the stairway with chairs, putting Big Papa's rocker at the foot for good measure. Next, Aunt Emily brought the lantern from its place on the kitchen wall, which Big Mamma placed on a chair near the door that opened into the hall. She raised an umbrella over this, draping a shawl so that not a ray of light penetrated. Next Big Mamma, as a final touch, rummaged her cedar chest for the little derringer that Big Papa had given her just before they set out for Texas. This she tucked under her pillow. Then she blew out her candle, knelt briefly by her bed and serenely went to sleep, for she knew the good Lord would watch over her household. However, Aunt Emily placed the ax where it would be handy.

Soon quiet settled over all the house, to be broken around midnight by the sound of a rock hitting the front door. The bed in the far room creaked; Big Mamma jerked off the enveloping shawl with one hand, grabbed the derringer with the other and reached the hall at one bound, with Aunt Emily with her ax not far behind. When a stealthy step was heard at the head of the stairs, Big Mamma sang out, "If you come another step, I'll shoot, and I always kill the hawks that bother my chickens." Dead silence, until another rock struck the front door, followed by the sound of hurried stumbling steps in the direction of the far room. Aunt Emily chuckled, "He'll find dem windo's nailed down good an' fast." Soon a prolonged creak from the bed in the far room. Long minutes passed, then a distant sound of horses galloping over the creek bridge, a mile away.

Big Mamma still kept guard, but Aunt Emily with the ax hugged in her arms soon snored. At the first peep of day, Aunt Emily was dispatched to the gin for Mr. Chatman, the ginner. He later said that he was aroused while she was yet a half a mile away by her scream of "Come quick, Miss Fannie dun kilt de robber." All excitement, with his pistol cocked in readiness, he reached the scene double-quick to find Big Mamma quietly removing the barricade of chairs. She calmly told him to stay with the stranger until she called them to breakfast, which Aunt Emily went at once to prepare.

Immediately afterwards Mr. Chatman began preparations to take the would-be robber to Austin, but to his eternal exasperation, this Big Mamma refused to let him do. In fact, they had some sharp words about the matter. Instead, Big Mamma took the stranger to the big room and after reading a suitable chapter from the Bible, she not only prayed over him, but had him ask the good Lord's forgiveness and promise Him never again to attempt any crime. Then she gave him the little Testament that she had read from, exacting a promise that he read it often. Next, she had Mr. Chatman return his pistol and had made Jess bring his horse, then bade him "Good Speed."

Mr. Chatman, still angry when next he saw Big Papa, greeted him with, "I do wish you had been here, Major, for then that robber would have gotten his desserts." To this Big Papa replied, "I doubt if anything would have been different." Mr. Chatman grudgingly admitted, "I reckon not so long as Miss Fannie is like she is, and you are like you are."

No, they never heard of the robber again. I just know that he stayed repentant, for Big Mamma not only believed in a literal Hell, but also that one was punished for all sins during life on this earth. Her descriptions along that line were very vivid. Anyway, the activities of highwaymen suddenly ceased in that part of Texas.

The obvious reason for a raid on only a fairly prosperous farm home in a sparsely populated community was that a few days previously Big Papa had sold a large consignment of sheep at Webberville. That small town, then as now, was a struggling settlement on the Colorado River. However, in those pioneer days it was an important trading center, especially for the many prosperous plantations on that river.

Had Big Papa not taken the money to re-invest in more sheep, the robbers would never have found it, anyway. It would have been safely stowed in a dark corner of the loft over the front bedroom, camouflaged by spread out potatoes and onions and other garden truck. The only access to said bank was by way of an unwieldy ladder, which Aunt Emily always carefully and immediately restored to its regular place in the distant barn. My mother gloating revealed to me that she knew of this hiding place for she had peeped one time and saw Big Papa toss up a bag that clicked when it fell. The secret was as safe with her as it was with Aunt Emily, for in those days children did not tell of things that they were not supposed to know, at least that was what my mother said.

My favorite story about Big Mamma happened after she had passed away. The Christian Church at Manor, Texas, was celebrating its fiftieth anniversary. This Church had begun life in the country, five miles distant, and was known as the Rock Church, of which the pioneer Hills were Charter members. It was built by that community for a school house and so used.

The anniversary was an old-fashioned affair, with dinner on the grounds, and everyone invited. The speaking followed the usual trend of extravagant praise for its founders. Toward the close of the program a person known locally as a "Hill-Billy from Tennessee" arose and said: "I've never made a speech in my life but I can't keep silent any longer, for I haven't heard no one mention the best and most important member of the old Rock Church, Aunt Fannie Hill."

Then he described the country-wide gatherings for big meetings at that church with its dinners on the grounds on Sundays. He further told how Aunt Fannie circulated, gathering up new comers and stray boys to eat dinner with her family. He added that she saw to it that they got as good a break at the fried chicken as the preachers. When he came to considering joining a church, he selected the Christian Church because "Aunt Fannie's Church was good enough for me."

"I am sure," he continued, "that Brother Addison Clark and Brother Campbell Hill were great preachers, yet I can't recall a single word they ever said, but I shall never forget Aunt Fannie's welcome to a homesick boy. I am just as sure as I stand here that when I cross over Jordan that she will be there to take my hand and again say, 'I'm glad to see you, Jim.'"

After that, in present day language, Big Mamma "stole the show." Had she been listening in, I am sure that she was bewildered by the praise, for she was a very humble minded person.

Worn out with so much living, Big Mamma passed away on June 12, 1896, at the age of sixty-five. A most fitting tribute was paid her by the minister who conducted the funeral services. He read without comment, Proverbs 31:10 to the end of the chapter. (Go read it.)

Amanda Burnam Holman (1823-1863)

By Emma Holman Scott*

On December 4, 1823, Amanda Burnam was born in a log cabin near the Colorado River in Texas. She was the sixth child of Jesse Burnam and his wife, Temperance. After Stephen F. Austin had established San Felipe de Austin as the capital of his colony, a road was made through Jesse Burnam's land to the old Mexican mission and fort, La Bahia (Goliad). As the Colorado River was too deep here to drive across, Burnam built and operated a ferry. This became known as Burnam's Crossing.

Stephen F. Austin returned to his colony in July 1823. He began to organize an orderly form of government dividing his colony into five districts. Each district was to hold free elections to elect an Alcalde and a Captain of the Militia. Jesse Burnam was elected Captain of the Upper Colorado Militia.

Although Amanda's father had been taking part in all the duties as a citizen in the Colony, it was not until August 16, 1824, that the thirteenth grant in Austin's first colony was given to him. It was awarded under a Mexican law in an unusual ceremony. Several witnesses, Baron de Bastrop, Commissioner for the Mexican Governor, and the surveyor met Jesse Burnam on his land. According to Records in the Texas Land Office, the Commissioner said:

---

* Granddaughter

121

Amanda Burnam Holman

> We put the said Jesse Burnam in possession of said land taking him by the hand, leading him about and then telling him in loud audible tones that by virtue of the commission and the power vested in us, and in the name of the government of the Mexican Nation, we put him in possession of said land with all their uses, customs, privileges, and appurtenances; for him, his heirs, and his successors, and said Jesse Burnam in evidence of finding himself in real and personal possession of said land without any opposition whatever, shouted aloud, pulled herbs, threw stones, set stakes, and performed the other necessary ceremonies, he being reminded of his obligation to cultivate them within two years, the term prescribed by law.

Amanda was not yet nine months old so the ceremony made no impression on her. If a Psychic had been among those present, he might have predicted that she would live the rest of her life within a radius of fifteen miles of her birthplace.

In the summer of 1827, Noah Smithwick visited in Captain Jesse Burnam's home. He described it as a comfortable pioneer station with cows, pigs, chickens, a large garden and fields of corn and cotton.

Amanda's father continued to improve the property. He built a blockhouse from which to fight any enemy attacking his family or settlers taking refuge in the cabins he had built within the log palisade surrounding his station. Jesse Burnam dug the first well and built the first brick chimney in Fayette County.

Amanda was a lively, fearless girl. She loved to ride on the ferry with her father or brothers. She helped around her home. Her little fingers soon became skillful in cleaning the cotton of all trash and seed and getting it ready for her older sisters to spin the thread to be woven into beautiful white cloth. She scattered grain for the chickens, gathered eggs, and watched the birds and wild game to keep them from destroying crops in both fields and garden.

It was customary in the autumn for neighboring families to go together on "pecan hunts." These were really occasions for getting in their winter supply of food. Deer, buffalo, and bears were killed and dressed to make plenty of jerky, or clothing. There were pecans, black walnuts, and hickory nuts to gather. Wild bee trees supplied an abundance of honey to eat and wax for candles. Amanda loved these camping trips. She made new friends among the children although they did not have many opportunities of seeing each other.

Until she was nine years old, Amanda lived a carefree, protected life. In May, 1833, her mother went on the ferry across the

Colorado to nurse friends ill of a fever. This was no ordinary fever; it was cholera. Cholera had been brought to New York by a ship from Europe, spread to the Mississippi River and down to New Orleans and across to Texas.

Floods prevented William Burnam, Amanda's oldest brother, from going after his mother for several days. When the flood subsided, he went and found his mother had died of cholera and been buried on the east side of the Colorado. It took some time for Amanda to realize that her mother was never coming back. Her family tried to comfort her.

Two important things happened to Amanda in 1834. The first school in Fayette County was established near Fayetteville on David Breeding's land. It was held in a log cabin with Mr. Rutland as the teacher. Although the school was fifteen miles from their home, the Burnam children attended. As there was no room for more boarders in the homes near the school, Jesse Burnam built a shed tent for the girls. The boys slept under the trees. Amanda, now eleven years old, had learned to read and write at home but this was her introduction to a formal education.

In August, 1834, Mary Burnam, Amanda's eldest sister, married William S. Townsend. The young couple established their home in the first section of the old Winedale Inn. Mary died in 1844 and her husband in 1846. The property was sold, and the house added to by later owners. Then it became a stage coach inn.

The tension between the Texas settlers and the Mexican government increased but Amanda did not realize the situation was becoming worse. One day several men rode up to Burnam's Crossing. One of them was the noted pioneer naturalist, Gideon Lincecum. His companions returned to the coast but Lincecum, anxious to study the flora of Texas, accepted Captain Burnam's invitation to be his guest. The naturalist stayed about two months making frequent trips to the prairie to gather specimens. Between these trips he talked to his host answering his questions on many subjects. Amanda enjoyed listening to these discussions without saying a word.

One day Amanda saw a man ride with great speed to her house. He had come to ask for volunteers to go help the settlers at Gonzales who were resisting a Mexican force trying to take a small brass cannon away. The cannon had been given to the settlers to protect themselves from the Indians. Amanda's father and two older brothers left at once. Under the command of Colonel John M. Moore, the Texans won. Their first battle of the Texas Revolution was fought successfully in Gonzales on October 2, 1835.

Events moved rapidly in the war after this but Amanda knew little about them as few travelers came by her home. Her father came for a short visit on his way to San Felipe for the Consultation of November 3, 1835. He selected a fresh horse and left.

In January of 1836, Amanda's father accompanied by Colonel James W. Fannin came to Burnam's Crossing. Jesse Burnam had been appointed to help Colonel Fannin raise and equip a volunteer army to meet the Mexican army at Matamoros. They stayed at Burnam's Crossing for two weeks while Amanda's father equipped many men out of his warehouse and gave them horses out of his own lot. Amanda admired Colonel Fannin as a brave and patriotic man. Upon departing, Fannin left a beautiful horse he had brought from Georgia to Texas. It was given tender care and a home there until it died of old age.

One day Amanda's father, tired and haggard, arrived bringing the sad news of the fall of the Alamo and of three weeks later the massacre of Fannin's men at Goliad. Many families were already at Burnam's Crossing eager to get on the east side of the Colorado. When General Houston arrived there, he stayed two days while his men assisted the settlers to cross.

Amanda's family joined what history has called "The Runaway Scrape." It had been raining for days, many were sick without food or shelter, and there were births and deaths among the refugees.

Jesse Burnam and his neighbor, W. B. Dewees, were camped with two hundred families about twenty miles from the San Jacinto battleground when news of the victory at San Jacinto and the capture of Santa Anna arrived. They joyfully started home.

A scene of desolation awaited them. Their homes were piles of ashes. There was no time to waste. Amanda's father built a shed tent for his family as there was urgent need to plant food crops for the coming winter. There were hunting trips to secure plenty of meat to make jerky and gathering enough nuts and honey to last all winter. Amanda, now twelve years old, helped in the house and garden.

Amanda's oldest sister at home, Minerva, died of pneumonia in November, 1836. The Burnams soon had a more comfortable house with a restored warehouse and cabins within a log palisade. They also ran the ferry again.

In January, 1838, Captain Burnam married the widow of Captain James Ross, who had fought at San Antonio and San Jacinto. Nancy Cummins Ross was a kind step-mother. With Jesse's five children living at home and the three Ross children, the house was full again. This was a wonderful relief for Amanda after the long lonely months of the past two years.

Two brothers came to Fayette County from Virginia in 1837 and bought land between the present town of La Grange and Weimer. Nancy Burnam married the older brother, George Tandy Holman, and a year later Amanda married Jerome Alexander and went to La Grange to live. Amanda's husband had fought at San Antonio and San Jacinto. He was the first Clerk of the District Court of Fayette County and owned a general store, a tavern, and large tracts of land.

In September, 1842, a large force of Mexicans under General Woll captured San Antonio and marched toward Gonzales. They were defeated at Salado Creek by a company of Texans under Colonel Mathew Caldwell. Another group of Texans under Colonel Nicholas Mosby Dawson, riding hard to go to help Colonel Caldwell's Company, were surrounded by a detachment of Mexican cavalry. Thirty-five were killed and fifteen were taken prisoners. Among those killed was Amanda's husband. Jerome Alexander had filed a will in the Courthouse at La Grange, leaving the bulk of his property to Amanda and their unborn child. One month later, Jerome Alexander II was born.

On December 12, 1844, Amanda married John Thompson Holman and went to live in Holman Valley near her father and sister, Nancy Holman. Her husband was a widower with one son, Natt Holman who was about the age of Jerome Alexander II.

When John T. Holman was an old man, he described his young bride, Amanda, as a beautiful woman. She had a happy, cheerful disposition and loved to have company. She was a fine horsewoman and often rode with him to inspect their farms.

John T. Holman took Amanda to visit her father in Burnet County sometime in 1859. She enjoyed visiting him and all of her brothers and sister. That was the last time they saw her.

The War clouds were gathering rapidly. Her brother, Bennett, and a nephew were killed in battle. While her husband was serving in the Confederate forces east of the Mississippi, their youngest child, Edward, died. She heard that her son, Jerome Alexander, had been wounded, captured, and sent to Chase Union Prison in Illinois.

The combination of grief and anxiety about her husband and children impaired her health. She died on November 10, 1863, not yet forty years of age.

Anna Raguet Irion

Anna Raguet Irion
(1819-1883)

By Helen Hoskins Rugeley*

Anna Raguet was born January 25, 1819 in Newtown, Bucks County, Pennsylvania, to Henry and Marcia Ann (Towers, *not* Temple as printed in *The Handbook of Texas* and elsewhere) Raguet. Some records show a middle name, Wynkoop (for her maternal grandmother, Anna), but it does not appear in the Bible Family Record in the Raguet Collection in the archives of Barker Texas History Center at The University of Texas in Austin. In that Family Record, Anna's mother is listed as Mercy Ann, her nickname in the family.

Henry Raguet's father, Jacques Michel (James Michael) Raguet, came to America from France in June, 1783. Although it is stated in *Writings of Sam Houston* that he had been on Napoleon's staff and fled to America when Bonaparte was banished to St. Helena in 1815, James Raguet was in America two years before that general received his first commission in the army of France.

A letter from the mayor of Commune des Riceys in the Department of Aube documents birth and death records of the Raguet family in France.

On August 18, 1780, James Raguet married Anna Wynkoop, daughter of Judge Henry Wynkoop, of "Vredenshoff" in Bucks County. Since this place was so small, the name of the

*Great-grandniece of Anna Raguet

nearest city, Philadelphia, is often used in the records. James Raguet was a merchant and postmaster of Newtown, in the same county. When his brother Claudius Paul died, James welcomed into his home Claudius's son, Condy Raguet, who became the idol of young Henry Raguet.

A veteran of the War of 1812, Henry Raguet moved from Pennsylvania to Ohio in the interests of Jonathan W. Condy, the maternal grandfather of Henry's favorite cousin, Condy Raguet, sometime before October 16, 1820, when Henry and Marcia Ann's daughter Catherine was born in Steubenville. By the middle of 1822 the family had migrated to Cincinnati, where it was increased by the births of James Condy, Henry Wynkoop, Claudius Morton and Augusta Amelia (twins), Mary Helen, and Charles M. in a ten-year period.

While residing in Cincinnati, Henry Raguet was elected a director of the Bank of the United States, but his personal enterprises in the mercantile business did not prosper, due to overextension of credit, so that he was forced to take bankruptcy in 1832. Mr. Raguet then went to New Orleans where he met Sam Houston and John Durst, who persuaded him to take a trip to Texas. In March 1833 the three men reached Nacogdoches. The economic prospects of the town convinced Mr. Raguet that he should settle there so he returned to Ohio and moved his family down. Anna was fourteen when she came to Texas. Her father soon became an active force in the community, serving as treasurer and later chairman of the Committee for Safety and Vigilance during the Texas Revolution, and as postmaster in 1837. Known as Colonel Raguet (an honorary title), he was a prominent merchant in Nacogdoches for many years, until his retirement in 1852. In 1873 he moved to Marshall to join his son Charles and died there in 1877.

Early in 1836 Col. Henry Raguet sent his family back to Philadelphia to escape the menace of the approaching Mexican army. This flight, in which so many families participated, was known in Texas history as the Runaway Scrape. No doubt the eight months' stay in Pennsylvania was a pleasant interlude in young Anna's life, a taste of the amenities of civilization again after three years of pioneer existence.

Being the first-born, Anna was "the apple of her father's eye," and he often took her with him on short business trips. In a letter to her husband in 1827, Mrs. Raguet wrote that Anna was still reproaching her for not being permitted to go with her father to Zanesville.

Anna Raguet blossomed into a beautiful and accomplished young lady. Some accounts say she was educated "in the best schools of Philadelphia and was fluent in several languages." Perhaps she was sent back there to school, but no such record has been found in Barker Archives. She was only about a year old when her parents moved to Ohio. There is a strong tradition that Anna gave lessons in Spanish to her father's friend, General Sam Houston (twenty-six years her senior), and entertained him by playing her beautiful gilded French harp. For several years he courted her, always closing his letters to her father with complimentary messages to or about her, calling her "the Fairest of the Fair," "the peerless Miss Anna," and "the brightest and loveliest star in Texas." He composed several flowery poems about her.

In the Barker Archives there is a letter to Colonel Raguet from General Houston at Columbia, Texas, dated December 31, 1836, which ends: "Take care of my 'great gem'," apparently referring to Anna. Someone in the family with little feeling for history has written a laundry list on the back of this letter!

As late as August 1839, after Houston had met his future wife, Margaret Lea, he sent Anna a snuff box said to be carved from a scrap of Old Ironsides, saying he believed "No fairer hand or more patriotic heart could receive or cherish the Gift. To me it is doubly endeared!!!" This incident is related in "A Famous Romance" in the 1962 *Year Book of West Texas Historical Association*.

In June 22, 1961, the *San Augustine Tribune* reprinted a *Houston Chronicle* feature story by historian Garland Roark. In the article Anna is said to have saved Sam Houston's life by throwing herself against an assailant who lurched from the shrubbery with knife in hand. Her quick action threw the would-be assassin off balance so that he could be disarmed.

In the same article, Roark stated that Anna played a role in creating "The Seal of Texas" at Houston's request. After the victory of San Jacinto, General Houston had sent Anna a twig or garland of oak leaves from the tree under which Santa Anna surrendered. The seal she designed, still used by the State of Texas, bears "the oak leaves of San Jacinto, symbolizing the liberties of Texas which are firmly rooted in native soil, and the olive branch, symbol of peace and strength, with the five-pointed star central."

This is a long-standing tradition; however, *The Handbook of Texas* states that the design was drawn by P. Krag.

Sam Houston often sent his letters to Anna by his friend, Dr. Robert Anderson Irion. Whether it was Houston's manner of getting his divorce, some aspects of his personal life, or the appeal of his John Alden that decided her is a moot question, but the final outcome was Anna's marriage to Dr. Irion on April 9, 1840 (license issued in Nacogdoches March 30th).

Apparently the genial merchant Adolphus Sterne played a part in this match which culminated in a wedding "at Roberts'," for in his diary (edited by Dr. Archie P. McDonald under the title *Hurrah for Texas!*) dated "Fryday the 25 Christmas" in 1840 he wrote: "made friends with Mrs. Raguet, who had not Spoken to me since the Marriage of her Daughter to Doctor Irion." In February 1844 Dr. Irion told Sterne that he was going to move into Col. Raguet's house, so the rift, if any, was mended. When the 1850 census was taken, Anna was still there, but Dr. Irion was away.

Their marriages did not break the friendship of the three protagonists, as evidenced by the fact that Houston's daughter Antoinette (who married Professor William L. Bringhurst) named a son Charles Raguet, and the Irions named their first child Sam Houston. The other Irion children were Harriet Durst (who married Lawrence Sterne Taylor), Julia H. (who married J. I. Heard), and Robert H. (who married Mary Helena Durst), and James Raguet (who married Ewing Calhoun Brownrigg).

Robert Anderson Irion was born, according to family Bible records, July 7, 1804, in Paris, Tennessee, to John Poindexter and *Maacha* (White) Irion. In 1929 the State of Texas erected at his grave a marker bearing the erroneous date of 1806, and *The Handbook of Texas* lists his grandfather, Philip Irion, as his father. Both of these sources also err in showing his marriage date as March 20th.

In 1826 Dr. Irion graduated in medicine from Transylvania University at Lexington, Kentucky. He came to Texas in 1832 after the death of his first wife, Ann A. Vick, in Vicksburg, Mississippi, leaving his daughter Ann Elizabeth with her maternal relatives. Moving from San Augustine to Nacogdoches, Dr. Irion temporarily abandoned his medical practice to become a surveyor and land dealer in partnership with George Aldrich. Irion served Texas as a member of the Committee for Safety and Vigilance, as commandant of Nacogdoches Municipality, and as a senator in the First Congress of the Republic of Texas until President Houston appointed him Secretary of State in June 1837.

After his marriage to Anna Raguet, Dr. Irion practiced medicine in Nacogdoches until his death on March 2, 1861. He was buried there in Oak Grove Cemetery, and was honored by the naming of Irion County for him in 1889. A historical marker, two miles east of Sherwood, honoring Dr. Irion gives his dates as 1806-1860 when they should have been 1804-1861.

Anna Raguet Irion was a member of Christ Church (Episcopal) in Nacogdoches until her removal, after her husband's death, to Marshall in Harrison County. She died in Overton, Rusk County, on November 7, 1883. She was buried near young Charles Raguet Bringhurst and her father and mother in Greenwood Cemetery, Marshall, Texas. The inscription on her gravestone reads: "Blessed are the pure in heart, for they shall see God."

Sister M. Josephine

Sister M. Josephine
(Ernestine Potard)
(1822-1893)

By Carolyn Reeves Ericson*

Sister Josephine won a place in the history of Nacogdoches by her devotion to the Church and her love for the people that she served.

This remarkable woman was born Renee Ernestine Francoise Potard on February 25, 1822, at St. Bartheleme, France, to parents who were well-to-do landowners of the area. Ernestine lived with them until she made application for admission to the convent conducted by the Sisters of the Holy Cross at Le Mans.

The Congregation of Holy Cross, originally founded by the saintly Abbe Basil Anthony Moreau, was a triple society of Priests, Brothers and Sisters patterned upon the Holy Family of Nazareth. The Sisters of Our Lady of Seven Dolors, generally known as Marianites, were separated from this their original congregation and were reorganized independently as the Sisters of the Holy Cross in 1841. The poverty of this congregation attracted the ardent soul of Ernestine, and on April 13, 1846, she bade farewell to her little world and entered the Convent at Le Mans. The following summer she received the holy habit and with it the name of Sister Mary of St. Joseph. While in the novitiate she was called to go on foreign mission work to Indiana where she completed her required novitiate and prepared herself for her future work by studying the language of her adopted country.

---

*Curator, Stone Fort Museum, Nacogdoches, Texas

The Sisters of the Holy Cross had come to the United States in 1843 and established their first Convent in Notre Dame, Indiana. Since that time they have been active throughout the country in educational, hospital and charitable work.

Sister M. Euphrosine, who went from Notre Dame to visit the Motherhouse in France in 1869, made the return trip to America in 1870 on the same ship with Bishop Dubuis and other volunteers who were coming to begin missionary work in Texas. The Bishop persuaded Sister Euphrosine of the great need for Catholic education in his diocese. It was arranged in due time for her to return with the Bishop to Texas. Sister M. Euphrosine, accompanied by another sister first established a small Convent and school in Corpus Christi. Her plans did not succeed for she was not well established when Bishop Dubuis told her he had made a mistake in giving her Corpus Christi, as he had promised it to the Sisters of the Incarnate Word. He advised her to join the colony of Holy Cross now in Nacogdoches.

During the Civil War the manpower of Texas was so completely depleted to furnish men for the Confederate armies east of the Mississippi that at Nacogdoches even the professors at Nacogdoches University were drafted to the colors, which left the college without a staff of teachers. The City fathers invited the Sisters of the Holy Cross to keep the college open in the dark days during the cruel period of Reconstruction.

The newly established Convent of Corpus Christi was accordingly moved to Nacogdoches in April, 1871 and a school was opened in the abandoned building of the once flourishing Nacogdoches University. The Convent was soon re-inforced by Sister M. Joseph (Potard) who came from the Motherhouse in Notre Dame. The new religious community was known as the Convent of the Agonizing Heart of Jesus. Sister M. Euphrosine, Sister M. Bernadetta, Sister M. Paula, Sister M. Joseph (Ernestine Potard) and Sister M. Joseph (Catherine Dunn) worked diligently to teach the long neglected children of the old town of Nacogdoches.

In September 1872 the Convent was moved to Clarksville, but Sister Josephine, whose heart had been won by the poor children of the old Spanish outpost, chose to remain among the Spanish-speaking. She realized if she left it would sever the last real contact the people had with their church. Many hours of doubt and prayer must have gone into her decision to remain behind. She must have realized the many days of loneliness and hardship she would face. But she asked permission to stay, and it was granted. For the final twenty years of her life, Sister Josephine labored alone for her Church in the Nacogdoches area.

After the decision was made to move the Convent to Clarksville, the Masonic Lodge of Nacogdoches prepared to assume the operation of the Nacogdoches University. William Clark, believing that some provision should be made to retain Roman Catholic patronage and to take advantage of the available teaching skills of Sister Josephine, moved that "Sister Joseph have the permission of the Lodge to teach in one room of the College building until the Lodge should want the same." The motion carried, and Clark, W. F. Hunter and A. H. Crain were appointed to inform the Sister of the decision, a remarkable example of cooperation.

Tradition is that after the Masonic Lodge assumed control of the University building, Sister Josephone began teaching in a log building which stood where the Redland Hotel now stands. She continued to teach in this log school house until January 1878 when she purchased a house and lot on South street, next to Banita Creek.

While teaching at Nacogdoches, Sister Josephine witnessed the sad plight and practically complete abandonment of the Old Spanish families living in the vicinity. These people were the descendants of the valiant pioneers who had helped established the missions of East Texas and were left alone in this isolated community after the Texas revolution. The treatment accorded those people by the incoming Anglo-Americans remains a vivid example of pioneer injustice. Without shepherd or church these people held steadfast to the religion of their ancestors, and the faith Father Margil had so labored to plant in East Texas was not to be doomed to extinction. Sister Josephine could not abandon these heroic children of the Church. She took up her abode with them, to teach, evangelize, catechise and lead these children of Margil.

She was now to live alone among a rude frontier people in a pioneer and backwoods country, and the overpowering American element, which surrounded them on all sides and blocked their every effort to expansion or progress, was most hostile to the Catholic religion.

In Nacogdoches she had been a Sister of the Holy Cross— were she now to take off her habit she would be disgraced in the eyes of all who had known her before, and therefore for her own

protection—a lone woman surrounded by most adverse circumstances—she was forced to continue to wear her religious habit
until her death. Time and time again every effort possible on the
part of superiors, who neither understood nor sympathized, was
made to prevail upon her to give up her habit.

On Sundays and feast days she gathered the people together
under a great oak tree and led them in their prayers and devotions; on week days she kept a little school and taught the Catechism to the children and prepared them for the Sacraments. She
rode a little mustang pony from farm to farm caring for the people
in their every need. No wonder she endeared herself to all who
knew her and came within her charm.

Sister Josephine taught in her home on the east side of South
Street until about 1889 when she went to the Church in the Moral
community, which had been organized in 1877. There a small
bare room at the rear of the building became her convent. Her bil-
lowing habit became a familiar sight along the dirt roads as she
traveled from house to house and community to community. She
taught the Catechism, as well as school subjects, to scores of children who would have otherwise had no opportunity for an education.

When Sister Josephine felt in need of spiritual comfort and
the company of other Sisters, she journeyed to Palestine to visit
Sister Flavienne, a sister of Providence. They were kindred spirits
and each was a remarkable woman. The distance to Palestine was
great and there was no railroad; so Sister Josephine was com-
pelled to make the journey of seventy-five miles on the back of her
pinto pony.

It was her custom to make most of her purchases while in
Palestine. On one occasion she had previously ordered by mail a
statue of the Blessed Virgin which was to be delivered in Palestine,
the most convenient point for conveyance to Nacogdoches. After
many disappointing delays she decided to take the statue with her
on her return trip to Nacogdoches. No one could persuade her
that it was an almost impossible venture, that the statue would
become heavier with each mile of the journey and her arms would
ache from the weight of it. She needed that statue to impress her
pupils and their parents with the love for God's Mother and for
instruction purposes. Nothing could deter her from carrying it and
carry it she did, at what agony one can easily imagine. This statue
is still preserved, not for its beauty, but for the lessons it teaches

and what it must have meant to the poor people for whom she bought it and for the suffering this remarkable woman endured in getting it to her loved children.

At Moral she had no bell to summon the people to the church services or the children to school or for any assembly she wished. She procured a large cow horn, such as was common in the early days in Texas, to call the farm hands to meals or for any other purpose when they were needed. It served her purpose and gathered the people for church services especially.

To Mrs. Carmel Y'Barbo, who lives in Nacogdoches, Sister Josephine was like a mother. Carmel's mother died when she was still a small girl and she would spend the week at the Church at Moral while her father worked. The Sister cared for her and made sure that she was fed and had clothes to wear. Carmel called Sister Josephine "Momma" because she was the only mother she knew. Mrs. Y'Barbo remembers Sister Josephine to be about 5'7" tall with a very proud erect carriage.

Sister Josephine lived until 1893 when age and infirmities had so weakened her that she at last consented to go to St. Joseph's Infirmary in Houston for treatment. Neighbors took a wagon and padded it with quilts for a comfortable bed for their beloved Sister Josephine. After she was in the wagon, she asked to be taken to the Moral playground. They called Carmel to come to the wagon to tell her "momma" goodbye. The child cried and the good Sister cried because she knew she would never see her again. It was a very sad parting. She was taken by wagon to Nacogdoches where she boarded the train for Houston. After a week of treatment in the Houston hospital she died on April 27, 1893. Father Hurth, at that time president of St. Edward's University, Austin was named executor of her will. He brought her mortal remains to the little cemetery plot at St. Edward's where the Sisters of the Holy Cross were buried before the present Catholic cemetery for the city was laid out. A simple cross erected by the Sisters of St. Mary's Academy in 1926 marks the last resting place of a truly great woman of Texas, a long neglected saint whose works live after her and whose children rise up to call her "blessed" for "they that instruct many to justice shall shine as stars for all eternity."

Sophie Tolle Koester and granddaughter, Fannie Eisenlohr

Sophie Tolle Koester (1826-1916)

By Fannie Eisenlohr Twitchell*

Sophie was a tiny and pretty adolescent recently arriving from Germany when she met Dr. Theodore Koester, a graduate of Heidelberg and official physician for the Society for the Protection of German Immigrants in Texas at New Braunfels in 1845. They fell in love, married in 1846, and had thirteen children of which only four lived to adulthood.

New Braunfels was named in honor of Prince Carl zu Solms-Braunfels' ancestral home. Prince Solms was a member of Adelsverein, an association of noblemen for the purpose of purchasing land in the free State of Texas and later to protect Germans in Texas. He bought land for the immigrants around Comal Springs where water was plentiful and the land fertile. Prince Solms returned to Germany and in 1847 the Adelsverein became bankrupt. He was succeeded by Baron von Meusebach whose special interest was Fredericksburg, named for Frederick the Great of Prussia.

The first houses in New Braunfels were log cabins, studding framework filled with brick, or huts of cedar posts driven into the ground and roofed over with a tent canvas or with ox-hides. In 1846-1847 there were eighty to one hundred houses in New Braunfels. The Koester's first house was of this kind. However, in 1859-60 a larger house was built nearby.

*Granddaughter

This new house is still standing. It was built by W. A. Thielpape, a local architect, for the Koesters. It is a two story house with a full basement of native limestone. The basement and first story walls are eighteen inches thick. The first and second floors contained five rooms while the basement had the kitchen, pantry, and storage rooms. Food was carried by the dumb-waiter from the kitchen in the basement to the dining room on the first floor.

In addition to the dining room the first floor also had a hall, a large living room, and the doctor's office. On the second floor were three bedrooms, a hall, and a maid's room. Later a bathroom was added. Between the largest and smallest bedroom were folding doors. When home-talent plays were given, the door between the rooms was folded back. The smallest room was used as a stage and the largest room held the audience.

The stairway was winding and fan-type, speaking tubes connected the three floors, and sash windows with weights made raising and lowering them easy.

Besides her children, Marie, Carolyn, Elisa, Emma, and Theodore, her husband and her church, Sophie loved this home built so lovingly for her comfort and pleasure. It was located at 421 South Seguin Street and until it was sold only a few years ago was occupied by some member of the family. It is now a real estate office.

On the new Koester house a sign indicated that Dr. Koester was an apothecary, baker, and physician. The bakery was run by German immigrants to whom Dr. Koester gave jobs. Like most physicians of that day, Dr. Koester preferred to prepare his own medicines. Sophie's brother, August Tolle, was a pharmacist and probably helped his brother-in-law.

Sophie was never idle. When she was not engaged with housework and caring for her children, Sophie knitted. She knitted exquisite lace for petticoats, tops of sheets and edge of pillowcases, and six-inch lace for the bottom of her window shades.

She insisted that her daughters and granddaughters knit. In order to encourage them to knit, Sophie would unwind the thread and insert a cookie, ribbon, small book, sox, or a note. When the child knitted thus far, she got a reward. One of her granddaughters still has Sophie's pattern books for lace and also for cross-stitching which Sophie brought from Germany.

Sophie also knitted baby jackets, petticoats, and drawers. Some of these are still in good condition. They are dainty and have ribbons run through parts either as a decoration or for a utilitarian purpose.

Sophie was an excellent cook and she taught this art to her daughters and granddaughters. Her old German molds are made of wood and the designs deep-set. These molds are still used on holidays such as Christmas, Easter, and birthdays. She was best perhaps with tin molds of men, women, children, angels, ponies, rocking horses, birds, etc. After the batter was baked, she used a thin white icing and then sprinkled colored sugars to show an apron, trousers, blouses, etc. The dough for these characters required much hand stirring (an hour or more). When the coloring was completed, these creatures (human or otherwise) were tied with a narrow ribbon and hung on the Christmas tree.

Sophie's butter was always molded in picturesque butter molds. She made her house a home by making herself a part of it. In large wooden trunks with round tops and iron handles, Sophie had brought from Germany delicate wineglasses, vases, and dishes. Most of the furniture in the Koester House was made in New Braunfels by skilled craftsmen. Her grandchildren have a number of fine pieces such as chests, desks, spice cabinets, wardrobes and beds.

When the second house was built, Dr. Koester had a duplicate made by craftsmen for his children to use as a doll house. This was an exact copy with furniture, mirrors, books, rugs, draperies, etc. The sofa was upholstered. The books had titles. Sophie's descendants still have many of these miniature things.

Dr. Koester died in middle age, leaving his widow poor. He always made a good living but unwisely lent money often to the immigrants without demanding a note. Seldom were the loans repaid. Sophie went to live with her married daughter, Marie Carolyn Koester Eisenlohr. Marie's (Mimi's) husband was Gustaf (Gustave) Eisenlohr, an uncle of Edward Eisenlohr, the well-known Texas landscape painter.

When she was about fifteen, Mimi became deaf from improper care of her ears during her frequent swimming each summer in the Comal River. Her father, unhappily, could do nothing to cure her deafness.

Sophie with her bright blue eyes and wearing a black cap trimmed with lace and ribbon meant much to her six Eisenlohr grandchildren. Although Sophie never learned to speak English,

143

her granddaughter's school friend came often to visit her. Henrietta or Fannie acted as interpreters. As long as Sophie lived German was the language spoken in the Eisenlohr home.

Sophie left the management of the Eisenlohr's home to her daughter but assisted her in her many duties. She was deeply loved by all her grandchildren, especially the Eisenlohr's six. She continued to do fine handwork and sewing for Mimi's children: Theodore, Henrietta, Fritz, Otto Hugo, Alfred, and Fannie.

Sophie died on May 26, 1916 before these United States entered World War I and never knew of the rupture between the land of her birth and the land of her adoption.

Mollie Jane Wilson Lay (1835-1875)

By Winnie L. Garvin *

When the Republic of Texas was a new frontier of hardships and ever present Indian dangers, yet a land of growing opportunity where people were struggling for livelihood and fortune, the subject of this sketch, Jane Wilson, came here with her family at the age of five years.

The advent to Texas of her father, Col. George Wilson, dates from the early days of the Republic. He was born November 27, 1806, in North Carolina, son of a Scotsman, later moving to Tennessee near Nashville where he married Elizabeth McCoy, and to this union five daughters and seven sons were born. He brought his family to Texas in 1840 from Missouri, and settled first in Lamar County, even before its political organization, where he was identified with the movement which gradually pressed back the Indians many times at the muzzle of the rifle. He was commissioned a Colonel by the first governor of Texas, J. Pinckney Henderson, in March 1847, and was Lieutenant Colonel in Young's Regiment at the close of the Mexican war.

He moved to Dallas County in 1848, settling near Cedar Hill, and was among the foremost men of the county during his active life. He became interested in politics and being a man of sound conviction and action, he was sent to the legislature in 1863 and in that body gave a good account of himself.

---

*Granddaughter

Mollie Jane Wilson Lay

MILITARY BALL.

—:—

You are respectfully invited to attend a **MILITARY BALL,** *at Lancaster, on Friday, the 22d inst., at 7 o'clock P. M.*

MANAGERS.

R. S. GUY,	N. K. GROVE,
WM. GREEN,	F. G. BLEDSOE,
MID. PERRY,	CRILL. MILLER,
JONES GREEN,	R. N. DANIEL,

Lancaster, Texas, Feb. 8, 1861.

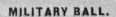

Two of Jane Lay's Invitations

He possessed an inquiring and inventive mind and, aided by his son, he invented and patented the pioneer gang plow, a wind mill and a traveling thresher, and at the commencement of the Civil War father and son were arranging to have Illinois manufacturers turn out the new inventions, but the unsettled condition of of the country for four years stifled the enterprise and it was not revived when peace was established.

Col. Wilson received a land grant for services rendered to the Republic, and was active in the Dallas County Pioneer Association which was organized July 13, 1875, being elected one of the vice-presidents at the fourth reunion in 1886.

Jane was born in Tennessee May 13, 1835, and was the fifth child in this family of twelve. In those days everyone in the family had his or her part in survival, doing daily chores such as caring for the crops and animals, or in household duties. The girls were always busy spinning cloth and sewing for the family, yet as they grew older there was time for social activities, as indicated by invitations received to balls and cotillion parties.

She must have cherished many fond memories, for she saved letters and other mementoes, and one quoted below is from a girl friend dated February 18, 1855. Waxahachie, Ellis County, Texas:

> Dear Jane: I seat myself this morning to inform you that we are all well and hope these few lines come to hand may find you enjoying the same blessing. I am in town in Nan's room, I am going home this evening. Jane, I wish you could have gone home with me from the wedding. I was very lonesome. I caught a beau in Dallas. He was a fine looking fellow. Jane, I have nothing of importance to write only I heard you were going to marry. Please save me a piece of the cake. I saw a great many of the boys last night that send their love to you and said you must come to town. I must close by saying excuse my bad writing and spelling. Come to see me. Give my love to all inquiring friends. Nan is going to write a little. Goodbye—burn this or hide it. Signed L. L. Singleton. P.S. Write to me as soon as you receive this piece of foolishness.

For the mode of transportation in those days, two of her brothers traveled extensively, and in one letter from Washington, D.C., dated May 20, 1857, her brother, Joseph, told of a grand exhibition to be given in Maryland where he expected to have some of his reapers and threshers that were being manufactured in Maryland. He also said that he expected a patent to be issued for sifting and burning bricks in Europe as well as one for a windmill.

This same brother wrote her on March 29, 1858, from the Palmetto House, Galveston, Texas:

> According to my promise I write to you again. I am getting on with my business here slowly but there were more patterns to make than I anticipated when I first got here. Galveston is a very quiet place yet and the spring trade still keeps off, though the time for it is here. I was informed this evening by a gentleman from up the country that the warm, dry weather, which has prevailed for some time past, has improved the roads and the grass so that hauling has commenced again. But from the threatening aspect of the weather, I am doubtful that the dry weather will not last long. It has been cloudy here today and the wind has been blowing a heavy gale from the South that has kept the restless ocean in great commotion and I can see from my window a heavy cloud in the North. I went to church twice yesterday. I went first to the Episcopalian Church and they have a very fine church. There was a large audience of good looking, well dressed people, and the pastor of the church read a a very sensible sermon. I went in the evening to a Methodist Church and heard an old fashioned sermon as long as the moral law, and I can't say much for the people.

William G. Wilson, another brother, wrote her on November 22, 1859, in which he mentioned the Mexican depredations on the Rio Grande and said,

> The news to Lockhart where I was staying a few days ago was that Cortinas had taken Brownsville and Corpus Christi and was advancing toward Austin with an army of 1,800 or 2,000 men well armed. This report caused considerable alarm. Circulars had been printed calling for assistance and scattered through the country. I was attending a Fair at Lockhart at that time. We had several war speeches and they raised a company of about thirty volunteers. Some of the people thought that the Mexicans would come to Austin and I tell you we had exciting times here. But news has come that it is a false report which is no doubt true. My candle is nearly out, so goodnight to all.

As women have always been fashion conscious, her brother Joseph knew that she would be interested in hearing about the latest fads and he wrote May 14, 1860:

> On Board the St. Lous Mail
> Packet Hiawatha
>
> I went right aboard off the Steamship Carlos Morgan. I had a very pleasant time crossing the Gulf. The weather was calm and clear and the steamer glided along as smooth as if it had been on a river. I went to one of the most fashionable churches in the city yesterday and to all the fashionable promenades in order to see the fashion and the beauty of the ladies of New Orleans, but there is such a variety of fashions that no man can tell what is fashion and what not. Hoops have decreased in size very little. Bonnets are about the same. You know how that is that when

a lady is walking toward you, you can't see her bonnet at all and the color of their bonnets and dresses is as varied as there are colors and they are every color from snowy white to sutty. Hats are worn considerably by young unmarried ladies, and they are of every color and size. I have no news to write. My health has improved considerably, though I have been troubled with the toothache until I had it taken out. Write to me at Washington.

One of her friends, an adventurous young man, wrote her on October 17, 1857, from Hagley, Cass County, Illinois:

We arrived at our journey's end on the 25th of last month after nearly six weeks of exposure and fatigue. We had considerable sport traveling, but more since we stopped. I went to a party the night we arrived here and have been to several since then. I have been to one circus and I'm going to another on the 21st.

I don't know when I shall return, but I expect to return single if nothing happens more than I am apprised of. I came very near falling in love with some of the pretty Indian ladies, but everyone I saw was somebody's wife, so my love availed me nothing. I have gotten acquainted with several young ladies here. They are very pretty and handsome but cannot compare with some few of those in Texas, the one which I am addressing especially.

Miss Jane, I would like to see you very much as it has been some time since I have had the pleasure of seeing you. Frequently in idle moments I catch my Thoughts wandering about the Cedar Mountain.

I must close. I would be very glad to hear from you as soon as you receive this, if you please. You will please excuse all mistakes, which I expect there are many as my mind is somewhat bewildered or charmed, thinking of one that is uppermost in my mine (Miss Jane . . .).

From a friend,
R.A.N.

P.S. "Thou hast each thought and dream of mine,
Have I in return one thought of thine?"

In her Album of Remembrance is a note from the daughter of one of the French Colonists at La ReUnion written in French:

Dear Jane: Who is so good and whom I love very much, receive as a souvenir this little token of gratitude, this little letter that I give you. Your face is so sweet and pretty that I shall never forget you as well as your family—these are the qualities of Mlle. Wilson, whom I shall always love.

From your friend,
Marie Bessard
Living near La ReUnion in Texas

In 1861 Jane was married to Jesse M. Lay who came to Texas from Alabama. The beginning of their courtship started at Little Bethel, near the settlement of Cedar Hill, where a Camp

Meeting was being held. As the people began to arrive a young man announced to his friends that he was going to ask the girl who came wearing the largest hoops to sit with him. Soon a wagon came to a stop and stepping down was a young girl, Jane Wilson, wearing a lovely dress with hoops of breath-taking size. The young man, Jesse M. Lay, and the girl, Jane Wilson, fell in love and were married. The dress, which is still in the possession of the family, was made of "lawn" material in a border print.

They lived at Johnson Station near Mansfield and when he served in the Civil War she stayed with her family at Cedar Hill. There were seven children born to this couple, four girls and three boys—Medora, Warren, Alston, Lorinda, Ella, Cora, and Jesse M. Lay, Jr., who died in infancy.

Jane died November 8, 1875, at the age of forty and was buried in the Johnson Station Cemetery. At the time of her death the oldest child was thirteen and the youngest, three. After her death the family moved to Parker County, near Weatherford, where the father reared his children to adulthood.

Although her life on earth was short, she had lived it to its fullest, and as one friend wrote in her Friendship Album, "She was a blossom that seemed more of heaven than of earth."

Rozalie Dusek Lesikar (1824-1922)

By Stacy Mikulencak Labaj*

Rosalie Dusek was born August 28, 1824, at Lanskrout near Cermne, Bohemia. Circa 1851 she married John Lesikar who was a weaver of wool, cotton, and flax near Cermne. The income from this was meagre, barely enough to feed their steadily increasing family.

The woven fabric lengths were carried to the market for sale. The "jahrmark," or market days, were set at the larger communities and towns. Rozalie would start walking at dawn to reach the market early enough to sell. With the money she received from the sales, she bought wool, cotton, and flax to take home for John to weave.

Their log house at Lanskrout was one of a cluster of six or seven such cabins hugging the steep hillside. The scarcity of good soil and of money as well as Austrian oppression caused John and Rozalie to decide to leave for America. The few coins they had were carefully hoarded to buy passage tickets.

The Lesikars had seven children: two daughters (Ann and Rozalie) and five sons (John, Josef, Vincent, Frank and Benjamin) and all nine left for Galveston, Texas, in a sailing vessel, arriving there, perhaps, in 1871. John, Sr., and the older children recalled vividly the raising and lowering of the ship's sails and the sailors struggling with huge sails. On the ship were many Italians who

---

*Collector of oral histories of pioneers and children of pioneers

never seemed to suffer seasickness; John thought this was due to the fact that they ate food highly seasoned with garlic. The ship's menu ran heavily to fish. Fish afterwards were associated in Rozalie's mind with seasickness. She could never eat fish again.

From Galveston the Lesikars made their way into Burleson County by wagon and oxen. Here was where some emigrants from Lanskrout had settled. Here were the Motls; Sefciks; Jan, Vince and Josef Dukatnik; and Ernest and Frank Bartek. Some immigrants had come empty-handed and a few indentured for the passage tickets.

The Lesikars' journey was slow and tedious. The roads were mere trails cut with an axe and only wide enough for a wagon. Stumps often protruded twelve inches from the ground. Low stumps were called "blind stumps" because they were almost on a level with the ground and so, dangerous to those in a wagon or on foot.

During the first year the Lesikars camped and cleared other people's land to make money while they looked for better farm land. They soon found out that stumps, left in a field, in no time sprouted long shoots around the trunk, which made them harder to cut out. They also learned that mesquite trees like pecan trees send roots straight down while elm trees have many side roots and are harder to clear away.

When they hired out, John and the older boys did the heavy cutting while the younger children and Rozalie whacked off smaller limbs, carried and stacked them in a big pile to dry and later to burn. The felled trees were cut into cordwood.

The Lesikars moved on to the Tyler Ranch in Williamson County still working for money and looking around for land that would make a good farm. They lived in cabins formerly occupied by slaves. Since a number of Czech families stopped here, there were not enough cabins to house them all. Several families occupied one cabin. In this the children slept, and bedding and perishables were housed. The parents slept under the trees with snakes and insects to keep them company. The men and boys were often hired to clear other people's land. If he were a boarder, he received $12.00 a month working from sunup to sundown.

In 1882 the Lesikars moved on to east Bell County and found the fertile soil they were seeking. However, this was timber-line country. Some of the tree trunks had the circumference of a barrel. The hardy mustang grapevines locked their tentacles upon the branches and trunks of the trees, creating a jungle. The younger children were warned to keep strictly in the clearings.

All winter long, no matter what the weather was, the sound of the axe and grubbing hoe resounded. Gradually the family cultivated the cleared land and planted cotton, corn, wheat, sugar cane, and many vegetables. When the cotton was picked, they took the harvested cotton to the gin. Cord wood was burned to fire the engine. Later, cotton seed was used for the same purpose.

There were plenty of grapes, hawthorn berries, blackberries, wild plums, pecans, black walnuts, and wild hogs, wild turkeys, prairie hens and prairie hen eggs to add to the family's diet. From the sugar cane he planted, John made molasses. It took a barrel of molasses to supply the family for a year. Sugar and coffee were hard to come by.

Rozalie baked bread daily after wheat had been planted, harvested, and ready for use. The loaves were generally large ones. One Czech family had a baking tin about a foot and a half in length and a foot wide. After looking at the tin, a neighbor ejaculated: *"Plechac, no ma duse, tak veliky"* (a tin, my soul, this big!). Always there were cornbread and corn mush. The corn was carried in packs on horseback to the mill to be ground.

Rozalie had little opportunity for a social life; her life was hard, gruelling, and monotonous. Busy with outdoor chores, helping the men in the fields and with children to be cared for and educated, meals to be cooked, clothing to be made and kept clean and mended, she was grateful just for a place to sit and mend.

When a neighbor or relative gave birth to a child, Rozalie would serve as midwife. This was about the only visiting she did. Generally, she took a length of calico to the baby's mother as a gift.

During the land clearing and before there were roads, a great drought came, a year and a half in duration, that tried the faith of all farmers. The land was parched, native grasses were as dry as shucks, and watering places dried up. Cattle had to be driven eleven miles to the river for water. Clothes washing was done with water caught in rain barrels as long as this lasted. Then the clothes and the washpot were hauled in a wagon to the creek. Usually, the washday was Sunday.

Water wells did not work all the time. Often the everpresent elm trees absorbed the spring water or made it unpalatable. Getting water for the family, the cattle and the horses was a continuing problem.

When the rains came in the spring, fall, and winter months, the roads often became impassable. When the Lesikars' son, Benjamin, died it took four horses six hours to take his body from Temple to Ocker for burial, a distance of eleven miles.

Rozalie worried when Saturdays came because her husband and oldest son did forced labor on the county roads. All the able-bodied men were required to help build the first public road east of Temple. She did not realize this road building was a community effort toward a mutual need but regarded this as feudalism all over again, one of the things which had caused them to leave Bohemia. Consequently, the children behaved as though their father and eldest brother were going to war. Later, a man could pay $1.00 for a replacement in Saturday's work.

Money was scarce. When it was needed, it was borrowed from a personal friend with no note nor signature required. The only time a Czech farmer had money was when cotton was sold. Then with his earnings, he bought more land. They were land hungry.

When John Lesikar found the property he wished to settle upon, he and one of his sons bought 100 acres along the Thornton Stone-Rutherford line for $5.00 an acre. An earthen-floor shack stood on the land. The land was entirely timberland awaiting the clearing of enmeshed trees, brush, briars, mustang grapevines and blood weeds. Before the complete clearing, the trees and underbrush offered the Lesikars some protection from cold blasts of the wind, frost and freezing. After the clearing the north wind swept across the unprotected land, taking the top soil along and forcing settlers to build windbreaks for their cattle and homes, to cover the walls of their cabins with old newspapers and periodicals, and to wear very heavy clothing. The winters were merciless.

When the Lesikars came from Bohemia, they had brought their Bible, their Kancional (book of sermons and prayers) and a hymnal and psalter. About 1876 the Protestant settlers in the area began meeting beneath the trees for a worship service. A pastor came only twice a year, so they were strictly on their own.

In November, 1892, the Protestant Czechs in the region officially organized and Josef Lesikar was named an elder of the

Czech-Moravian Brethren Congregation at Ocker. The Brethren dated back to the great reformer, John Huss. The church was incorporated and dedicated by the Reverend J. Juren and the Reverend Adolf Chlumsky of Brenham.

Hard labor faced the Lesikars at every turn and yet most of them lived to a ripe old age—in fact, far surpassing the allotted time of man. In her old age, Rozalie lived with Josef and his family. She died on October 1, 1922, at the age of 98 years and four days. She was buried with those she loved in the Ocker Cemetery.

Elizabeth Gaertner Levy

Elizabeth Gaertner
Levy
(1849-1925)

By Marguerite Meyer Marks*

Elizabeth Gaertner, daughter of Clara Moss and John Gaertner and granddaughter of Betsy Isaacs and John Moss, was born July 8, 1849, in London on Ashley Street. Elizabeth was descended from a line of Sephardic Jews who had fled Spain at the time of the Inquisition, settling in England by way of Holland.

In the heritage Elizabeth Gaertner brought with her to America converged many of the strands that, woven together, created the pattern of American life. The liberal attitude of Holland and England encouraged the transplanted Spanish Jews to settle and give of their gifts. Moving on to the New World, these Jews took with them their treasure of culture and moral stamina which they added like shot gold to the warp and woof of the burgeoning American Way.

Elizabeth's girlhood was a happy one of glamor and excitement made more so by the romance and marriage of her widowed Grandmother to Rufus Isaacs whose son was to become Lord Reading, Viceroy of India. That Ashley Street held lovely memories becomes obvious when years later she named one of her sons Ashley. Reared in the Victorian Age, Elizabeth's manners, her morals, her culture, and her dress reflected the dominating Queen.

---

*Granddaughter

After John Gaertner died his widow, Clara Moss Gaertner, took Elizabeth and her other children: Emma, John, David, Isaac, and Alfred to New York to make a new life. Elizabeth's heart was torn at the time of the Civil War when John joined the Northern Army while David fought for the Confederacy. To her dying day, Elizabeth cherished the small Bible David wore over his heart and which he claimed saved his life in battle.

One of Elizabeth's stories recounted how New York buildings were draped in solemn black at the time of Lincoln's death, while the melancholy funeral march echoed through the still streets as the cortege rolled by.

Shortly after the tragedy of the Civil War, Elizabeth with her mother, Sister Emma, David, and Alfred moved to Galveston. Brothers Isaac and John remained in the North. Isaac was the first oculist ever to remove an eye from its socket, perform the necessary operation, and then return the eye to its place.

The travelers from New York found Galveston picking up its spirit in the renewal of shipping and the grain industry. That force, combined with the educational background of its citizens, made the island city one of the early industrial and cultural centers of Texas.

As a young woman, Elizabeth had charm, quick wit, and a beauty of her own. It is no wonder Alphonse Levy, a typical Frenchman with a goatee, was attracted to her. He had done his stint in the Battle of Galveston (behind a barrel he always joked) and was making his way as an ambitious merchant in the wholesale grain and grocery business.

Elizabeth and Alphonse were the first couple to be married in the new Temple B'nai Israel, July 7, 1871. According to faded yellow clippings, it was a grand ceremony amid June roses, bright-eyed bridesmaids with a radiant satin-garbed bride as beautiful as her own blossoms.

The Alphonse Levys took their place quickly in the social life of the Harmony Club, the spiritual life of the Temple, the cultural and business life of the fast-growing community. Their home became and was ever a place of ingathering, the center of much activity.

Elizabeth's famous Sunday dinners became the drawing card for Alphonse's French compatriots among whom was the well-known priest, Father Le Moinier. They came to share the joys of speaking their native tongue, discussing affairs of the day, and relishing the delicious soup ladled by Elizabeth from her generous and hospitable English tureen of muted blues, gold and ochre design.

A story told in the family of Elizabeth's early married life throws light on her spicy sense of humor, by which she played a trick on her devoted bridegroom. At a masked ball at the Harmony Club, she went with Alphonse in one costume only to change to another, using her disguise to flirt with and tantalize her bridegroom to distraction. Neither would tell the end of this escapade when Elizabeth unmasked and Alphonse found his bride once more.

A favorite relative of Elizabeth's was Cousin Maurice Levy, a debonair past-eighty gentleman. His English accent still rolled trippingly off the tongue. His toupee held tight to his bald head. His gold-headed cane cut the air as he walked straight as a die down the street. He would ask: "How old are you, Lizzie?" And she would answer: "Same as you, Maurice. Old as my tongue, a little older than my teeth."

All her life, Elizabeth was known as a meticulous housekeeper. Her featherbeds and pillows were a formidable sight, waving on the clothesline, while her china, silver, and dark inlaid furniture, some still in use, shone like mirrors. She had a passion for order and quickly noted if anything was missing from its place.

When their three boys and three girls arrived in rapid succession, Elizabeth dedicated her time to their rearing. She instilled in her children a sense of Victorian morality she had been reared to respect, a love of books and music, a deep devotion to Judaism as a way of living and serving mankind. During their growing-up years, Elizabeth, with a nurse, took the children to Mackinac Island or Charleroix to escape the hot summer. Alphonse joined the noisy, active brood at vacation's end to escort them on the long train ride home.

Example as well as precept was Elizabeth's code. Her compassion and keen sense of social service made her mother and grandmother to many not born to her. To her there were no Jewish measles or Catholic mumps. She stretched out her hand and her heart to all. True, she practiced the Lady Bountiful type of social welfare as it was done in those days by taking baskets of food to the poor, sewing shrouds, and nursing the indigent sick. No interfaith organization *per se* existed in Elizabeth's day, yet as she made her way to poor Irish Catholics, Protestants, or Negroes in trouble, she became a prototype of what was to come on a larger scale. She went about those low slung roofed houses with an ease, a grace that blessed man's dignity.

Elizabeth's closest friend for well over a half a century was Agnes Erhard, a staunch German Episcopalian. The two lived across the street from each other on Avenue K and 17th Street. They exchanged recipes and gossip, reared their large families side by side, sharing one another's joys and trials. To this day, the grandchildren of Agnes and Elizabeth recall this special bond between two great matriarchs who loved and respected one another and commanded respect from the world.

When tragedy struck down Alphonse in a train wreck and when her son, Mannie, was caught in the vortex of the Great Galveston Storm, buffeted about all night by the swirling waters, injured past nursing to health by Elizabeth, and doomed not to live out his full life, the strength within asserted itself. These were nature's calamities. These were from the outside. Grief-stricken, she was not defeated. As Job, she rose from her afflictions to create life anew.

With more zeal than ever, she devoted herself to her remaining family and those in need about her. She encouraged her daughter, Estelle Meyer, when she led the Jewish community to abandon provincial Sisterhood in order to ally itself with a larger National Council of Jewish Women. She was the first to see the need of a Mothers' Club and helped Estelle achieve that goal in the city's schools. She encouraged her grandchildren to go to college in order to broaden their lives to that they could serve with more understanding.

As the ideas and need for social service grew, Elizabeth never ceased to grow herself. She added her strength to those working with the incoming Russian immigrants pouring into Galveston to help them find jobs and housing and to learn the language of a new land.

When Elizabeth in the twilight of her life was stricken by paralysis, she never failed to cheer those who cared for her. Unable to speak, the twinkle in her eye communicated, carrying outward her great spirit. She never knew self-pity. Elizabeth continued to be the center of the busy home. Tenderly cared for and loved by her daughter, Estelle; son-in-law, Herman Meyer; and their children, Alphonse and Marguerite, she who had mothered the world was now mothered. Friends came and went away cheered by this invalid of indomitable spirit.

Elizabeth lies buried beside Alphonse in the Hebrew Cemetery in Galveston. She was a deeply human woman, a woman of valor whose spirit lives on in her grandchildren and great-grandchildren to light their way. Hers is a spirit remembered by all those whose lives touched hers. Years have passed but the memory of my Grandmother Elizabeth lingers on to pervade my life.

Mildred Satterwhite Littlefield

Mildred Satterwhite Littlefield (1811-1880)

By David B. Gracy II*

Mildred Terrell Satterwhite was born in Wilkes County, Georgia, on June 12, 1811, into a family of wealth, position, and heritage. Her parents, both representatives of long and distinguished lines, belonged to an enclave of affluent, respected, influential Virginians who left their native state shortly after the American Revolution and moved south. These Virginians nourished the ideals and styles of the high born. Women, whom the men prided themselves in insulating from the vulgar, real world, were the ornaments of this exclusive society. They were expected to marry within the circle to sustain the economic strength and to maintain the social aloofness of the group. On December 19, 1826, then, fifteen-year-old Mildred wed John Henry White, a son of a neighboring Virginia family.

For twelve years, the Whites lived in the region of their birth. But in 1838, after the virgin fertility of the up country had been exhausted by successive plantings of tobacco and then cotton, they moved to Panola County, Mississippi. The following year John Henry White died.

In a day when women were expected not to manage alone, Mildred, twenty-seven years old and the mother of six children ranging in age from one to ten, took complete charge of the plantation left to her and her children. The domestic duties of the place

---

* Great-great-grandson

163

she managed herself. To direct the work of the slaves in the fields, she naturally hired an overseer. The plantation prospered.

On September 16, 1841, Mildred married her overseer, Fleming Littlefield. To this union Mildred bore four children. For nine years the Littlefields lived on their plantation in Panola County increasing their stores. By the census of 1850, they owned real estate valued at $8,000 and 46 slaves. Ranked among the upper 20 percent economically, the Littlefields enjoyed comfort but not leisure.

Mildred's choice of a husband outside the Virginia circle would have been difficult enough for her kin to accept, but her selection of an overseer was unthinkable. Overseers as a class ranked at the very bottom of the social scale, an unspannable distance beneath the high-born Satterwhites. The ill feeling grew deeper as the years passed, until December, 1850, when a gun fighter was sent to assassinate Littlefield. Fleming, in front of his own home, met the assassin and shot him dead. Then, fearing a murder charge, he fled.

Mildred, the children, and the slaves followed Fleming to Texas, where within a year they settled on their own plantation along the Guadalupe River in Gonzales County near Belmont.

About a year later, just when everything seemed to be progressing well, Fleming died of pneumonia on January 8, 1853. Forty-one years old, Mildred again faced the world a widow. But this time to assist her were children who had reached their maturity. The oldest, Thomas Jefferson White, who had helped her move to Texas said that he could not think of his mother coming out by herself.

More importantly, she had her own vigor, fortitude, endurance, and native ability. "Old Misstus," one former slave testified of his years on her Gonzales County plantation, "could look in your eye and tell you what you was up to. . . . Whatever she told you you was going to do, you did it, and whatever she told you was going to become of you, it did." Imposing in physical as well as mental stature—she weighed upwards of 200 pounds and was "too short and thick to be a Southern belle"—Mildred bossed her own plantation and her minor children's with unquestioned authority.

On these Mildred produced cotton and corn as well as livestock, and she maintained her economic stability through the poor crop years of mid-century. Her net worth, ten years after leaving Mississippi, totaled approximately $55,000.

Devoted as she was to the efficient management of her properties, Mildred was equally concerned with her family. "Grandma always liked to have the family around," one granddaughter testified. "The more she had, the better she liked it." Her eldest Littlefield child, George, wrote that she "was a mother carrying the confidence and love of her children." Daughter Sarah Dowell demonstrated it. She had left home and married precipitously in defiance of her step-father. After Littlefield's death, Sarah implored her financially inept husband to accept "the benefit of her (Mildred's) advice and aid." He did not, and Sarah eventually sued for divorce. "If Dowell gets judgment," Mildred wrote defiantly in the only letter of hers that has survived, "I intend to scatter things miterly." Sarah won and lived the rest of her life on her mother's place.

Of Mildred's sympathetic understanding for one within the family circle, a grandson recalled the time that Mary Kaufman, the tutor Mildred hired during the Civil War, was driving to school in one of Mildred's buggies with one of her grandchildren. A slave driving Mildred's own wood wagon clipped Mary's sulky, shattering its shaft. Mary worried what the old lady's retribution would be. But Mildred, "one of those old-fashioned talking womans," as the grandson described her, said simply, "It couldn't be hoped (helped), and there ain't no use grieving about it, you couldn't hope it."

Her concern reached beyond her kin. Being quite wealthy "before the War, she had ample means and opportunity to show her kind and liberal spirit," her obituary reported, "and right well did she improve her opportunities." After the Civil War erupted, fifty-year-old Mildred, like most women on both sides, supported the war effort unstintingly.

As cloth became scarce following the Federal blockade of Southern ports, Mildred erected spinning jennies and looms in her home, took her own cotton and wool, made dyes from moss, weeds, and minerals from the earth on her place, and created "pretty, rich, soft, firm, strong, comfortable cloth of all kinds and in as many colors as Joseph's coat." Then with her youngest child and often a grandson with her, she rode to the neighborhood schoolhouse to join other ladies from the Guadalupe bottom in a sewing circle. The grandson marveled at her dexterity, remarking that she had the "most fitting hands to work." Often when completing a pair of pants, she sewed a coin, sometimes as large as a $20 gold piece, into a pocket. The thought of the duty she was performing, one grandson wrote, "was a great pride and joy to her." At home she never turned away a Confederate soldier needing a meal or a place to rest, nor spurned soldiers' wives or widows. Many were the notches cut on her barn door accounting for barrels of corn "Granny," as Mildred was coming to be called, gave them.

At the war's end, she had her overseer assemble the slaves before her and read the order freeing them. "She did not pout, she did not fool about it. She did not cry. She did not say all was lost. She did not cower. She was not small about it. She did not leave the poor negroes to find out they were free from others. She told them they were free, she no longer owned them, they could go and work for whomever they pleased. Standing there erect . . ., she bid slavery so far as she was concerned on this earth, a final and complete farewell, forever; kept her faith . . . lived a regenerate citizen for a re-united country and died a devotee to its solidity and worth as loyal as she had ever been to the Confederacy, States rights and the Stars and Bars." Nor did she abandon the commitment made to one of her brothers years before to provide and care for two of his elderly slaves for the rest of their lives.

The record of Mildred Littlefield's activities after the war is scanty. She turned over the management of the plantation to her son George, holding back, as a mother must, a few responsibilities for her other Littlefield son, William. This fretted pragmatic George, who was much the better businessman of the two. But George easily assumed his mother's role as the focal point and strength of the family. Having learned well what she taught him of business, he amassed a fortune in the cattle trade and banking. And from the first, he employed family members—those on the White as well as on the Littlefield side—in his several enterprises. They helped him expand his operations; he provided them security. He used his wealth to educate his nieces and nephews (as his mother had done with her grandchildren), to assure that the legacy his mother intended for each one was delivered in full, and to provide for those less astute with money than he. With George in charge, Mildred could afford to devote herself less to economics and more to her family and friends.

A Christian, if not a regular church-goer, Mildred never slackened her concern for her neighbor, both those in the country and those in Gonzales, where she moved to be near George and where she spent the last decade of her life. "Only a month or two before her death," the author of her obituary wrote, "she arose at midnight and, throwing around her the waterproof coat of her son, went out into the night storm to wait upon a neighbor lady who was dying."

On Tuesday morning, June 8, 1880, Mildred Littlefield died of apoplexy, three days short of her sixty-ninth birthday. Only five of her ten children survived her. But the "large number who attended her burial attest the warm place she held in the hearts of the community, and the great feeling manifested by her former slaves who were present show how kind a mistress she had been. Many mingle their tears and sympathies with the children and grandchildren she leaves."

Elizabeth McDonald Lockwood

Elizabeth McDonald Lockwood (1825-1872)

By Jean Lockwood Williams *

Elizabeth McDonald was born in Texas April 29, 1825, a daughter of John McDonald and Jemina Jett. After her mother's death, Elizabeth was reared by a maternal aunt, Mrs. Elizabeth Jett Berry.

Her father, John McDonald, a native of Louisiana, was a veteran of the War of 1812, fighting under Andrew Jackson at the Battle of New Orleans. John McDonald had moved to Texas in 1806. He was a descendant of Scot immigrants who came early to the United States.

Elizabeth McDonald married William R. Lockwood on December 15, 1842, in Tarkington's Prairie, Liberty County, Texas. She was a small, energetic young lady with light brown hair and hazel eyes. Her husband, a native of Connecticut, had come to New Orleans in 1821. After spending a year or two on a whaling expedition, he came to Texas in 1823 or 1824 on a tour of exploration. He eventually settled in Houston, Harris County, where he engaged in cutting and shipping wood to Galveston Island.

The acquisition of a home-farm for the young couple came in several stages. First, they secured 160 acres of land in Harris County about ten miles north and eighteen miles east of Houston (Survey 1858 in State Land Office). Second, on July 7, 1862, the

* Granddaughter

Lockwoods purchased 180 acres from James Berry. Third, Mrs. Elizabeth Jett Berry died a few months later and left one-half of her estate to her niece, Elizabeth Lockwood.

This sizable estate was lived on by members of the Lockwood family until the house burned after Elizabeth's death in 1872. Many family records, pictures, and books were lost. In 1910, my father, Henry Lockwood, with the legal help of Baker, Botts, Parker, and Garwood of Houston, settled the estate, so he could distribute the purchase price to the heirs of William R. Lockwood and Elizabeth Lockwood.

William R. Lockwood was a skilled workman in both wood and iron. In his early married life, he gave his full attention to the trades. However, in 1852, he took up farming and stock-raising and continued in these activities until his death. In early days, William was elected sheriff of Harris County, but he refused to serve having no taste for public office. He was a Democrat in politics, a member of Masonic Orders, and a zealous supporter of churches.

William and Elizabeth Lockwood had eight children: Hannah Jane, Elizabeth, William, Mary Ann, Frank, Henry, Warren, and Elam. Stories told me by my father indicate a very happy family life with a successful father and an understanding and sympathetic mother who took care of the family with love and industry.

The two older daughters, Hannah Jane and Elizabeth, were a great help with the younger children. The second daughter, Elizabeth, although blinded probably by measles, was able to do many useful things. Also she is said to have removed warts by rubbing them and praying with the patient. Elizabeth passed her method on to my father, Henry Lockwood. He was known throughout the community for doing this service free with all who came to him.

The Lockwood boys were skilled in riding and hunting. They liked to hunt bears with their father along Buffalo Bayou. The bears were generally large. The meat was used for food and the skins tacked up and dried on the farm walls. They became laprobes or rugs. The boys also liked to catch raccoons and opossums which they brought home as pets.

Elizabeth taught her daughters the household skills: sewing, cooking, canning, preparing jellies and dairy products, and the care of chickens and turkeys.

Elizabeth's aunt, who had reared her, lived on a dairy farm adjoining the Lockwood Farm. She helped the family as a grandmother would. The Berry family burial plot on Mrs. Berry's land became the burial place for the Lockwoods too. The Cemetery is now in the center of a large cemetery in Brookside, Harris County, and situated near the Chapel.

Elizabeth Lockwood saw that her family was well fed with the produce from the farm, the game obtained from hunting, vegetables from the garden, the natural yield of the pecan trees and wild fruits and berries, bountiful milk supplies, beef and pork slaughtered on the farm by her husband and cut up, smoked and stored or made into sausage. My father talked often of eating hoecake, an unleavened pancake fried on top of the stove but originally cooked outside on a hoe over an open fire.

Every morning hot oatmeal was served in the Scot tradition, together with sausage, eggs, hotcakes, cornpone or biscuits. The children were told that oatmeal was good brain food.

Pecans were greatly loved. Large toe-sacks of pecans would be gathered or bought. The children divided the pecans among themselves, took them away, and hid them for safe keeping. Some of the pecans were buried around the yard and were dug up as they were wanted for eating. Some never dug up sprouted and formed a wide circle of beautiful pecan trees around the home place.

Also close to the house were magnificent oak trees, several feet thick, branches almost as thick, and filled with Spanish moss.

My father recalled that the family went to church, picnics, dances, and fiddlers' contests. He himself played the fiddle for dances. He probably had learned to fiddle from other fiddlers. During my childhood, he played "Dixie," "Yankee Doodle," "Skip to My Lou," "Old Dan Tucker," hymns, and a folk song I have never heard and which I gave to Bill Ownes for his book on native Texas songs. It concerned a young man's farewell to his "little pink" as he left to fight in the War of 1848 with Mexico.

Elizabeth died in 1872 five years after her husband. Her four younger children took measles. While nursing the younger boys with the help of her blind daughter, Mrs. Lockwood came down with "black" measles and died.

The four younger children, all boys, went to live with a married sister, Mary Ann Sternenberg, who was only twenty-one years old when her mother died. Mrs. Sternenberg taught her young brothers to be independent, self-reliant, honorable men. They were soon self-supporting in farming; clerking in a mercantile house; engaging in the lumber business; and mining in New Mexico, California, and Alaska.

Elizabeth lived a short life of forty-seven years. She bore and reared eight children, helped her husband build and run a large farm, and was a good neighbor, wife, and mother. Like other pioneer women, she worked hard but had the satisfaction of seeing her children and the land grow to make Texas the great State it has become.

Sarah Ellen Eaton McCallister (1830-1888)

By Fay Lockhart Mays *

"My mother had a hard life," Great-uncle "Matt" McCallister told me. He was speaking of Sarah Ellen Eaton McCallister seventy-eight years after her death. He was one hundred and three years old at the time, a merry, alert, affectionate little leprechaun of a man we visited in 1966 in Albuquerque, New Mexico. He was the only person who had actually known her and could tell me of her from his own knowledge. I valued his treasured memories, and told him of my searches of county and census records and wide correspondence with relatives to learn all I could of the Eaton and McCallister families.

He had no picture of her to show me, but he told me that she had brown eyes, that his father had blue eyes, that they were near in age, that they raised cattle for a living. Sarah was a small, slender woman with dark hair and fair complexion. When I was lucky enough to borrow a picture of his parents, I made a copy and sent it to him. By then he was one hundred and four, and at long last living in a rest home. His son-in-law wrote me that Great-uncle Matt wept when he saw the picture, because his family had meant so much to him. He lived on to one hundred and six years!

It was a hard life, indeed, for Sarah, yet she succeeded in taking care of her large family while her husband served in the

* Great-granddaughter

173

Sarah Ellen Eaton McCallister

Confederate forces and after his death. How she was sustained by faith and family is her story, and the reason I write it.

Sarah Ellen Eaton was born near Palestine, in Crawford County, State of Illinois, November 25, 1830. She was the eleventh and last child of Richard and his wife Mary (Polly). Family legend has it that she was of Welsh descent, but we have no proof. We believe that he was the son of Benjamin and Malinda Eaton and that he was born in 1782, probably in Hampshire County, present West Virginia. The Eatons lived in Kentucky until after 1802, then settled in present Illinois about the time of the War of 1812.

Why did Richard Eaton come to Texas? I think his reason was the same as that of most pioneers who thought they could better themselves by acquiring more land. It was not through religious persecution nor through poverty, for they were doing well before they came. Richard owned land and a grist mill, had been appointed ensign in the local militia, and had served on the grand jury. The Eatons were devout people, as well as brave. They were influenced to come to Texas by Rev. Daniel Parker, who had visited this area in 1832 and had learned that the Mexican government would not permit organization of any Protestant church here, but that a previously formed church might stay organized after coming in.

Daniel Parker organized the Pilgrim Predestinarian Baptist Church in Crawford County, Illinois, in July, 1833 and persuaded several families to come to Texas with him. Richard and Polly Eaton, with daughters Elizabeth and Rachel, met the ox-drawn caravan in Claiborne Parish, Louisiana, in October, 1833, so state the church minutes. I do not doubt that the younger children, including three-year-old Sarah, came with them.

This very first Protestant church of Texas held its first meeting in Texas January 12, 1834, near the town of Anderson, in Grimes County. Soon the group divided, some going to Fort Parker, near Goresbeck, and the original church to Fort Brown, in Houston County, later to Elkhart, in Anderson County.

Minutes of the church show that Richard Eaton was a very active member and was ordained as its first deacon. The congregation met in his home several times between 1841 and 1843. He helped supervise construction of the log churchhouse, of which a replica stands today about three miles from Elkhart. In the adjacent cemetery lies Richard's daughter, Lucinda, whose husband was Dickerson Parker, hero of San Jacinto and son of Rev. Daniel Parker, who is buried there also.

Because of danger from Indians, the church held no regular meetings from April 2, 1836, to February 25, 1837. During this period some of the settlers were driven from their homes briefly. Sarah's brother, Richard, a boy of thirteen or fourteen years, was sent for help on a dark and stormy night. He slipped through the Indians and brought soldiers who enabled the people to return to their homes.

Sarah herself joined the church "by experience" on May 18, 1844. The setting for her growing up was wholesome morally and socially. Only persons of good character were welcomed into the Stephen F. Austin Colony. The church had high standards of conduct for its members, sometimes stepping in to settle personal infractions that would go uncensured today, perhaps. Sometimes there were reprimands. One man repentantly confessed that he had had too much to drink on election day and had "acted wrongly." On another occasion, after an embarrassed delay, church officers effected a reconciliation between Polly Eaton and a sister member, "M.L.," of whose levity Polly had complained. This incident leads me to believe that Polly would have set very high standards of conduct for her daughters and would have taught them that they owed obedience to church, parents, and husband.

Minutes of the church show that "on Saturday August 15, 1845, Richard Eaton, cister (sic) Mary Eaton, and cister Sary E. Eaton were dismissed by letter." They were moving to Limestone County, where they settled about one mile east of Thornton. Richard Eaton had been granted in 1834 two and one-half labors of land in present Robertson County; in 1835 he received twenty-two and one-half labors in present Limestone County, and in 1838 one labor in present Anderson County. He had plenty of land to share with the nine of his children who came to Texas. Those who came were Malinda, Mary M. (Polly), Elizabeth B., Lucinda, Rachel, Richard, Daniel D., Jesse, and Sarah Ellen. The two who did not come were Absolum (sic) who moved to Kansas, and son Squire, who died unmarried in 1833, leaving his property to his brothers, sisters, and parents.

Sarah's mother Polly died between 1845 and 1850. By the time the 1850 census of Limestone County was taken, Richard had married Charity, widow of his brother Stephen. Richard died about 1855 and is believed buried with both wives in Eaton cemetery, near Thornton, though their graves were unmarked.

Before she was eighteen years old, Sarah was married to Alabama-born David Crockett McCallister, son of Michael and Hannah McCallister. She and David gave a deed March 20, 1848. The census record shows many members of the same family lived near each other, even after beginning families of their own and living in separate dwellings. Pioneers needed each other, and Sarah had the comfort of living among her own people. In the same enumeration were her sister Malinda, now married to her cousin Benjamin Eaton; sister Mary Thomas; sister Elizabeth Welch; brother Daniel D., who had married Dicey McCallister, now doubly Sarah's sister-in-law; Brother Jesse, and sister Rachel Culp, that fearless woman who rode horseback, dodging Indians in darkness when called to aid the sick. Rachel's great-granddaughter is Oveta Culp Hobby, first director of the Women's Auxiliary Army Corps and mother of our present Lt. Gov. William Hobby, Jr. Besides her Eaton siblings, Sarah had many of her husband's relatives as neighbors. The life was difficult; lonely it was not.

David and Sarah's first child was Mary Ann, born July 4, 1849. Then came Hannah, my grandmother, and Angeline, all born in Limestone County.

David bought one hundred seventy acres of land in Coryell County (organized 1854) from G. W. Robinson on February 17, 1858. He made another purchase of land from Mary Eadens May 10, 1860. Sarah's brother Richard also bought land in that county October 6, 1860.

The 1860 census of Coryell County shows David and Sarah, now with four little daughters: Mary Ann, eleven; Hannah, nine; Angeline, seven; Melissa, four ("Melisey C" sounded like "Elizabeth C." to the enumerator). There was a two-year-old son George W. A son at last, after four daughters! Not named in the census was baby son David, born August 14, 1859. All were living near Raney's Creek in the home of David's sixty-nine-year-old parents. David had real estate worth $700 and personal property of $1500, probably consisting principally of livestock. In the same neighborhood lived Madison McCutchen, county judge, whose eldest son William would eventually grow up to marry Hannah McCallister and know me as their granddaughter.

In 1861 the fear of Indians caused some settlers to abandon their homes in the western part of Coryell County. My grandmother Hannah told my mother how she and her sisters worked in their vegetable garden without seeing an Indian hidden in the brush nearby. They were unaware of his presence until he told them, years later, how often he had watched them. This was after he became friendly with the family.

Then came the Civil War. I have read in the Texas Archives of David's enlistments in 1863 and 1864 and two muster rolls. But of Sarah's service I learned from a sketch written by my mother.

> David McCallister, handsome on his big black horse, was a man who laughed in the face of any danger. He was generous to the point of giving away his own homespun blankets and clothing to less fortunate companions in arms. Then he sent home for more, and his wife and daughters sometimes sat up all night spinning and weaving to make him more blankets and clothing.

Since these little girls were so young—from seven or eight to fourteen or fifteen, I hope they did not have to do it very often, or that they took turns at loom or spinning wheel. The daughters learned some other crafts, too, and one was dyeing fabric with native plants. I value a quilt Hannah made of pink calico and brown pieces in the Log Cabin pattern. The brown material was dyed with cedar bark, my mother told me. David was a real hero to his wife and daughters, who gave their help eagerly.

David McCallister died of a heart attack in late 1868 or early 1869, when in his early forties. Sarah was a widow at age thirty-eight. In June, 1869 she gave birth to David's posthumous child, Sarah Ellen, named for her mother, and their tenth child. In twenty years of marriage they had had ten children. All lived to adulthood except one infant son who had died unnamed.

In November, 1869 Sarah appeared before the county court of Coryell County and was granted letters of administration on her late husband's estate. Her inventory of their community property showed one hundred eighty-five acres of land in Coryell County, six head of horses, three hundred eighty-five cattle, one yoke of oxen, and household and kitchen furniture. The three eldest daughters were married by 1869, or thereabouts. Hannah and Angeline and their bridegrooms lived near their mother, and I believe the new sons-in-law, William McCutchen and "Ham" (Alhambra) Reeder were of help to Sarah and her young children.

The 1870 census showed widowed Sarah as head of a large household. Malissa, fourteen; George, twelve; and David, eleven, attended school. At home were James M. (James Madison, nicknamed "Matt") age seven; Henry, five; and Sarah E., one-year old. The mother was more than equal to her responsibilities, however, for not only did she care for her own six children, but she had in her home at the same time eight children of her widowed brother Richard. These Eaton children were approximately the same age as the McCallister children, ranging in age from fifteen down to two, and the three oldest were in school. This may have been a temporary arrangement, as Richard took another wife the next month. He was a faithful member of the primitive Baptist church and was much in demand as a vocalist and singing teacher. Sarah was on the roll of members of Salem Primitive Baptist Church, which was constituted in 1871.

The year 1880 found Sarah in Coleman County, near Santa Anna. She was listed as a cattle raiser, and once more was living next house to William and Hannah McCutchen. Now her sons were old enough to be of some help to her. George, twenty-one, was listed as "keeping stock." Madison was seventeen, and not in school, for he had only three months' schooling in his long life, yet was to succeed financially in the days to come. Henry, thirteen, and Sarah, ten, were in school.

Sarah died in late 1888 and is buried beside her husband in Coffee cemetery, about eight miles north of Gatesville. May she rest in peace.

What is my heritage from this pioneer woman? I never saw her. I do not remember her daughter Hannah, my grandmother, who died when I was only one year old. I believe Sarah Ellen Eaton McCallister passed on to her children, who passed on to their children, a way of being cheerful in adversity, of working hard, and of faithful following of Christian principles. Just as she did, my grandmother taught her children to love each other, as my mother taught hers. I have held those same ideals before my own children and grandchildren. I trust they will hand them down to their descendants, for in this month of April, 1975 my first great-granddaughter has just come into the world!

The Sanctificationist group, photographed around 1895. Martha White McWhirter is second from left in front row.

The Sisterhood opened the Central Hotel in Belton, Texas, on May 10, 1886.

Martha White
McWhirter
(1827-1904)

By Eleanor James *

During the last century and a quarter many stories have been told in Belton, Texas, about Martha McWhirter, founder and leading spirit of the sanctificationists, the longest-lived of Texas communal societies and the only known woman's commune. The tone of the town's talk about Mrs. McWhirter has risen to rage in certain decades, has fallen into whispered rumors in others, and is rising again in amazed admiration in these days of many focuses upon woman, her rights, and her abilities.

In 1827 Martha McWhirter was born Martha White, daughter of a planter in Jackson County, Tennessee. At sixteen she joined the Methodist Church, and two years later she was married to George M. McWhirter, born in 1816 in Wilson County, Tennessee. They came to Texas in 1855, homesteaded in the five-year-old County of Bell, first on Salado Creek near the present Armstrong community, and then moved into Belton, the county seat, in 1865. The county census for 1860 listed George M. McWhirter as farmer, and named the following children who, like their parents, had been born in Tennessee: Emma (1846), Ada (1850), and John (1852). The 1870 census (which lists George as retired merchant) adds the names of children who had been born in Texas: Nannie (1865), Robert (1866), and Sam S. (1868); Emma's name no longer appears since on December 2, 1869 she

---

* Researcher, Bell County Historical Society

had married J. J. Pond. That the census ten years later names no McWhirters may be due to accident or inefficiency, or it may reflect the community's sense that Mrs. McWhirter had withdrawn herself and her family from the community. Later accounts of Mrs. McWhirter refer to her having mothered twelve children; some of them no doubt had died in infancy, possibly even before the move to Texas; and some may be represented by four small rough-hewn and unlettered stones on the McWhirter family lot in North Belton Cemetery where lie George M. McWhirter, who died in 1887, the son John, aged twenty-nine, and a grand child, two-year-old Mary Pond.

As I begin to piece together that which can be known and told in brief about Martha McWhirter and the band she formed and led, let me mention that we are fortunate that she was studied and chronicled by so scholarly a reporter as Professor George P. Garrison of the Department of History of The University of Texas, who spent two weeks in the summer of 1892 at the Central Hotel, daily observing Mrs. McWhirter and her then definitely communal organization of Sanctificationist women; that court records and the Belton *Journal*'s coverage of certain divorce and other cases between the years 1877 and 1883 are extant; and that when in the 1940's I began to follow up my interest in the tales told about Martha McWhirter and the "Sancties," my grandmother, my father and aunts, and a number of delightful elderly citizens related their clear memories of the mass of stories which had not been set down and would otherwise now be lost.

Along with many Belton citizens, the Methodist McWhirters were active in the Union Sunday School, the religious center of the town before denominations began to build separate churches, the first being the Methodist in 1870. Opposing the sectarianism which most Methodists upheld, the McWhirters retained their leadership in the Union Sunday School. Actually it had been several years earlier, in 1866, as Martha revealed later in testimony in a court case, that a strong religious experience had moved her to change her life and thereafter the lives of many other women.

As Mrs. McWhirter recounted it, it was after the death of her brother and two of her children in 1866 that she became convinced that God was chastising her and calling her to take thought of her life and of the evils around her. On her way home from a church revival meeting one evening at the end of a dry and mercilessly hot August, a Voice asked her to question herself and to see if the events of the meeting did not seem to her the work of the devil. She says that all night she had prayed and struggled against the suggestion. In her kitchen at her dishpan the next morning she experienced what she could only describe as a pentecostal baptism through which it became clear to her that the Voice had been God's and that she was called for a particular work. Henceforth she professed sanctification.

It is hard at this distance in time to tell how closely the views of Martha McWhirter corresponded to any of the then-current Methodist beliefs on Sanctification, or the second blessing, and the call to special service. She declared in court that she had read all the writings of Wesley upon the subject. Never in years to come did she seem to have any interest in other groups professing such doctrine, and it would seem that she did not set out to form a separatist group; she took God's leading as it came. If she can be called the founder of a group, she was one who seems never to have set down in writing any sort of charter or rules to live by. Regarding the name, she said they just called themselves Christians; other names were labels the town applied to them in scorn. As will be shown, a group of women formed around her, and she took these women as what God intended her to work with.

A few principles that she constantly supported with all her force can be set down, but they were not announced at the start. From the testimony she was called upon repeatedly to give, however, in the divorce cases or property suits in which her family and other members of her group became involved, from as early as the early 1880's to the last long interview that she gave for *Ainslee's Magazine* in Washington near the end of her life, three points seem basic. Sanctification came from God; although one could pray for it earnestly, God sent a conviction of that state only to the worthy. God spoke through dreams and visions; it was thus that He had spoken to her and to other Christians and thus that He had revealed His will to them. Within the statements of St. Paul in I Corinthians 7:12-15 she found her belief that if sanctification came to one already wed to an unsanctified partner, the sanctified partner should exert every effort to keep the marriage peaceful; that the unbelieving spouse should become sanctified was desirable; however, if the unbeliever made trouble or left the sanctified mate, that mate was no longer under bond to live with him or to take him back, but could take no second mate. Children should be brought up by the sanctified parent.

Her following came to Martha McWhirter in this way: she had been a member of a small interdenominational group of women who on a weekday would meet in the home of one member or another to pray and to seek guidance. One sorrow that many of these frontier townswomen shared was the frequency with which their men would become drunk and overbearing. Another was that nearly all the women felt bowed and humiliated at being unable to own property, even when they had brought it into the marriage; and they felt galled by the necessity of begging their husbands for money even for food and the running of the households. Mrs. McWhirter had shared with the prayer-members her sense of sanctification and had from time to time imparted the dream-leadings of God on practical problems. Most women prayed that they too might be convinced of sanctification; they prayed that they be given patience and strength. To Martha McWhirter was given the leading that they could help one another by building up a common fund, from the little money that came their way through sale of eggs and milk and butter; as the nest egg of their fund one unmarried sister, a teacher, brought her savings of twenty dollars.

To most of the beliefs of Martha McWhirter and the gradually emerging group of Sanctified women, the town at first was indifferent. But men long accustomed to controlling their women-folk through the purse felt the strangeness of passive resistance when the slowly but steadily growing common fund became known. When money at home was denied in a legitimate case of need, the wife went to her sisters and their joint savings. One sister and her child, long brutalized by a husband who drank, fled to the McWhirters' and were taken in there to live; Mr. McWhirter agreed that Sister Pratt could work out her board and the child's by helping Martha.

The beginning of their laundry work came when a Sanctificationist's neighbor complained that she could find no decent laundresses among the colored folk. The group prayed and decided that humility being good for them and money being needed, they would agree to go out in small groups and do laundry, or gather at some sister's house to do the work. The first court case against the group arose when a nasty-tempered husband caught the women washing on his premises; he gashed his wife's head, but found three other women fighting back. Ironically, *he* preferred charges, and the four sisters paid the levied fine of $100 from the fund.

Male dissatisfaction grew; other women, whose husbands had not been more than living under the same roofs with them, declared themselves their husbands' servants and asked for wages, or claiming desertion, moved together into property which little by little the group had begun to collect. In the settlements of wills, widows who received the homesteads would turn their houses over to accommodate the sisterhood's common need of shelter. The McWhirter house, the old limestone headquarters of the group, standing today on the bluff over Nolan Creek, grew too over-run for Mr. McWhirter to put up with. He did not hold with what his wife was doing but seems to have trusted in her motives; eventually he let her arrange rooms for him to live in on the north side of the courthouse square above a store building he owned. It was there that he died, alone, in 1887.

The degree of animosity which people felt for her Mrs. McWhirter says she first fully realized when the town blamed her for her husband's dying alone and when it saw her and her religion as the cause of the divorce of her daughter Ada from her husband, Ben Haymond, in 1887. Martha testified that it had never been a peaceful marriage, and that the three children—Hattie, George, and Emma—had known more security after 1879 when Ada, her sanctified daughter, came bringing the children home to their Grandmother McWhirter to be brought up in the Sanctificationist headquarters. The father had sold their home in Belton and had gone away to Central America from 1881 to 1889. Once home, he had tried to force Ada to renounce Sanctification and return to him; thwarted, he had based his divorce suit on a claim that the hotel which the Sanctificationists now ran was not a fit moral home in which to rear his children. He had lost his suit, but Ada had counter-filed and had won her divorce. The testimony of townspeople on both sides revealed the involvement of the emotions of the town. It is significant that no evidence of anything personally dishonorable was produced against Martha or Ada McWhirter or any Sanctificationist woman.

Everyone in Belton had always acknowledged the forcefulness of Martha McWhirter; they said that there would have been no Sanctified women but for her leadership and that the group would last only as long as she did. What they held against her most was her rigidity in backing wives who had left their husbands for the order. The town was split wide open as woman after woman left home and husband, taking with her the daughters and even the small boys; for these were wives, mothers and aunts from the best families in town and from the leading churches. They were "read out in meeting," and had their church letters taken away; but they prayed for strength and stuck together. The 1880's saw the group grow to fifty members, its largest size.

That decade also was lively with tales such as of the night a posse of husbands clattered up the stone walk to the McWhirter porch, called out that they wanted their wives, and sent one intentionally mis-aimed bullet through the paneled door, just to frighten them. But women who had stood up to the scorn of neighbors, deacons, and elders, were not frightened by a bullet (still embedded in the hall paneling, it is said). One man from a near-by town lured his small son off the "Sancty" premises, hid him out during the day and kidnapped him, taking him home with him.

The story richest in both near-tragedy and near-comedy concerned the two Dow Brothers, Matthew and David, newly arrived from Scotland to become carpenters in the town, who asked Mrs. McWhirter for membership, having belonged to a Sanctified group at home. This was too much for the Belton men; however outrageous they considered the acts of the women, they were, after all, ladies, and they could not be fought. But *men* in the Sanctificationists! The Dows were taken out on the old Waco road, beaten and warned to get out of the group and out of the town. When the men would not leave, they were tried for lunacy, apparently out of the concern of the more law-abiding citizens lest further violence occur, and were whisked to the asylum in Austin. Obviously sane, the men were kept at the asylum only overnight.

Thereafter, work was found for them in Austin until what the Belton *Journal* headlined as "The Late Unpleasantness" simmered down. One rather suspects that Martha McWhirter may have been the writer who informed the British Consul in Galveston of the deprivation of two British subjects' freedom. The *Journal* printed both the letter of protest from his honor the British Consul, Arthur T. Lynn, to acting Texas Secretary of State Bowman, and the latter's reply that a grand jury in Bell County would try and suitably punish the miscreants as soon as the mob could be identified.

Not as dramatic as this international near-incident, but more pathetic, was another insanity case involving a member of the Sanctificationists. A widow Johnson, whose unsanctified husband on dying had left her a life insurance policy worth two thousand dollars, was declared insane at the instigation of a brother-in-law who had eyes for the money. Martha and the sisters prayed for guidance in trying to right the injustice to their friend who had been held for several years. In a dream one sister was told that the governor should hear of this; Martha McWhirter wrote Governor Ireland, and in no time Sister Johnson was free to return to the group, bringing with her the ninety dollars she had made during her years in the asylum where she had been employed as a seamstress.

Despite the at first bitter opposition of the town to the Sanctificationists, Mrs. McWhirter and her loyal group quietly prospered. Work was as instrumental as dreams and visions to their growth. Sisters hired out as practical nurses and as silent but very excellent cooks. Others wove rag carpets to sell. Two sisters cut cedar posts and firewood, with the help of their boys, and carted it to town to regular customers. But the center of their projects was the hotel. From a boarding house converted to their use when the widow Henry inherited her homeplace, the women built on and improvised a fairly commodious if ramshackle hotel, famous for its good farm-fresh food. They bought the machinery for a steam laundry and installed it on the back of the Henry block, in the building used at one stage for the Methodist meeting house. This laundry served for their needs, for the hotel linens, and even for the laundry of the townspeople also.

In answer to the combined prayers of the Sanctificationists God must have prompted Martha to use her almost unsuspected financial talents when they constructed the big, plain three-story light brick hotel, called the Central Hotel, quite the finest in the county. It was the central concern of the group and their real money-maker when Professor Garrison stayed there in the summer of 1892, enjoying its good meals and clean beds and observing the sisters. Talking with Mrs. McWhirter elicited fairly tight-lipped replies, but as his article in *The Charities Review* (III, 1893) says, the communism that had been growing gradually for fourteen or fifteen years in this group which was cut off by religious views from their fellows, had for the past five years been a well-developed commune.

He commended the remarkable arrangement by which the women, under Mrs. McWhirter's leadership, rotated their duties, in kitchen, as waitresses and chamber maids, and on the farm near town from which they brought the poultry and garden produce for their well-run dining room. He reported the centrality still of dreams as guidance, mentioned that the daily prayer meetings still existed, remarked on a sort of group-sensitivity which Mrs. McWhirter said they had developed so that ideas seemed to come to all of them, and privately deduced from observation that it looked as if the religious motivation was in second place to the economic. He admired the firm control that seemed to meet with little opposition. He marveled that one sister had become a fairly competent dentist, while another cobbled to keep their shoes mended and even to make some of them.

He noted that there was no special costume or habit of the religious sort; instead they dressed plainly in dark colors, most wearing, as did Mrs. McWhirter, the long skirt and basque waist that had been in style some years before. There were some little girls growing up around the hotel, grandchildren of the sisters, and one or two who had been intrusted to these good women to raise.

Garrison's report listed some leading magazines and papers the women subscribed to, and he noted that there was a piano on which hymns and decorous songs were played. At that time the adults numbered thirty-two, all women. Mrs. McWhirter, when asked, said that they had no objection to men as members, adding that few, however, had cared to try to live after their pattern. At the time of Garrison's visit, a man served as hotel clerk, one as engineer of the laundry, and another as carpenter for the community; but they did not seem to be members of the Sanctified group.

Garrison saw Mrs. McWhirter as an intelligent woman with surprising breadth of vision. That she and the sisterhood might learn by seeing something of the world, in the summer of 1880 Mrs. McWhirter had rented a house near Central Park in New York and sent the whole group in three divisions, each gone for about six weeks. They had traveled up by rail and returned by boat to Galveston. The total expense she figured at about three thousand dollars.

Judge George W. Tyler, in his *History of Bell County* (Naylor, 1936) adds details invaluable as they came from one who had known both Martha and George McWhirter. He recorded that George, as a member of the Belton Chapter of the Royal Arch Masons, had served as Grand High Priest of the Grand Chapter of Texas in 1878-9. He admired the forebearance of Mr. McWhirter, a man of substance and sound judgment, who had never lost faith in his wife's integrity although he disapproved of her Sanctificationist activities. It was his will, leaving Martha not only the widow's half of his twenty-thousand-dollar estate, but making her executrix for his will that may have turned the tide of the town's opinion grudgingly in favor of Martha.

That the tide was turning in their favor appears in several ways. The town admired their financial prosperity, and although people had at first talked against the big brick Central Hotel, they came to be proud of the fact that it drew many boarders and overnight travellers who came through central Texas. For a time the women leased two hotels in Waco and ran them. According to what Mrs. McWhirter later told a Washington interviewer, she was the first woman to be admitted to Belton's Board of Trade, a forerunner of the modern chamber of commerce. When a railroad was being built in the vicinity and the town was raising capital to induce the line to send a spur into Belton, Mrs. McWhirter is said to have contributed five-hundred dollars in the name of the group to purchase necessary land right-of-way. A now weathered cornerstone of Belton's old limestone and brick Opera House on the southwest corner of the courthouse square shows the name of Mrs. M. McWhirter among the six or seven names there, the only woman's name among them. These facts seem to lend credence to Mrs. McWhirter's reiterated statement that it had not originally been her group who withdrew from the town, but the town that had isolated them for their beliefs.

But she was growing old, as were the other women; and their celibacy had meant that the years of the group must be numbered. This fact never seemed to concern them greatly; Mrs. McWhirter, when asked in interviews, would say that God would lead them, as He had always done. There had been a restless feeling common to the women and discussed in their meetings, that they should leave this well-known place for another time. Small groups had traveled to other cities, including San Francisco and even Mexico City, where one reporter says they talked with President Diaz about possibly residing there. But in the end, the collective feelings of the group settled upon Washington, D.C. as the place for their last home.

Figures vary as to how much money the sisters were worth collectively in 1899 when they sold or leased their holdings in Belton; there is little proof of the sum of $200,000 that is sometimes given. But George Tyler, one of the last Belton residents to talk with Mrs. McWhirter, visited with her in Washington in the big house at 1437 Kenesaw Avenue; he wrote that they had paid $23,000 in cash for the place and had spent several thousand more in renovating it to their needs when they had arrived in 1899.

Two young men from Belton attending college in Virginia paid Belton's respects at the funeral of Martha McWhirter in the spring of 1904. A brief obituary in the Belton *Journal* reviewed the course of the Sanctificationist group in the town and called her its founder and leading spirit. In the last known interview with Mrs. McWhirter, reported in an eight-page story in *Ainslee's Magazine* (September, 1902) Margarita Spalding Gerry described in some detail the large, immaculate, but rather austere grey house in what had become the suburb of Mount Pleasant, complete with a large garden, chicken yard, and orchard trees, that was almost a farm home to Mrs. McWhirter and the thirty women who still carried on their quiet, pleasant, if spartan existence. She spoke of two grandchildren and one great-grandchild of Mrs. McWhirter who were with them at the time. The remnant of the religious observances of the group was the prayer-meeting; but each woman otherwise was free to attend any church she desired.

One could wish that Mrs. Gerry had devoted more of a word-picture to the seventy-five-year-old leader, for pictures of the group are few and faded. But the tone of the writer suggests that she found a great admiration for the strong-spirited old lady. She assesses the elements of her business success as ". . . a shrewd insight into character, a quick grasp of conditions, honesty, and a firm belief in the virtue of cash transactions." Of the total woman, Mrs. Gerry writes:

> Belief with her is action. She says that is no religion which is not practical. At the same time, she is a mystic, trusting implicitly in the revelations that come to her and to them all. Whatever may be the attitude toward this question, one can but reverence the strength of faith which has transfigured her. It has led them through tragic experiences, ruined homes, hardships, persecutions, and crushing griefs. . . . They have no definite plans for the perpetuation of the colony; in fact they seem scarcely concerned about it. When the time comes the revelation they are awaiting will lead them.

Perhaps, after all, one needs no better portrait of Martha McWhirter.

Juana Navarro de Alsbury (circa *1816-1888)*

By Glenn Scott*

Suzanna Dickinson has been popularly referred to as the only survivor of the Alamo, and her child was patriotically christened the "Babe of the Alamo." Actually, there were at least ten Mexican women and a half dozen of their "Babes" inside the besieged walls right along with her. One of these women, Juana Navarro de Alsbury (also Alsberry), was born the daughter of Jose Angel Navarro II, the only son in the prominent Navarro clan of North Mexico who did not side with the Texians. Juana's uncle, Colonel Jose Antonio Navarro, one of the signers of the Texas Declaration of Independence, fought with Sam Houston and later served both in the government of the Republic and the state legislature.

When the death of his wife Concepcion Cervantes had left Jose Angel with two small daughters, Juana and Gertrudis, his sister Josefa had adopted them. Josefa's marriage to Juan Martin Veramendi, who later became vice-governor of Coahuila and Texas, had interlaced the responsibilities and financial interests of the two most powerful families in the region. Consequently, Juana, Gertrudis and the Veramendi's daughter Ursula grew up in extravagant surroundings—mansions at Saltillo and San Antonio and a summer home at Monclova.

It was this affluence that attracted many eligible bachelors. The legendary knife-brandishing Jim Bowie became a Mexican

* Teacher-student-journalist in Austin's Alternative Community

*Juana Navarro de Alsbury and Gertrudis took refuge in a west room
of the Alamo during the siege*

citizen, joined the Catholic Church and pledged a lavish dowry, which some historians have insisted was half figment and half imagination—all for the golden hand of Ursula. A year after Ursula's wedding, Juana married Alejo Perez, a member of the de Leon Colony which had settled in Victoria County in the 1820's.

As a settler in good standing, on March 23, 1833, Perez was officially granted his one-fourth league of land, located on the east side of the Guadalupe River. He also had a house in San Antonio which faced north on St. Mary's and Market Streets.

Juana and Gertrudis spent the summer of 1833 in San Antonio, rather than accompanying the Veramendis, Ursula, and her two infants to Monclova. Had they gone they almost certainly would not have returned alive. Sweeping across the Southwest that year was an epidemic of cholera, a disease which made no exceptions for extravagance. In three days Ursula, her two babies, her mother and father were dead; and back in Victoria, Alejo Perez succumbed to the same disease.

The epidemic left Juana re-orphaned, widowed, responsible for her younger sister, and pregnant. With her father off in Mexico as an officer in Santa Anna's army, there were three choices open to this young woman: enter a convent, re-marry, or remain the helpless dependent of her dead husband's relatives. From what little information is available, it seems that Juana opted for the latter, living in the Perez house in San Antonio for the next two years. According to one source, Juana had already given birth to a daughter named Encarnacion, who apparently died in infancy. In 1834, Alejo, Jr. was born, the child that Juana carried into the Alamo a year and a half later.

Juana remarried in January, 1836 to Dr. Horace Alsbury, who had come to Texas with Charles G. and Harvey Alsbury to settle in the Stephen F. Austin colony. (In these frontier years, the title "Doctor" was a rather loose term that rarely indicated more than a rudimentary training in medicine.) The three men had petitioned and received one and a half leagues of land in Brazoria County in August, 1824.

The same month of Juana's marriage to Dr. Alsbury, San Antonio residents heard of Santa Anna's army crossing the Rio Grande. Many Anglo-Americans discounted this as rumor, but others, especially Mexicans who remembered the pillage and rape of 1813 at the hands of the Spanish Royalist Forces, began a hasty evacuation eastward. Colonel Travis, believing it essential to make a stand rather than retreat toward Nacogdoches, sent Dr. Alsbury and another man to convince Fannin to bring his forces to the Alamo. Dr. Alsbury left his bride of a few weeks, her baby and fifteen-year-old Gertrudis in the care of Jim Bowie, with the promise to send for them as soon as he could provide a safe place.

On February 23, 1836, when Santa Anna's army was sighted outside San Antonio, Bowie took the women into the old fort and, according to Walter Lord, installed them in a room on the west wall of the Alamo, separate from the other women and children who stayed in a room at the southwest corner of the church. During the first days of the siege Juana and Gertrudis attempted to nurse the ailing Bowie, but the Rodriguez memoirs explained that Bowie refused their help for fear they would catch his typhoid-pneumonia. On March 6, Juana and Gertrudis spent the final hours of the battle in their room guarded by a Mexican boy and a wounded man named Mitchell. Neither woman was armed. Just before dawn, when Santa Anna's soldiers were over-running the old mission (according to some witnesses, it was so dark and the smoke so thick that even after the last Texian had fallen the Santanistas kept up a frenzied gunfire for over fifteen minutes), Gertrudis opened the door to tell the soldiers to stop firing into the room as it contained only women and children.

Over the din of battle the soldiers yelled curses at her, and one man tore the shawl from her shoulders. Gertrudis tried to reclose the door, but several men rushed in the room demanding her money and her husband. She replied, "I have neither money nor husband," a particularly revealing statement, since at that time, a woman without a husband or guardian indeed had virtually no other means of generating income.

The Santanistas turned toward Juana and bayoneted the wounded Mitchell, who attempted to defend her. At this point the Mexican youth put himself between her and the soldiers and met the same fate. Spotting her trunk, they broke it open and appropriated her money, clothes, and the watches Colonel Travis and other Texians had entrusted to her. One officer ordered them out of the room, and then steered them in front of a cannon where he instructed them to wait until he brought "El Presidente." In a few minutes a second officer hurrying by was evidently so struck by the incongruous picture of two women with a baby standing in front of a cannon in the midst of strewn bodies, choking smoke and ricocheting bullets, that he stopped to ask Juana what they were doing in that particularly precarious locale. When Juana repeated the first officer's orders, the man roared incredulously,

"President the Devil! Don't you see they are about to fire that cannon? Get out of here!"

As the two women were stumbling over the shadowy bodies in the courtyard, a man's voice called out to Juana, *"Cunada* (sister-in-law)! Don't you know your own brother-in-law?" He was Manuel Perez, the brother of her late first husband Alejo. According to some sources, Perez placed the women in the charge of Bowie's slave Sam, who escorted them out of the Alamo. Others claim there was no such slave belonging to Bowie in the mission. Regardless, it seems doubtful that anyone other than a military escort could have led them safely out of that early morning chaos. At about 8:00 a.m. Juana, Gertrudis and the other women survivors arrived at the home of Ramon Musquiz, a prominent merchant and fence-sitter on the question of Texas Independence, where they waited for an interview with General Santa Anna.

Little is known about Juana after that most famous and dreadful morning of her life. Her husband, Dr. Alsbury, according to John S. Ford, had intended to move his family to East Texas, but instead joined Sam Houston's raw recruits for the Battle of San Jacinto. Whether or not Juana and Gertrudis did join Alsbury later in East Texas is not clear. Evidently, he was serious about leaving the South Texas region because on December 4, 1836, he sold his land in Brazoria as well as the 640 acre donation for active duty at San Jacinto to a Robert Peebles.

In 1842 Dr. Alsbury was killed in a gunfight, whereupon Juana married Juan Perez, the cousin of her first husband. Juana applied for and received a pension for her services at the Alamo in 1857, despite several sworn testimonies that she had left the mission on March 4, two days before the fall, under a flag of truce ordered by Santa Anna at the request of her father Jose Angel. Juana died in San Antonio on July 25, 1888.

Gertrudis married a prosperous businessman, Miguel Cantu, in the San Fernando Cathedral in San Antonio in 1841. The couple moved to Calaveras, Texas, near Elmendorf, where Gertrudis died in 1895.

Juana's son, Alejo Perez, Jr., who John S. Ford testified "was a respectable San Antonio citizen," married Antonia Rodriguez in 1853 and had four children. Years later, after Antonia's death, Alejo married Florencia Valdes on March 18, 1916, at the astonishing age of eighty-one.

Anna Hurd Palm

Anna Hurd Palm
(1808-1878)

By Amy LeVesconte*

Anna Palm, a widow with six young sons who settled near Round Rock in 1853, was responsible for naming this community Palm Valley and for establishing Palm Valley Lutheran Church.

Anna Hurd was born, educated, and married in Berkeryd, Sweden, now a modern industrial center. Her husband was Anders Palm, a civil engineer in the King's service. During the ensuing years she bore him six sons: John, August, Carl, Andrew, William, and Henning.

Anna's pleasant, orderly life in Sweden was interrupted by letters that told of the success of Swante Magnus Swenson, her husband's nephew. He had left Sweden for New York in 1836. Soon after Texas Independence, he came to Columbia, Texas, at the mouth of the Brazos River. He first found work in a store but after a few years he began to drive a supply wagon to the plantations in East Texas. There he met Dr. Long who asked him to manage his plantation. A few years later Dr. Long died of pulmonary consumption, and soon after this, Swenson married the widow and became a man of wealth and owner of slaves. He increased his wealth by buying large tracts of land which the State had given to soldiers as pay or to railroads as an incentive to build more tracks. He sold the land to new settlers at much higher prices.

* Retired college professor

When Swenson visited his home in Sweden in 1847, he convinced his uncles that they should move to Texas. One of his uncles, Swante Palm, had come earlier. In July, 1848, the families left Sweden in a small sailing vessel. Their party consisted of Anders Palm, Anna, his wife, and their six sons; Gustav Palm, his wife, and children; Swenson's mother; three maid servants; six men servants; a mechanic; and a boy.

In addition to the large human cargo the small ship carried heavy steel rails destined for the Charleston Railroad Company in South Carolina. As they neared America, a violent storm struck the ship and the rails shifted to one side; the ship was in great danger of capsizing. The captain gave up hope but Mrs. Swenson, a strongly religious woman, went up to the bridge to pray, holding up her arms to God in supplication for their safety. As her arms tired, others helped her hold them up. The storm passed and the ship was able to enter New York harbor with no loss of life. As a result of this experience, the Captain anchored the ship in the harbor and used it as a seaman's mission during the remainder of his life.

The Palm party transferred to a schooner that took them to Galveston, Texas, and from there went on a steamboat which landed them at the foot of Main Street in Houston on November 22, 1848, after four months of travel.

S. M. Swenson had arranged to be notified of the arrival of the party. A rider carried him this news and he sent a prairie schooner and mules to bring his relatives and the others of the party to his plantation near Richmond, Fort Bend County.

While waiting for the schooner, the party, none of whom spoke English, was comfortably quartered at the Washington Hotel at the foot of Main Street. Here they were the center of attraction. The boy of the party, G. A. Forsgard, many years later recalled:

> The two-horse wagons we brought from Sweden attracted much attention. So did our large chests of clothing and implements, and also our big double-barrel muzzle-loading shotguns that every man brought along to defend us against Indians and to kill buffaloes with.

The land which was intended for Anders and Anna near Richmond was being cleared by the Palm family when Anders died of a fever and was buried in Fort Bend County. Anna, left a widow during her first year in a foreign land, moved with her six sons and others to New Ulm in Washington County, seeking a more beautiful land. During their sojourn in New Ulm, Swenson visited his aunt and cousins. When Anna complained that she had not had a coffee bean in the house for six months, Swenson told her to send her son, August, to San Felipe and he would see that she obtained some coffee. Of course, all coffee was green in those days and had to be roasted and ground as needed.

While on this visit, Swenson suggested that the family sell their land in New Ulm and move to higher land in the valley of Brushy Creek near Round Rock where he owned large tracts of land. The area was relatively free of malaria; it was near Austin where he planned to open a mercantile establishment; and it was near Kenny's Fort where his sister and her husband, William Dyer, were settled. The Fort would offer protection from Indians if this were needed.

Anna and her family, accompanied by some of the young men and women who had migrated with her, moved in 1853 to the area now named after her, Palm Valley. They liked this location with its water, mesquite and oak trees, and plenty of grass. Squirrels, rabbits, turkeys, and quails, as well as fish, were plentiful. The small animals were trapped since powder and lead were scarce and guns were only used to kill deer, bears, cougars, and buffaloes. Wild grapes, plums, berries, walnuts, and pecans were also abundant.

During the first two years the party camped in their wagons and tents while the men and boys started to clear the land for farming and to fence it in to protect it from live stock and wild hogs. As they found time, they began to lay the foundation for a house. Each night they stored their live coals for the next morning to save rekindling them with flint and tinder. It was a triumph for them when they raised wheat and oats to use for bread in place of the corn to which they were limited at first.

Anna's grandson, Rufus Palm, Jr., wrote in a manuscript found in the Austin Library Archives:

Anna Palm, the matriarch of our branch of the family, deserves the highest measure of admiration, respect, esteem and gratitude. With Spartan determination she set about learning a new language, new customs, and a new way of life. Pioneer days were full of hardships, disappointments, tragedies and sacrifice. Her youngest son, Henry, died in early youth. Her second son, August, was sent to Austin where he worked as a clerk for his cousin, S. W. Swenson, and later became a wealthy merchant. All of the boys had the best schooling possible for the times and conditions, and all five of them responded with a will and vigorous enthusiasm. They came from a family which realized the importance of education as a tool for a better way of life. They were encouraged in this by their kinsman, Sir Swante Palm, who was a polished scholar.

In 1861 all of Anna's sons except Henning, who was too young, enlisted in the Confederate Army. Henning died in 1863 and when his mother was asked where she wished him to be buried, she answered: "Under the tallest oak tree, there." He was buried under this oak near their home, and thus began God's Acre.

When her sons returned from the war and communications were restored, Anna wrote her nephew, S. M. Swenson who was then in New York, and asked him to donate the ground where Henning was buried along with enough acreage for a cemetery, church, and school. Swenson authorized his uncle, Swante Palm, to do this. Swenson deeded twenty-one and four-fifths acres to Arvid Nelson, Daniel Hurd, and C. A. Engstrand as trustees for a Swedish Lutheran Church and school to replace the cabin then in use. A wooden frame building, constructed from lumber hauled from Austin, was completed in 1872. This was the original Palm Valley Lutheran Church.

Anna and her family continued to prosper and to take an active part in the Palm Valley community. Four of her sons acquired large farms. Carl became a salesman for the Bremond Mercantile Company in Austin and later became a prosperous and influential business man. August was the first man to raise cotton in Williamson County; he also built the first cotton gin there. In Austin he was influential in helping the State recover from the Civil War. When the State had decided to close the Blind Institute and the Insane Asylum because it had no money, August borrowed $50,000 from S. M. Swenson which kept the two places functioning. Later he was repaid in a different curency which gave him seventy-two cents on the dollar. When officers came from the North to oversee Reconstruction, August gave a banquet in his home for them to create a feeling of friendliness.

All of Anna's five sons were active in their church and community. When she died in 1878 after a long and painful illness, *The Austin Statesman* wrote:

Her life has been one of usefulness and has been spent in doing good to others. She leaves a large circle of relatives and friends who mourn her loss.

Auguste Mentzel Raven (1809-1887)

By Pansy Nichols*

Born December 14, 1809, in Gotha, Germany, she was christened Johanne Freiderich Auguste Mentzel. On February 7, 1830,
she was married to Ernst Raven of Hanover, Prussia.

For the first eight years of their married life, the Ravens lived
in Saxe-Coburg, Gotha, where Ernst was a bookbinder at the court
of Ernest I, Duke of Saxe-Coburg and Gotha. A story in an old
Austin, Texas newspaper says, in part, "There, in spite of the oft-
quoted stiff, formal etiquette of German courts, Mr. Raven found
himself on terms of easy familiarity with the family and with (then,
of course, a youth) the present prince consort of England."

One day in his father's library Prince Ernest, elder brother of
Queen Victoria's future prince consort, asked the young bookbinder to make "a beautiful cover" for a certain book. The book
was to be a gift for the prince's current girl friend—and he handed
Ernst half a dozen jewels with which to decorate it.

When her husband reached home that evening Auguste was
alarmed. "Suppose you lost one of those stones!" she said. "Or
. . . oh, Ernst, suppose a thief came in the night and stole them all!
What would we do?"

No such catastrophe occurred, but many years later in Texas
Auguste told her grandchildren that she did not rest easy until the

* A great-granddaughter

201

Auguste Mentzel Raven with two granddaughters

book, with each precious stone safely embedded in its handsome binding, was in the prince's own hands.

In 1838 Ernst and Auguste Raven left Germany, en route to the Republic of Texas with their four children: Gustave Herman Leopold, age seven; Bertha Amalie Therese Eleanore, age five; Louise Emma Therese (who would become this writer's grandmother), age two; and Christian Heinrich Hugo, age one year. The family stopped in Baltimore, Maryland, where they resided for five years, and where two other children were born—Julius in 1841 and Anna in 1843.

Anna was less than a year old when the family resumed their journey to Texas. But due to the serious illness of Julius and Anna aboard ship, they stopped in New Orleans where both children died and where they were buried. At journey's end in Galveston Auguste herself, exhausted from nursing her sick babies and desolate over their deaths, was gravely ill.

A further blow awaited her. When the family's household goods were unloaded it was discovered that sea water, seeping into the ship's hold, had damaged most of the furniture and had ruined some prized oil paintings. Auguste was heartsick over it all, but she was even more distressed over Ernst's reaction to the loss of their paintings. For a few moments her usually calm and patient husband had gazed despairingly at the soggy canvasses in their twisted frames; then, with well-placed kicks, he furiously completed their destruction.

Ernst's uncharacteristic action may have led Auguste to determine that he should never know how intensely she sometimes longed for the relatives and friends (and a few of the amenities) they had left in Germany. She was aware that he grieved bitterly for Julius and Anna, the memory of whose lonely little graves she herself found almost past bearing. It distressed her to think that her husband might now be regretting his optimistic, but far from impulsive, decision to exchange the security of their well-ordered life in Germany for the uncertainties they faced in this raw, new Republic of Texas.

However, homesick and frightened though she was, Auguste did her best to make her husband and children comfortable and happy in each of the two communities in which they lived between 1844, when they reached Texas, and 1848, when they were permanently settled in Austin. They lived first in Caldwell, Burleson County, where her son Fernando was born; then in

Cameron, Milam County, where her last child Ione was born.

Besides the vicissitudes experienced by other pioneer women, Auguste was handicapped by a language difficulty. When the family reached the United States Ernst had said, "Now that we are in an English-speaking country, we will speak English." He himself was perfectly at home in that language, and the children had learned a surprising amount from playmates on their voyage across the Atlantic; but Auguste's languages were German and French. She learned English eventually, but she never mastered the pronunciation of certain words such as *thimble*. Her daughter Ione once said, "We would show Ma exactly how to place her tongue and lips, but to the end of her days that word always came out *t'imble*."

The family was finally comfortably at home in Austin at an address designated in old city directories as "near the corner of East and College Avenues." There, in a house affectionately known among their friends as "The Ravens' Nest," Auguste looked forward to raising her children in comfort and relative safety.

After he moved his family to Austin Ernst established a book-binding business. He became active in various civic enterprises, and for a time was an alderman of the city. A Knight Templar, he was secretary of his masonic lodge, another member of which was Sam Houston, who was a frequent visitor at "The Ravens' Nest." Auguste made all of Ernst's friends and business associates welcome; but her own interests lay chiefly in homemaking and the care of her children.

She grieved over the loss of her eldest daughter Bertha, who died giving birth to her first child, which was stillborn. She was pleased over Herman's marriage to Mollie Hamilton (who eventually bore fifteen of Auguste's thirty grandchildren), and over Louise's marriage to the young South Carolinian, Thomas Jefferson Campbell, come West to seek his fortune. In later years she welcomed Fernando's wife, Evelyn, and Ione's husband, Neil McCashin, a Union soldier stationed in Austin after the War.

She rejoiced at the birth of every grandchild. She had six when Texas seceded from the Union, and her sons, Herman and Hugo, and son-in-law, T.J., joined the Army of the Confederacy. During the anxious years that followed she and Ernst were busy looking after their minor children, Fernando and Ione, their grandchildren, and the mothers of the latter.

The following item appeared in an Austin newspaper on April 17, 1861:

> Mr. Ernst Raven, long a resident of this city, we are pleased to learn, has received the appointment from the Duke of Saxe-Coburg and Gotha as Consul for the State of Texas. Mr. Raven is an old citizen of Texas and we are glad to see that he is thus honored by the appointment to this important trust. His office will be located in this place, and we doubt not, will prove a great accommodation to his German fellow citizens in this state.

(The appointment was made by the man for whom Ernst Raven designed the jeweled book cover that had troubled Auguste so long ago—Prince Ernest had become Ernest II, Duke of Saxe-Coburg and Gotha, at his father's death in 1844.)

Auguste was occasionally able to be of assistance to Ernst in connection with his duties as Consul for Texas, especially where women and children were concerned.

There is a little grave in Austin's Oakwood Cemetery marked by a stone on which these words are engraved: "Rudolph Heffter —Born June 25, 1871—Died June 30, 1871—Son of Mary L. and H. A. Heffter." The Heffters were German immigrants traveling through Texas. Born in Austin, their baby lived for five days. They had little money and only a limited knowledge of English, and someone referred them to Ernst Raven for help. Auguste did what she could to comfort the parents; and Ernst, as Auguste hoped he would do, provided space on their own cemetery lot for the baby's grave, and ordered a stone to mark it.

Microfilm copies of old newspapers at Austin's public library record accounts of Ernst Raven's involvement in various affairs of his time, but Auguste is mentioned only twice. One item was a brief, dignified announcement of her death. The other was a fulsome account of Ernst and Auguste's golden wedding anniversary, celebrated at Turner Hall on the night of February 7, 1880. The reporter who covered it seems to have had an inexhaustible supply of superlatives—which he used with abandon. He commented on "the beautifully decorated and brilliantly illuminated hall"; described one part of the entertainment as "truly sublime"; spoke of "the groom of seventy-six summers, still erect and vigorous, with the bride of seventy at his side"; "two hearts that beat as one," etc., etc.

At all of that Auguste could smile, but portions of the last two paragraphs (which follow) certainly caused her, and Ernst as well considerable annoyance:

A notice of this occasion would be incomplete without the magnificent display of presents referred to. They were too numerous for special mention, and many of them were elegant in the extreme, embracing a wide variety of things, among which may be mentioned the silver service presented by the Turners. There were also several interesting relics from the Faderland. One of these was a Bible 184 years old. Another was a cup presented to the grandparents of Mrs. Raven at their golden wedding in 1820. The presents were worth more than one thousand dollars. The supper, which was liberally partaken of, was provided at great expense by Mr. Raven.

Mr. and Mrs. Raven have lived in Austin for twenty-five or thirty years. For many years he carried on a bookbinding business in this city, from which he retired seven or eight years ago, having laid up a nice little fortune for himself and those dependent upon him.

Ernst and Auguste made only one trip back to Saxe-Coburg and Gotha to visit relatives and friends. They enjoyed seeing those who were there, but many were gone—some forever—and there were other disheartening changes. They returned to Austin with a trunkful of gifts for their grandchildren—and the firm conviction that, in spite of their early hardships, their emigration to Texas had been a good thing.

Auguste died on August 7, 1887. The following notice appeared in the *Austin Daily Statesman* on August 9, 1887:

The many friends and acquaintances of Mrs. Augusta Raven, widow of the late Ernest Raven, will be grieved by her death which occurred Sunday last at the advanced age of 77 years. She was an old Austin resident, having moved here with her husband in 1850. Here they reared a large family of children; and children and grandchildren gathered to do sacred honor to the loved and venerated one yesterday. Mrs. Raven was held in high esteem by all who knew her, as was amply and warmly evidenced by the large concourse of friends who followed her remains to their last resting place yesterday.

Rebecca Kilgore
Stuart Red
(1827-1886)

By Mabelle Umland Purcell*

Rebecca Jane Kilgore Stuart, the second daughter of William Stuart (or Stewart) III and Mary Cummins, was born on October 2, 1827, on her grandfather's farm in West Middlesex Province, Pennsylvania. Her father was the grandson of Lt. William Stuart of Revolutionary War fame and a descendant of the Stewarts of Green Hill, near Letterkenny, County Donegal, Ireland. Her mother was of staunch Presbyterian stock. Being the seventh daughter of a seventh daughter, Mary Cummins was thought to have special healing powers and people came from miles around to be healed of scrofula, wens, and other tumors by the touch or massage of her hands.

The William Stuarts III had three sons one of whom drowned in boyhood and four daughters: Elizabeth, Rebecca, Virginia, and Mary. After twelve years of marriage, Mary Cummins Stuart died. William Stuart III remained a widower. He had one financial failure after another and discouraged, migrated to California where in 1849 he died and was buried on Mt. Shasta.

Elizabeth, Rebecca's older sister, attended Steubenville Female Seminary for a time but withdrew in order to care for her young brothers and sisters. Rebecca borrowed money from the Reverend Charles C. Beatty, President of the Steubenville school, and graduated there in 1849.

---

* Wife of a grandson.

Rebecca Kilgore Stuart Red

Rebecca began teaching in Kentucky immediately on gradua-
tion in order to repay her debt to Dr. Beatty. She was attractive,
dignified, and had many admirers. To the latter she turned a cold
shoulder.

The Reverend James Weston Miller, D.D., valedictorian of
the 1840 graduating class at Jefferson College, Cannonsburg,
Pennsylvania, went to Houston, Texas, first as a missionary and
later as first pastor of the First Presbyterian Church. He married
Elizabeth McKennan, a Steubenville graduate. Since the climate of
Houston did not agree with him, the Millers moved to Gay Hill,
Washington County, Texas, where he served as pastor of the
Prospect Presbyterian Church and organized a female seminary.

After Mrs. Miller died in childbirth, Dr. Miller went to Pennsylvania where he married Elizabeth Stuart and returned to Gay Hill.
Dr. Miller's new wife, Elizabeth (Lizzie) Stuart was an excellent
choice for him as she could instruct the girls in domestic arts.

Dr. and Mrs. Miller persuaded Rebecca to join them on the
boat trip down the Ohio and to become principal of the prospec-
tive school. This she was glad to do as she often said that she was
treated as an "upper servant" in Kentucky by the Southern
women.

On February 17, 1853, Live Oak Female Seminary was
opened in Oak Lodge, the commodious home of the president.
By September 1854 there were twenty-seven day scholars. As
there was need for a boarding school, two dormitories were added
to the school complex. There was a waiting list since provision was
made for only sixty boarders and fifty day pupils.

At the urging of his sister, Mrs. Thomas Stahworth Hender-
son, Dr. George Clark Red had come to Washington-on-the-
Brazos to practice medicine. Being a staunch Scotch Presbyterian,
Dr. Red went to a meeting of the Brazos Presbytery held in Chries-
man School, first public school building erected in the Republic of
Texas, and named for Horatio Chriesman, Surveyor General for
Stephen F. Austin's Colony. Here he met Rebecca. On his return
home, he wrote her a letter proposing matrimony.

Rebecca showed the letter to Dr. Miller and asked him to
advise her. He replied: "I'd think a long time before I'd turn down
a man like Dr. Red." She accepted the proposal with the understanding that she be allowed to educate her two young brothers.
The Reds were married on January 11, 1854.

The young couple lived at Oak Lodge the first year. Dr. Red purchased a fifty-acre tract adjoining the Miller property. In a letter dated September 1, 1854, to her aunt, Clarissa Stuart, Rebecca wrote:

> I do not know when I will quit teaching, for above all other employment I like it best. I expect to teach the balance of this year and next year. By that time I suppose Dr. Red will have our house builded and will want to go to housekeeping, and of course I will not object. . . . Dr. R. . . . has commenced to build an office on it, he will not commence the house until next year.

In addition to being the school physician, Dr. Red taught the physical sciences, using his office as a laboratory for experiments. The students delighted in this variety.

In 1860 Robert C. Stuart II, Rebecca's younger brother, married Frances Blake, an alumna of Hartford Female Seminary who had studied with the great naturalist, Louis Agassiz. She joined the teaching staff of Live Oak Female Seminary.

The outstanding faculty of Oak Hill Female Seminary attracted the elite of that part of the State as patrons. Friends in Houston sent their daughters to be educated by their former minister. The intelligentsia of the area were thrilled at the location of such a school nearby. The first three Justices of the Texas Supreme Court; Judge Abner Smith Lipscomb; Chief Justice John Hemphill; and Judge Royall T. Wheeler, were patrons. And so were some members of the Texas Legislature; the Post Master General, Honorable John Rice Jones; and Reverend Harry Lee Graves, first president of Baylor University, and Judge R. E. B. Baylor for whom Baylor College and University were named. Reverend Graves on retirement moved to Gay Hill. Judge Baylor, a bachelor, lived across from the Seminary and educated eight great-nieces there.

Except for a short period during the Civil War, Mrs. Red continued her teaching at Gay Hill for twenty-three years. She educated her four children (William, Lel, and the twins, Samuel Clark and Harriet) along with the other scholars.

Rebecca's brother, Robert C. Stuart II, had moved to Austin after the completion of the railroad and built a stone warehouse on the Chisholm Trail. He dealt first in hides and tallow and then became a successful cotton merchant. When Dr. Miller retired in 1875, Mr. Stuart persuaded Rebecca to come to Austin and establish her own school.

Mr. Stuart supervised the erection of the handsome building near his own home in East Austin. Vacation at Gay Hill was during the winter months, so Rebecca did not complete her contract until December. Mrs. Robert Stuart gathered a group of children in the fall of 1875 and taught them in her own home. These students became the nucleus of Stuart Female Seminary, which formally opened in January, 1876.

Some students from Live Oak Female Seminary, daughters and relatives of others, followed Mrs. Red to Austin. At least two families moved to the Capital City in order to continue their daughters' education under Mrs. Red.

Mrs. Lee Joseph nee Lillian Thornton, one-time regent of Texas State College for Women; past president of the Texas Federation of Women's Clubs; and an ex-student of Stuart Female Seminary recalls:

> The students were drawn from some of the best families in Texas. Typical was our room, Number 5. There was Anna Forsgard, daughter of a wealthy and prominent Presbyterian family in Houston; Adriene Tyson, of an aristocratic Louisiana French family; Josie Rawls, daughter of a Colonel in the Confederate Army; Kate Benson, daughter of a civil engineer, native of Boston but a resident of Uvalde; Emma Johnson, daughter of the editor and owner of "The Houston Post," and grand-daughter of Gail Borden, and I, a daughter of a physician and surgeon whose practice covered much of south-central Texas.

Mrs. Red is remembered as a scholar of great dignity who commanded the respect and confidence of her students. She was sound in her teaching, able to share her learning, and especially interested in the various sciences. Her English classes were impressive. She was somewhat austere which may have been necessary in the control of students "bubbling with vitality."

The education of the Red children had been supervised by their parents to prepare them to be instructors in the family school, and results showed they could not have had better mentors.

William Red was a scholarly teacher of Latin whose classes attracted many students. Lel Red was destined to carry on her mother's work in the Stuart Female Seminary. Samuel Clark Red was a faculty member of the Seminary. However, in 1883 when the University of Texas was opened, he entered and became the lone member of the first academic class in 1885. Later he attended Jefferson Medical College in Philadelphia and had a distinguished career in medicine in Houston. Harriet Red was an artist. She studied in Europe two years. Her place on the faculty of the Seminary was the head of the Primary Department. It was due to her artistic skill that a portrait of her father exists. Dr. George C. Red was unwilling to submit to the vanity of having a photograph made.

Dr. George Clark Red retired as a practicing physician but continued as a science'instructor in Stuart Female Seminary until his death on August 6, 1881.

In 1882 the cultured German Catholic family of Alfred E. Ritz came to Austin and settled near the Seminary property. Mrs. Ritz, a former pupil of Franz Liszt, was a very talented musician. Mrs. Red employed her to head the music department. The daughter, Maria (Mrs. Victor Schmidt), taught French and German. A younger daughter, Helene, after returning to Germany for further study, succeeded her mother in 1894 as piano instructor.

Among the art teachers were Miss Fannie Speed, Miss Janet Downie, and Mrs. Maggie Stiles.

Colonel Ashbel Smith was President of the Board of Trustees of the Stuart Female Seminary. When he was selected the first Chairman of the Board of Regents of the University of Texas, he served in both capacities until his death in 1886. Another trustee was Judge Zachary Taylor Fulmore, first County Superintendent of Travis County.

Miss Lel described by the Reverend Robert L. Dabney, Professor of Philosophy, The University of Texas, as the most intellectual woman of her generation, was admirably fitted to succeed her mother as principal when Mrs. Red died in 1886.

Dr. Miller frequently said that he thought he had done some service to Texas as an educator but never a better one than finding and bringing to Texas such a teacher as Rebecca Stuart Red.

Rebecca Stuart Red has a number of material memorials. The first doll presented by the Alpha Chapter, Delta Kappa Gamma Society, to "the pioneer teachers" collection represents Mrs. Red. Her name is inscribed on a beautiful scroll painted by J. Coleman Akin, that was prepared in commemoration of the Centennial of Texas Public Education in 1954, and unveiled in the Hall of Fame at the Dallas State Fair. Her old home in Gay Hill has been purchased by Col. George P. Red, a grandson, and restored so well that it has won an historic marker.

All of the property of Stuart Female Seminary was given by Rebecca's heirs to the Presbyterian Synod of Texas, U.S. The Synod donated the property to the Austin Presbyterian Theological Seminary which held its first classes there in 1902. The property was recorded as a Texas Historical Site in 1972 and was awarded a commemorative marker by the Texas Historical Commission in 1973 on the sponsorship of the Austin Colony Chapter of the Daughters of the American Revolution.

Certainly, the hundreds of young women who passed through the doors of Live Oak Female Seminary and Stuart Female Seminary exemplified the training of a past era, when educators stressed religious training and character building along with academic attainments.

Large statue brought by the Rzeppas from Poland and now in St. Mary's Church in Panna Maria.

Tecla Rzeppa
(1802-1880)

By T. Lindsay Baker*

On the morning of September 16, 1802, in the tiny Upper Silesian village of Stare Tarnowice, at the southeastern tip of the Kingdom of Prussia, a little girl was born to Polish peasant parents. On that morning Johanna, the wife of Sylvester Dostrach, the parish organist, bore this child whom they named Tecla. The infant was baptized in the parish church of St. Martin that very day. Little is known about Tecla's childhood and adolescence, but it is known definitely that on November 18, 1823, at the age of twenty-one, she married in her home church a young man by the name of John Rzeppa, a native of the nearby county town of Toszek. The couple remained in Upper Silesia for the next quarter century, but then they made a decision which dramatically altered their lives—the decision to immigrate to America.

As early as 1854 Polish peasants from Upper Silesia had begun immigrating to Texas. There they founded the settlement southeast of San Antonio named Panna Maria, which today is recognized as the oldest Polish colony in the United States. The early years of settlement at Panna Maria were times of great trials for the European settlers—as one colonist recollected a decade later:

> What we suffered here when we started! We didn't have any houses, nothing but fields. And for shelter only bushes and trees . . . the church

---

*Authority on Polish settlers in Texas and Research Associate, History of Engineering, Texas Tech University

we had been promised in Europe wasn't there, nor even one poor hut,
nothing at all for us to live in. . . . There was tall grass everywhere, so that
if anyone took a few steps, he was soon lost to sight. . . . The crying and
complaining of the women and children only made the suffering worse.
. . . How golden seemed our Silesia as we looked back in those days!

Conditions indeed were hard, but the Polish immigrants were
pious folk who found in their Catholic religion a security beyond
that of the temporal world. Soon after their arrival they began
gathering building materials for a church and within three years it
was built.

Tecla and John Rzeppa, one of the older couples in the
village, contributed probably more than their part to the church.
Their first major donation to the religious structure was a large
Christ figure which they had carried from Prussian Poland when
they immigrated to Texas. On Friday of Easter Week, March 21,
1856, Rev. Leopold Moczygemba, founder of Panna Maria,
dedicated a large cross upon which this figure had been mounted.
According to the memoirs of a priest who served the parish in the
1860's, people who entered the church generally paused to say a
prayer before this crucifix in memory of their homeland. One
woman, her mind confused by her longing for home, one day
knelt before the crucifix. She noticed that, like herself, the figure of
Christ had his head bowed in the direction of the faraway land
from which she had come and she cried aloud, "Oh, Lord Jesus! I
see that you too long for the old country. You too have your poor
head turned toward Europe!" This same figure, now mounted on
a modern cross, remains standing today beside the entrance to St.
Mary's Church at Panna Maria.

Tecla and John Rzeppa made a second large donation to the
construction of the first Polish church in America. They brought a
bell from St. Martin's Church in Stare Tarnowice. Most likely
Tecla's father, the organist there, assisted in its removal. The current parish priest at Stare Tarnowice recently complained that a
century before one of the bells from his church disappeared.
Undoubtedly this missing bell is the one which Tecla and John
Rzeppa carried to Texas. After the Panna Maria church was
completed in 1857, the Polish bell was hung from a small tower
over the choir of the church. It was used there for nearly a quarter
century and then in the 1880's it was transferred to a new church
building. Since that time the Rzeppa bell from Stare Tarnowice
has hung in the tower of the church at Panna Maria and today it
still can be heard ringing several times daily.

When Tecla arrived in Texas in the middle-1850's, undoubtedly she wore the folk dress common in Upper Silesia. The best description of this dress comes from Lyman Brightman Russell, who moved to the Panna Maria area about the same time. Later in life Russell recalled the Silesian peasants as wearing:

> ... the costumes of the old country, many of the women having what at that time were regarded as very short skirts, showing their limbs two or three inches above the ankles. Some had on wooden shoes. ...

The unusually short skirts of the Polish women apparently created some excitement among the male Americans, because in June 1855 Father Moczygemba wrote home advising, "Don't take any country dresses for Hanka, because she will not need them here. Our country dresses are the reason that the native people make fun of us and they cause sin." The wooden shoes Russell described were the *holzschoen* worn by Silesian peasants in Europe. These solid wooden shoes, similar to Dutch shoes, continued to be worn by people at Panna Maria until the early twentieth century and by peasants in Upper Silesia until World War II.

The American Civil War increased problems for the Silesian Polish immigrants to Texas as it did for all people in the South. Although no Silesian have been identified as slave holders, they were as surely drawn into the conflict as any other non-slave holders in the state. Settlers in all the Polish settlements attempted to evade the Confederate recruitment and conscription officers, thus securing for themselves reputations for disloyalty to the Southern cause. In reality one of the Poles' purposes in coming to America had been to escape conscription into the Prussian army in Europe. They simply did not want to fight in anyone else's wars.

Tecla's husband, John, was one of the Poles at Panna Maria who chose to fight on the side of the Union in the war. Although his military service record has not been located, it is known that he survived the conflict and returned to Panna Maria by 1865. In that year he was recorded as a livestock owner at Panna Maria with his brand shaped like a key and his cattle's ears marked with circular cuts in their centers.

Even though most of the Polish soldiers returned home from the Civil War, the problems of the Silesians did not end with the conflict. Immediately after the close of hostilities, Texas experienced probably the greatest civil disorder in its entire history.

Confederate civil government was replaced by a Union administration operated by Northern appointees which nullified many acts of the state government since 1861 and disenfranchised all men who had supported the Southern cause. Bands of freed Negroes, deserters, and assorted riffraff passed back and forth through the state with little or no restraint. For some time frontier areas like that around Panna Maria remained havens for outlaws.

Surrounded by lawless men with no legally constituted authorities to hold them in check, the Unionist sympathizing Poles became the objects of attack from revenge-seeking, lawless Southern element. William W. Gamble in San Antonio wrote to the Secretary of State of Texas about Panna Maria:

> The persons & property of these industrious people are entirely at the mercy of the lawless desperadoes who inhabit this county, their colony is in danger of being broken up, and the local Civil Authorities appear to connive at their persecution.

One of the settlers at Panna Maria recalled that one night during the post-war unrest, a party of thieves broke into the store operated by John Kuhnel. After stealing what they could carry away, they proceeded to attack the proprietor. At this moment John Rzeppa, who had a reputation for marksmanship, came to his rescue. When the miscreants heard his rasping order behind them, they turned to see the "business end" of a heavy rifle leveled at their middles. Rzeppa did not have to repeat his order for them to depart.

Tecla Rzeppa lived on at Panna Maria into later years which were less violent and troubled than those of her first twenty years in America. She died at the age of seventy-seven years on January 21, 1880, and today her grave marker is seen easily at St. Mary's Cemetery in Panna Maria.

Anna Salazar de Esparza (circa *1806-1849*)

*By Glenn Scott**

Present in the Alamo during its siege and surviving its fall was Anna Salazar de Esparza and her four children. Her husband, Gregorio Esparza, was one of the defenders. Gregorio had entered the volunteer Texian army in October, 1835 and fought with Juan M. Seguin's company in the assault on Bexar, the old San Antonio fort.

Anna, who was probably thirty years old; her three sons (Enrique, Manuel and Francisco); and a baby girl Maria de Jesus lived at the Esparza house on La Calle de Acequia now Main Avenue. However, Anna and the children were temporarily staying at the home of her friend Ramon Musquiz when Santa Anna's army was sighted in late February, 1836. Gregorio and a fellow volunteer, William Smith, had planned to send their families by wagon to safety in Nacogdoches, but the wagon did not arrive in time. On February 23, with Santa Anna's army just outside the city, Gregorio raced up to the Musquiz home to get Anna and the children. The front entrance to the Alamo was already barricaded, but Anna and the children were slipped into the mission through a chapel window.

Seventy-one years later, Enrique Esparza, Anna's oldest son, was interviewed by *The San Antonio Express*. The distinguished looking, bearded caballero of eighty-two years repeated once

---

* Teacher-student-journalist in Austin's Alternative Community

Anna Salazar de Esparza's eldest son, Enrique Esparza, 74 years after the fall of the Alamo

again his recollections of the most historically important day of his life: March 6, 1836. Enrique, who was eleven then, claimed that his mother had seen her husband killed and had rushed to where he had fallen by the cannon he had been firing. Senor Esparza remembered his brothers and sister clutching at his mother's skirts amidst the darkness and the smoke and the screams of the dying.

Finally, at daylight when the shooting had stopped, all the women and children were escorted to Ramon Musquiz' house. At 8:00 a.m. Anna Esparza left the room where the group was being guarded to go into the kitchen to prepare some breakfast for the infants and children who were very likely in serious need of food. Senor Musquiz came in the kitchen and ordered Anna to return to the room. Anna, hotly retorting that she did not care whether she was under guard or not, added that she was going to fix something to eat for herself, her children, and the others since Santa Anna had not seen fit to provide food for his prisoners. Musquiz tried to silence her with promises that he would bring them some provisions from his store. When the food finally did arrive about two hours later, Enrique remembered that he ate heartily but his mother sparingly.

Anna's husband had a brother Francisco who fought in Santa Anna's army. Like many families during the Civil War, Mexican families were often split over the issue of Texas independence. Francisco received the General's permission to find Gregorio's body and to give it a Christian burial. All the other bodies were heaped on a pyre and burned. Evidently, the body was buried quickly and quietly in the *camposanto* near Milam Square because Enrique admitted he had not been present at his father's burial. Sometime later Gregorio's remains were moved to the first San Fernando cemetery.

At 3:00 p.m. on March 6, the prisoners were presented to General Santa Anna in the Military Plaza. Juana and Gertrudis Navarro were interviewed first. Enrique recalled that when his mother came before Santa Anna she was given two silver dollars and a blanket "as he had given all the other women."

It seems that Anna and her children lived in or near San Antonio for the rest of their lives. According to Enrique they were ranchers for many years near Pleasanton and built a church and school in the area. In February, 1848, as the heirs of one of the Alamo defenders, the Esparzas were officially granted one league and labor of land. The next year, Anna Salazar Esparza died, evidently without re-marrying, and only a few months later, her daughter Maria de Jesus followed her.

The surviving sons, all residents of Atascosa County, were granted additional tracts of land by the State of Texas: 1920 acres on April 24, 1854; 316 acres in Bandera County on September 29, 1868; and 1351 acres in Bandera County on April 10, 1872.

One of Enrique's five children by his marriage to Gertrudis Hernandez was Sister Claud, one of the founders of the Incarnate Word community in San Antonio.

When interviewed in 1907, Enrique, Anna's only surviving son, had returned to San Antonio to live out his old age only a short distance from where he had been born on La Calle de Acequia in September, 1824. He died in 1917 at the age of ninety-three and was buried at Losoya, Texas.

Emilie Ploeger Schumann (1822-1896)

By Elinor R. Houston*

My great-grandmother was born Antoine Theresa *Emilie* Valeska Ploeger, the fifth child of Ottilie *Adolphine* Charlotte Sack and her husband, Friedrich Ploeger in Paderborn, Germany, on June 6, 1822. (The names italicized were the ones used by the family.) She was brought up in a family well educated and in comfortable surroundings. She was married on December 8, 1848, to Carl Friedrich August Heinrich Potthoff and the next year a daughter, *Ottilie* Adolphine Wilhemine, was born on August 8th. The marriage was ended by the death of her husband in September, 1849. In 1852 the widow decided to emigrate to America.

Several members of her family had already gone to Texas. One brother had settled in Bastrop in 1843 and established a medical practice there. Another had gone to Round Top, Fayette County, and was in business. In order to provide for herself and small daughter, my great-grandmother learned tailoring and the fashioning of hats.

After packing the huge wooden chests used by immigrants to convey all their possessions, Emilie sailed from a German port to Galveston, Texas. The voyage took three months.

On board was a young man also on his way to pioneer in America. He was *Bruno* Willibald Heinrich Schumann, a watchmaker and jeweler from the Black Forest region in Germany. Dur-

---

* Great-granddaughter

Emilie Ploeger Schumann and her daughter, Ottilie Pothoff

ing the long voyage, Bruno was attracted to the little girl, then became friends with her mother. They fell in love.

After arriving in Galveston, Emilie and Bruno were married on January 4, 1853. They settled in Round Top where they lived until after the Civil War. On May 3, 1856, a daughter was born who was named *Ellen* Marie Adolphine Schumann. She was my grandmother.

During the Civil War my great-grandfather worked as a non-combatant in the cap factory which was located in Austin, Texas. The factory turned out caps for Magruder's Army. The ammunition caps were stamped out of lead strips about an inch wide leaving a row of crosses in the strip. Some of these strips were always hung on the family Christmas trees in memory of those days of the misery and deprivations in war time.

While her husband was in Austin, my great-grandmother sewed for others to keep her family in food and the barest necessities. My great-grandmother told of a woolen skirt, re-dyed each fall with hickory bark, which always turned out the same ugly shade of brown. Shoes were hard to find and expensive, so copper toes were put on to keep them from being worn off as quickly by small scuffling feet.

All clothing was made at home: socks and children's stockings were knitted by hand. Men's clothing was not very different from today's but women's was much more elaborate. There were chemises, drawers, corset-covers, numerous petticoats, and dresses with long skirts. The skirts and bodices were fully lined, waists were boned and elaborately decorated with lace or embroidery. Most of the undergarments were trimmed with hand made knitted lace or embroidery, some in intricate designs. Some had crocheted or tatted borders or rows of tucks above the borders.

Toward the end of the War, my great-grandmother had only one needle left for her sewing machine. She would not let her daughters use the machine; for if the needle was broken, she would be unable to sew what was needed.

Much of the time, artistry and effort went into maintaining the clothes of a family. Everything became scarce and nothing was wasted. Floor coverings were made of small scraps of material, either cotton or wool, hooked or looped onto sacking or burlap. These rag rugs were warm if not always bright and colorful.

All during the time my great-grandfather was in Austin, his

wife saved whatever she was paid in gold, spending only the Confederate paper money. He brought gold he had saved and, after sending the girls away, they hid the gold in an old iron pot under the floor boards of the cabin and covered the floor with a rag rug. They had between them saved $1,000.00 with which to start a jewelry and watchmaking shop when the War was over. For a number of years Bahn and Schumann were partners in a jewelry business on Congress Avenue in Austin.

In 1857 my great-grandfather bought the property in Austin on which he later built his home. The address was 309 East Eleventh Street. The house stood until a few years ago when it gave way to a high rise building.

The family home with a small front porch was a one and a half story clapboard, four rooms and a hall on first floor and two bedrooms upstairs. All windows had wooden shutters painted gray as was the house and surrounding picket fence. On the east side was a lattice and shutter enclosed porch which was called "Die sommer-frische" ("the summer holiday resort," literally translated).

The house was built on sloping land so there were three terraces divided by stone walls with stone steps from one level to the next. There were flower beds and shrubs on the first level. The next one had a wisteria arbor around a large oak tree. Vegetable gardens were planted on the two lower terraces. A deep underground cistern, fed by rain from the tin roof, filtered through charcoal, was enclosed in a small garden house, two sides of which were latticed.

A lawn, fig trees, fruit trees, and a large grape arbor filled much of the back yard. In the early days a carriage house and stable, also a shed for storing wood were in the far end of the yard. The basement was divided into a wine cellar; a deeper, darker room for storage of vegetables and preserved food; a shop; and another store room.

The home was the birthplace of the first grandchild, Elfriede Jessen. Otillie, the elder daughter, had married Adalbert C. Jessen, a professor in Brenham, Texas, on June 19, 1872. Ellen, the younger daughter, married Johann Friederich Reichmann on June 21, 1873. Her first child, a daughter, named Emmy (the diminutive form of Emilie) was born on April 27, 1874. Five other grandchildren joined the growing family group.

After they were established in Austin and had a circle of friends, my great-grandparents kept up with books and periodicals by a sort of circulating book club. It was referred to as "Die Mappe" (translated "The Portfolio"). In this way, they were able to see and read many books and magazines in their native language. There was always music, always literature both in English and German, and always handwork. The latter included such things as carved picture frames, beaded footstools, yards of fine embroidery and lace, objects made of silver and gold, an ingenious contraption for a shower bath, miniature furniture for a doll house, cradles for grandchildren, and endless other things.

These forbears brought with them family customs and traditions. There were many varieties of cookies and special dishes that were served at certain times, such as Christmas Eve. Many seasonings were used, grown in the gardens and dried for winter use. They had onions and chives but never garlic; parsley and summer savory but never sage. Grape leaves and dill went into pickles packed in stone jars in the deep cellar. Bay leaves for savory stews came from trees in the garden.

My great-grandmother died in Austin on November 4, 1896, at seventy-four. Her husband had died on December 12, 1893. They are both buried in the old west part of Oakwood Cemetery in Austin. Pioneer, in the true sense, Emilie Schumann built something lasting and beautiful in an alien land.

Louise Ormsby Stanuell

Louise Ormsby Stanuell (1859-1909)

By Katherine Weisiger*

Louise, one of the eleven children of Henry and Julia Hamilton Ormsby, was born at Dublin in 1859. Her English forbears had settled in Ireland 600 years before her birth. The story of her life is a dramatic one. It tells how she, the daughter of the Chief Justice of the Supreme Court of Ireland, was tutored in the ancient Killeny Castle; was presented at the Court of Queen Victoria; came to Texas as a bride; and lived in a small house on a sheep ranch on the Kendall County prairie.

As a girl in Dublin, Louise studied music, played tennis (she won a championship), enjoyed the social events of the era, sang in choir groups, and skated on frozen ponds with other young people. She lived the pleasant, sheltered life of a young Victorian lady.

Then she met Athill Stanuell, an exciting young man who had just graduated in engineering from Trinity College in Dublin. He and five of his friends had read in English newspapers of Kendall County, Texas, where acreage could be obtained and horses could be purchased. The young men were polo enthusiasts and eager for adventure.

In 1883 Athill sailed from Ireland to New York and traveled on to Kendall County, Texas, to look over the situation. Later he returned to Dublin and to Louise with wondrous stories of the new

---

* Member of Bicentennial Book Project, 1971-1975, Austin Branch, AAUW.

land. Deeply in love, Athill and Louise talked long hours and made plans.

Louise was slender, of average height, with violet-blue eyes, fair skin, and dark hair. Like the young ladies of her day, Louise had been carefully reared for marriage.

To the women of that day, bishops, barristers, and husbands were formidable. When Louise was young, Mrs. Ormsby used to say to her: "Don't disturb your father!" When she was allowed to come to the breakfast table, young Louise, fascinated but silent, watched her father as he neatly clipped the top off his boiled egg in its cup.

In 1886 in Harpool, England, Louise and Athill were married by her brother, the Reverend Edwin Ormsby, Canon of Durham Cathedral.

From England the young couple sailed to New York and probably to Galveston, Texas. They traveled across the country to San Antonio where they stayed at the Menger Hotel. After resting and buying supplies, they went to the frame house Athill had built on land he had bought, he thought, from a Texan. Later he found the sale to be fraudulent, as were many in those pioneer days.

Athill and the five young men (one of whom was an Episcopal priest who became their rector) quickly established a community near Montell, Uvalde County. Athill and several of the others had invested in sheep while the remainder invested in bees, goats, and cattle.

Louise helped to establish the Church of the Ascension where the young people's social and religious life centered. Her music, wit, and humor helped the first difficult days to pass.

She loved the prairie flowers but not enough to plant and care for them in her own yard. A helper, Mrs. Rowan, was engaged by Athill to help Louise with the housework before and after Harry, their first child, was born.

One day Mrs. Rowan was busy filling the lamps with kerosene from a can in the kitchen. Accidentally she snapped off the head of a match. It flew toward the open can of kerosene near the baby Harry's cradle. In the explosion that followed Louise and Athill's young son was burned to death before anyone could save him. In this fire, they also lost their home.

Saddened, Athill and Louise built on their land a concrete house with walls two feet thick. Their house was the only one in the area with water piped to the kitchen door. A windmill was added to help irrigate the vegetable garden.

A piano came from somewhere and again there was music in the home. Violet, the little daughter born in 1889, remembers that her home was always filled with singing and laughter. As Violet grew, her parents taught her to sing, to play the piano, and to read. From her father Violet learned to paint with water colors. He also helped to plant a little cactus garden near the carriage house. Although Violet received no toys except at Christmas and these were quickly worn out, and had no child with whom to play, she does not remember ever being lonely.

The nearest neighbors were the Stirt brothers, half a mile away, and an Irish gentleman named J. D. Tracy, who owned a goat ranch. As a treat and at rare intervals Violet was taken to visit a neighbor. One day she was sent to a neighboring ranch. On her return, Violet was shown something in a basket. Athill smiled and held her on his lap. Violet asked: "What's that? Pick it up!" Her father laughed and hugged her. "It's your little brother, Stewart, born while you were away." She had never seen a baby before— only tiny lambs.

Although there were both cattle and sheep ranches in the area, Violet recalls no traditional quarrels between cattle and sheep men.

Another brother, Ainsley, came to join the family. When Violet was about six years old, Athill was advised that the dry, hot, dusty air of the prairie was detrimental to his health. It was suggested that the family go to the coast for a while.

They settled in Galveston expecting to return to their ranch, but they never did. Later when Athill wished to sell his property near Montell, he discovered that the Texan who had sold him the land had never owned it.

After a short time in Galveston, the cotton firm by whom Athill was employed transferred him to Houston. This was when the streets of Houston were paved with cedar blocks and mule cars carried people across town from the Main Street.

Ainsley died and was buried in Hollywood Cemetery in Houston. Harry, the brother Ainsley and Violet had never known, had been buried in the churchyard at Ascension Church in Montell.

When Violet was twelve, she and her family went to England on a French ship, La Salle, that had been chartered by the Cotton

Firm. The Stanuells had a pleasant trip but were happy to return to Texas.

In 1909 Louise died in Houston and Athill died five years later. Both lie with Ainsley in Hollywood Cemetery. Life went on.

Stewart became a successful business man like his father. Violet, after marriage and early widowhood, in 1931 was appointed the first Director of Child Welfare in the State of Texas. Her son, Joe Greenhill, a distinguished alumnus of the University of Texas, is Chief Justice of the Supreme Court of Texas.

Eva Catherine Rosine Ruff Sterne (1809-1897)

By Gloria Frye*

Eva Catherine Rosine Ruff Sterne was born in Eslinger, Germany, on June 23, 1809, to John Eberhard Ruff and Elizabeth Margaret Eberspacher Ruff. At the age of six, her parents brought her to the United States. The Ruffs landed at New Orleans and took a river boat up the Red River. Yellow fever broke out on the boat and Mrs. Ruff died. Mr. and Mrs. Placide Bossier, a couple whom the Ruffs met on the boat, consented to care for Eva Catherine, her sister, Anna Marie, and a brother, Jeremiah. Some say that both parents died, and other accounts state that the father took Eva Catherine to Natchitoches, Louisiana, where she was adopted by the Bossiers, wealthy French Catholics. All accounts reveal that she was raised by the Bossiers who owned a large plantation near Natchitoches.

On June 2, 1828, at her plantation home, Eva Catherine Rosine Ruff married Adolphus Sterne, a man who immigrated to America from Germany at the age of sixteen and later joined the early colonists in their struggle against the Mexicans; who took part in the Fredonian Rebellion, the Texas Revolution, and the Cherokee War; who served as alcalde and postmaster of Nacogdoches; who was a member of the first Grand Masonic Lodge of the Republic of Texas; and who, at the time of his death, was a member of the Texas Senate. There are several accounts as to

---

* Special Collections, Librarian, Stephen F. Austin State University, Nacogdoches, Texas.

233

Eva Catherine Rosine Ruff Sterne

how Adolphus Sterne met Eva Catherine Ruff. Isaac Sterne, Adolphus' brother, lived in the community near Natchitoches, so it is likely that on one of his trips there, Adolphus met and courted Eva. Others say that she met her future husband while visiting in Nacogdoches. At any rate, these two German-born people of different religious backgrounds, he with a Jewish father and a Lutheran mother and she, a Catholic, met and married. Adolphus was twenty-eight years old when he married Eva Catherine, nineteen.

The couple settled in Nacogdoches. Adolphus became a leader in the community and Eva the most respected and beloved woman in the city. They had seven children: Eva Helena Eugenia, Charles Adolphus, Joseph Amador, William Logan, Placide Rusk, Laura Theresa, and Rosine. Eva Helena married Thomas C. Barrett of Virginia. Laura married Major E. W. Cave, well-known editor 'and later Secretary of State under Sam Houston. Rosine married William A. Ryan. As far as can be determined, William Logan was the only child who did not live to adulthood.

During her long residence in Nacogdoches, then the gateway to the United States, Mrs. Sterne entertained more distinguished guests in her home than any woman in Texas. General Sam Houston, J. Pinckney Henderson, David S. Kaufman, Kenneth L. Anderson, Thomas J. Rusk, David Crockett, and many other distinguished Texans, as well as Mexican officers, were frequent visitors in the Sterne home.

Recognizing the requirement of the constitution and laws of Mexico, that a prerequisite to citizenship and to holding office was to support the Roman Catholic Church, General Sam Houston was baptized into that church and had Mrs. Sterne as his sponsor. The baptismal service took place in the Sterne home. After General Houston and other members of the convention signed the Declaration of Independence at Washington-on-the-Brazos on March 2, 1836, he sent Mrs. Sterne a beautiful set of jewelry with the request that she wear it on each succeeding anniversary of that day. She did so until the death of Adolphus. But, when she attended the ceremonies for the laying of the corner-stone of the capitol at Austin on March 2, 1886, she again wore the jewelry. That was the fiftieth anniversary of the Declaration as well as being another important history-making event.

Not only was the Sterne home famous for its hospitality, but Mrs. Sterne, being a devout Catholic, also made it the center of

Catholic activity for the entire area. Visiting priests made the home their headquarters. It was also the rendezvous of the women and children of the surrounding country during the perilous times when the men were on duty and under arms. Much of the social activity of the community took place in the Sterne home. Because Mrs. Sterne had a real love for Texas, San Jacinto Day was always celebrated in great style. There were banquets, dances, and card parties. Charles Adolphus said that his mother was one of the most graceful dancers that he had ever seen.

In Adolphus' diary many references are made to his wife. On June 2, 1842, he wrote, "This is the fourteenth anniversary of our Marriage and but few Clouds have darkened our nuptial Hemisphere—my wife is *now* as *dear* and as *lovely* in my sight and my Heart thrills with as much enthusiasm as when I first called her mine—may the great ruler of the Universe vouchsave to end our union with as much harmony as it has begun and is now." A son, Charles Adolphus, described his mother as being a very attractive woman of medium height and having black curly hair and blue Eyes.

In addition to her duties as wife, mother and hostess, Mrs. Sterne found time to be an amateur horticulturist. The Sterne house was built on thirty acres which provided space for a vegetable garden, a flower garden and an orchard. The gardens contained many rare and beautiful specimens of plants, collected and cared for by Mrs. Sterne.

After the death of Adolphus in 1852, Mrs. Sterne remained in Nacogdoches for seven years. Then she moved to Austin. In 1874 she moved to Houston to live with her daughter, Mrs. Rosine Ryan. On March 1, 1897, she died at her daughter's home. There is a story told of her dying. She had sunk into unconsciousness. Extreme Unction had already been administered. The blinds were drawn, and only one bright sunbeam pierced the gloom in the room where she lay. Suddenly the sound of her labored breathing ceased. She, who for weeks had been unable to move, sat up, her blue eyes wide open and a sweet smile making her face look young and girlish. Upward she extended both arms and called softly in a youthful voice, "Dolph." Then she fell upon her pillow and died. She is buried beside her husband in the Oak Grove Cemetery in Nacogdoches, Texas.

The Sterne house is still standing today. In 1869 Joseph Hoya bought the house from Mrs. Sterne. Later his descendants donated the property to the city, and it is now the Hoya Memorial Library and Museum. Many interesting relics of the Sterne family are preserved in the museum. The house is one of the outstanding landmarks of Nacogdoches. Not only does it represent the political, social and religious activities of a period when Texas was struggling for her independence, but it also represents Nacogdoches hospitality as established by the graciousness and friendliness of Mrs. Adolphus Sterne.

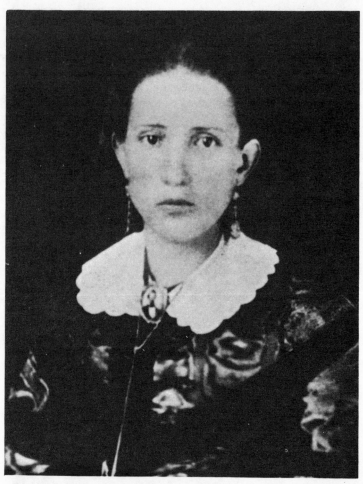

Eveline Greenwood Stoneham

Eveline Greenwood Stoneham (1835-1926)

By Lois L. Stoneham*

Eveline Greenwood Stoneham was truly a representative Texas woman. Her life span of over ninety years covered a period of time in which Texas, her native state, lived under the flags of Mexico, of the Republic of Texas, of the United States, of the Confederacy, and again under that of the United States. She was the daughter of one of Stephen F. Austin's colonists, Franklin Jarvis Greenwood, and his wife, Mary Montgomery Greenwood, and the granddaughter of two others, Henry Bailey Greenwood and William Montgomery.

Eveline was born December 14, 1835, in the turbulent months just prior to Texas Independence. Her early life was typical of that of other pioneers. While she was still a child, a mere babe in arms, she participated in the famous "Run-away Scrape" when the Texians fled before General Santa Anna as he made his march across Texas after the defeat of the Alamo patriots. She claimed to "remember" how she was caught up in her father's arms, riding in the saddle before him, as the family left its home on Grimes Prairie, about fifty miles north of the present city of Houston. She also "remembered" how the family stacked the "valuables" in a dry ravine and covered them over with brush to save them from the scavenging army. Fortunately her family did not have to go beyond the Sabine into the United States to safety.

---

*Granddaughter

They with hundreds of others were turned back at the Trinity River by the good news of the victory at San Jacinto, in which, she was always proud to recall, twenty-one of her kinsmen had fought. Before returning to their home, the Greenwoods visited the battle-field to see their kinsmen, and Eveline claimed that while there they saw the captive Santa Anna.

Eveline's childhood held many noteworthy experiences with the friendly Indians—and some not so friendly! Once her parents left her with the old slave woman while they went on a short visit to her grandparents who lived about a mile away. The old Negro was outdoors ironing, and the young Eveline was toddling around under the old woman's watchful eye when three silent Indians appeared on the path that went by the house. The Indians stopped, spoke to one another in inaudible tones, and approached the place where Eveline was standing mute with terror. The old slave began screaming for them "to leave dat little white child alone," but they completely disregarded her. One of them picked up the near-hypnotized child and placed her on a convenient stump. Taking out a hunting knife from his belt and skinning a big leaf from a nearby Spanish mulberry bush, he placed the leaf under her little bare foot and traced around it with the knife. He, then, put Eveline back on the ground, replaced his knife, and with his friends left as quietly as he had come. A week later, the Indian returned and presented her with a pair of little moccasins that fitted perfectly.

At another time, Eveline was playing in the yard alone. From some bushes just outside the rail fence came a low whistle. She looked up to see an Indian, half-hidden there, beckoning her to come over. In his hands he held a beautiful little basket filled to the brim with wild plums. "Me give you this for an ear of corn," he whispered. The plums looked luscious, and Eveline ran to her father's corn-crib, chose a good ear of corn, and made the exchange gladly. On succeeding days her Indian trader returned, sometimes with berries or other fruits, but always with the same greeting, and Eveline made more trips to the corn-crib. When her father heard of her trading, he was somewhat amused; he told her, however, that the corn crop was short and that she must make no further exchanges so Eveline's bartering came to an abrupt end.

Eveline had her own adventure with the noted Sam Houston, who often on his trips between Houston and Huntsville, spent the night at her father's home. On one such trip, the family and their guest were sitting around the blazing hearth-fire, and Houston was relating one of his stirring adventures. It came time for her to go to bed, but she wanted to hear Houston's story to the end. The five-year old Eveline, however, was firmly put to bed. After her mother had left her, Eveline slipped quietly out of bed and tip-toed to a safe hiding place behind the door, where she could listen undetected. There she stood until sleep overtaking her, she toppled over with an ominous thud. Her father and General Houston, thinking that an Indian was skulking behind the door, caught up the tongs and snatched a pistol from the mantel and advanced on the door. They found only a sleepy, disobedient little girl in a nightgown. Her father scooped her up into his arms, laughingly, and put her back in her bed.

When she became old enough to go to school, Eveline left her father's home on Grimes Prairie and went to stay with her sister, Mrs. James Lawrence, who lived a few miles away in the town of Anderson. Here she attended the famous Patrick Academy and met her future husband, John Stoneham.

At recess, the boys played baseball. Eveline, entranced by the handsome John, would run to pick up the stray balls. John was a newcomer and fifteen years old. When he left to return to Alabama to visit his sister, Eveline pined away, thinking he might never come back. He did, however, and when she was a grown-up lady of seventeen, she married him.

John Stoneham, a native of Brooklyn, Alabama, had been orphaned by both mother and father within a month from a virulent fever. He had been brought to Texas by his uncle, George Stoneham, who bought the Widow McIntyre's Mexican land grant in 1844. John was placed in school at the academy until he finished his courses. When he became of age, his uncle and guardian gave him his patrimony—a five hundred acre black land farm and his portion of his father's slaves from the Alabama plantation. Two years later he and Eveline married and moved into their new home, a large, two-story plantation-type home about five miles from Plantersville.

Through the early years of marriage, Eveline was the typical Southern plantation mistress, in charge of a large number of slaves to teach and to administer to in their illness. When it came time for her first child to be born, Eveline knew it would be a hard labor. John went for the doctor, Eveline's own brother, Dr. Thomas Benton Greenwood. Before the two could return, a Texas blizzard swept down suddenly, hindering them from arriving in time. Eveline, with the pains upon her, was taken by her faithful old Negro slave to the kitchen—detached from the big house as was usual in those days for safety—and there on a cot in the warmth of the old kitchen and attended only by old Lyddy MacDowell, her slave from childhood, as midwife, she brought forth her first-born child, Joseph. When her husband and the doctor arrived, they were met by a *fait accompli!*

During the 1850's and the years of the Civil War, Eveline and John were rearing a family and amassing land and coping with the problems of the war. Eveline bore twelve sons and two daughters; of these fourteen children, eight of the sons grew to manhood. She had bequeathed some of her amazing stamina to each; for all lived beyond the age of sixty-five years. John, meanwhile, was buying land. Before the oldest son reached his majority, John had acquired more than three thousand acres. It was then that Eveline understood completely his obsession with land. He was hoping to be able to pass on to each of his eight sons the same patrimony of five-hundred acres black land farm as his uncle had passed on to him.

The war years were strenuous ones for the family. John and his two brothers, Henry and Joe, had volunteered their services to the Confederacy and reported to camp at Hempstead. John, however, suffered the first of a series of heart attacks during maneuvers. After he recovered, he became a procurer of supplies for the army and was kept busy going over the county buying up stock and produce. He was also managing, not only his own plantation but that of his brother Joe also and looking after Joe's family. When this brother was killed in the Battle of Mansfield, Louisiana, John's responsibility for the family became even heavier. Eveline, too, was busier than ever. Her medical knowledge was second only to that of her physician brother, and when he left for the army, she was sent for as an able substitute. She could mix medicines, making dosages of calomel and rolling them in little papers (There were no capsules in those days). She knew the value of massage and sat for hours giving relief to those in pain.

Eveline had been thoroughly grounded in pioneer cooking lore. She preserved eggs for Christmas cakes by packing them in salt. By the time they were needed, there would be several dozen in the big earthen churn, all ready and all perfectly preserved for the fourteen cakes that she always made for the Christmas season.

242

She smoked sausages, hams, and spare-ribs, but she also knew how to pack the little "patty" sausages in lard—even as she had packed the eggs in salt. She supervised the blanching of the corn in ashes to make lye hominy and liked the taste of it! She presided over the mixing of the white paint for the house. She had so much white lead put in that after almost forty years, the south side of the house really never needed painting. She entertained in the old Southern tradition which meant that her home was always open to near relatives (and far ones), all visiting presiding elders and circuit-riding preachers, and any guest, whether they be invited ones or uninvited.

In 1886, when the youngest of her children was seven, John and Eveline moved from "The Old Place," their two-story plantation house to "Stoneham Oaks," which was to be their retirement home. It was built in the town of Stoneham, which was named for John, who had donated land for the railroads, the school, and the Methodist Episcopal Church, South. This house, while large, had only three bedrooms instead of the eight in the big house, but it had a beautiful living room papered with a golden floral design, the pride of Eveline's heart. Imagine her feelings when the wagons rolled up with the furniture and she found John's beloved old uncle already set up for housekeeping in it!

The uncle lived there until his death about twelve years later (Such was her hospitality!). The older boys and a local carpenter added two new rooms to take care of the "expanded" family. Newly-invented window screens were installed and lightning rods bought to protect the house from the elements.

Though their eight sons were either married or off at college, John and Eveline still were as active as ever. He managed a large mercantile business, his farms, and a cotton gin. She supervised the landscaping of the home. Dozens of young red oaks were set out to line the avenue to the house. Black walnuts, cherry laurels, and white cedars were set in strategic places, and sumac was planted to turn a brilliant red in the fall. In her yard she placed lilac, cape jasmine, bridal wreath, japonica, wistaria, Virginia creeper, and three shades of the graceful crape myrtle, which she allowed to grow into trees. In the big pasture, she scattered variegated phlox, and for the beloved uncle she saw that his favorite fragrant four-o'-clocks proliferated in the side-yard where he could enjoy them best.

Eveline and John were devout Methodists. When the new church was built in 1894, it received generous financial support from them. It was to have been dedicated that year, but on the day of its proposed dedication, John Stoneham was buried. It was another year before that ceremony of dedication was performed. In her eighties, Eveline's sight began to dim. It was characteristic of her that, when she realized her approaching blindness, she set herself to memorize all of her favorite Bible quotations. In her last years, she spent much of her time sitting in the swing on the front porch with one of her grandchildren beside her to "keep her entertained," but it was she who did the entertaining, regaling her demanding audience with stories of her childhood days. In that swing she did much character-building, too. She taught her grandchildren, in turn, those Bible passages she had stored up in her mind.

In April of 1926, Eveline Greenwood Stoneham died at the home of one of her sons at Yarboro, Texas, where she had been visiting. She was ninety years old at her death. Hundreds of relatives and friends attended the funeral service and they brought many lovely floral offerings to bespeak the love they held for this strong and courageous pioneer woman. One especially beautiful and appropriate floral piece she would have cherished most highly—a huge Texas star, woven of the Texas bluebonnet that was then in bloom over her beloved hills. She was laid to rest in the cemetery at Stoneham, land that was given to the little community by her father long before the Civil War.

Encompassed in the ninety years of the life of Eveline Greenwood Stoneham lay much of the history of Texas as colony, independent republic, and state. Embodied in her character were the traits of strength, independence, and courage, those particular attributes that represent the finest virtues of the Texas pioneer woman.

Sissie Thompson Sylestine

By Marion McMurrey*

The Alabama-Coushatta Indian Reservation lies deep in the heart of East Texas where the woods are thick and there are many springs. Here it was that Sissie and her brother, Charlie Thompson, and their parents were born in the 1800's.

In the early part of the 18th century, the French had come to Alabama and had sailed up the Alabama River in order to establish a fort. There they found the Alabama-Indians living much as has been described by early writers. The French established a fort "Toulouse." This fort was only a mile from the Indian Village and the Indians were friendly from the first. They brought fruit and farm products to sell to the soldiers.

In the fifty years with the French the bond of friendship grew very strong. The Indians had previously learned quite well the Spaniard's cruel treatment. Because of the kindness of the French they learned to trust them. The English, on the other hand, they had learned both to fear and dread—more by hear-say than by actual knowledge we think.

In 1763 the French ceded all their lands to the English. The French soldiers at the fort knew that they must leave and they decided to leave quietly in the night so that they need not witness the grief of the Indians. When the Indians went to the fort the next day and realized they were to fall into the hands of the hated English a

*Retired teacher of the Big Thicket area

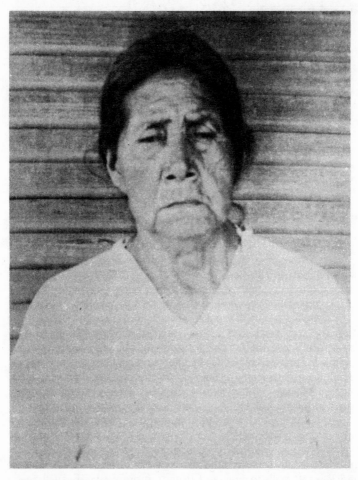

Sissie Thompson Sylestine

great wail arose. A council was called immediately and it was decided they would follow the French. They burned their houses
and the fort (which they had helped to build), cut down their fruit
trees, got into their canoes, and drifted down the river to Mobile
where they found their French friends. Their Chief Tomatha Lee
Mingo, grief-stricken over the homeless condition of his people,
sickened and died. He was given a military funeral by the French
and was called "King and friend of the King of France."

From Mobile the Indians migrated to New Orleans, still following the French. They established themselves in a village on the
Mississippi River about 100 miles north of New Orleans. It was at
this time that Chief Colebe Sylestine, who often went with the
French, helped to encourage the Indians to push westward. They
were appearing in Texas in the early part of the 19th Century. At
first they came for the purpose of hunting and fishing, gradually
staying longer and longer on the trips, finally building a village on
what is called "Horse-pen Creek." In Tyler County this was good
rich land—later bought by a white man. The Indians were driven
from their homes and were not allowed to take their corn and
stock. One of the white men even occupied the Chief's house.
After this they moved to land near the birthplace of John Henry
Kirby.

The Coushatta Tribe, better known as Koasati, were neighbors of the Alabama; both are Muskhogean stock of the Creek
nation and their languages are closely related. In their moves and
wanderings they came, sometime after 1795, to the Trinity River
in Texas, one group occupying a site on the river bank near the
present town of Shepherd in San Jacinto County.

In 1836 General Sam Houston camped with the Indians
overnight. He told them of the trouble with Mexico and the uncer-
tainty of the outcome and advised them to go back to Alabama.

Loving peace, they went to Louisiana for two or three years
and then came back and settled in Liberty County, from which
they were driven. For several years they wandered around from
place to place. At Governor Houston's suggestion the chiefs of the
Alabama Indians held a council with their white neighbors in Polk
County in 1853 and petitioned the Texas Legislature for 1280
acres in the vicinity of Livingston. In 1854 their request was
granted. The Coushattas by marriage and by special permission of
the Alabama people came in 1854 to live with the Alabamas on
their land. In 1928 the United States government added 3071

acres of land in Polk County to the Alabama-Coushatta's holdings and gave this in perpetuity.

Sissie Thompson married Washington Sylestine, son of Chief Colebe Sylestine. Washington and Sissie had several children. One of these was Bronson Cooper Sylestine who was born in 1879.

Crops were grown on plots of ground allotted them by the chief of the tribe; for the land was considered community property. Although the soil was poor, corn, peas, peanuts, potatoes and sorghum cane were raised and hay baled. Some stock was kept, but the best meat was obtained from hunting excursions to the Big Thicket where deer, bear, and small game could be obtained.

Before 1881 the Alabamas believed in a great, good Spirit but used charms, dances, and ceremonials to propitiate the evil spirits. Then the Presbyterian missionaries came and did away with native dances and ceremonials. There was complete silence in the church, a sort of funeral solemnity except for the hymns sung and the sermon given in English. The congregation stood for the prayers which were said in the Alabama dialect. However, the Indians liked the change, and when the church bell rang, they would come eagerly from their homes among the trees.

It was many years before women were allowed to speak English, and even in 1975 the Alabama dialect is not used in speaking to the whites. The Coushatta language (a type of Choctaw) is used instead. Only in the privacy of the Indian home was the true tribal language spoken.

Bronson, the son of Sissie and Washington Sylestine married Mozanna Thompson, daughter of Red and Jennie Thompson (no kin to the earlier Thompsons). Bronson was to become Chief of the Alabama-Coushatta tribe in 1957 and to hold that place until 1968 when he died at the age of 89.

Bronson and Mozanna had six children—three girls: Emily, Martha, and Cora, and three boys: Edwin, James Ludwell, and Clem (named in honor of adopted white Chief Clem Fain, Sr. of Livingston and Austin). These grandchildren of Sissie and Washington have done work outside of the reservation. Clem works for the Sam Houston Electric Co-operative in Livingston and Cora, a graduate of Southwest Texas State University at San Marcos, has taught Special Education in the Livingston schools and has, also, taught at Incarnate Word College at San Antonio. According to

Cora, Mozanna has been the power that has pushed her children to do their best in their station in life. When she married, Mozanna went to live in a log house, later in a white frame house, and now lives in a red-brick house in a beautiful setting of large oak trees. She is now 88 years old and seldom speaks of her early years and of her mother-in-law, Sissie Sylestine, but memories must linger with her still of those early days.

Sissie and her husband lie in the Indian graveyard by the church. They are buried in traditional manner, prone and with their heads to the east. In earlier days, the Alabama buried their dead in a sitting position and placed on their graves material things that they had loved or that they might need after death.

Nancy Tevis
(1796-1876)

By Reid W. Tevis and
Nancy Snyder Speer*

Noah Tevis of Scotch ancestry and his wife, Nancy, of French ancestry, emigrated from Tennessee through Louisiana to Texas as colonists. Traveling by covered wagon, they with their seven children, arrived in the Beaumont, Texas, area between 1824 and 1826. According to County Records and a letter written by Nancy, the Tevises arrived in the latter part of 1825.

They settled on the western side of the Neches River and applied to Lorenzo de Zavala for a land grant on January 16, 1835. An old document in Jefferson County Courthouse in Beaumont contains Noah's letter stating among other things that he, a native of the United States of the North, had been attracted by the liberal provisions of the colonization laws in Coahuila-Texas.

Tevis' application was approved and in the Field Notes of Arthur Henrie, Noah was admitted as a colonist and received a half-league of land situated on the west bank of the Neches River with its sixth corner on the bank of Tevis Creek. This was all the vacant land found in the locality where Noah had his house and field (arable land and pasture land). Tevis, in turn, promised that within a year he would build lime and stone monuments in every angle to the land, live there, and cultivate the property. The land grant (2,214 acres) was received January 16, 1835, and was

*Great-grandson; educator and compiler.

recorded as Tevis Bluff (now the city of Beaumont). Noah and Nancy were the first white settlers in what is now Beaumont.

Noah Tevis died on December 6, 1835, leaving to survive him his wife and eight children. Afraid that Noah's death, and because years earlier a stranger who had been their guest now threatened to take the land, Nancy wrote General Houston for counsel and aid, and she had her eldest son, George Washington Tevis, carry the letter to the General at Columbia, Texas. This was six months before San Jacinto.

The letter is beautifully written and states that Noah and Nancy had lived at Tevis Bluff for a decade. In February, 1830, a stranger, who said he was about to be married, had been told by Noah that if the man would come back with his family in the course of a year, he would give him a piece of land to settle upon. The stranger did not return until July, 1835, more than five years later. In the meanwhile Noah had laid half of his headright upon the same tract of land and "did (reside) and ever had, for these ten years back, resided on it." On this frail foundation the stranger had a few days prior tried to take the land from her unless she paid him $2,000.

Nancy retained the headright and no more trouble was caused by the stranger (his name was not mentioned in her letter). She, her children, and two Negro slaves left her in Noah's will, continued to improve and develop the property. In the spring of 1836 most of her neighbors (there were about fifty settlers there in 1836) left for the United States to escape the invading Mexican army and because they were afraid of the Alabama-Coushatta Indians who had settled in the area. However, Nancy Tevis took no part in the Runaway Scrape. For several weeks hundreds of people camped on the Neches River waiting for news of General Houston's defeat or victory. She gave the campers such help as she could. After what seemed a long time, George Washington Tevis on horseback brought the good news from San Jacinto. This made the little out-lying settlement have one of the happiest days in its history.

Nancy was kept very busy with the affairs of her husband's large estate and keeping her eye on their eight children: George Washington; Andrew Jackson, Napoleon Bonaparte; Roland; Noah, Jr.; Mary (married Gilbert Stephenson); Delilah (married Pierre Le Mans); and Le Visa (married Daniel Chesher). Le Visa was the only one of Tevis' children born in Texas.

The first marriage in the community was that of Mary Tevis and Gilbert Stephenson on November 27, 1832. This took place in the Tevis' log house with large logs blazing in the fireplace. Afterwards there was a feast and the table groaned under its weight of venison, wild turkey, and ducks out of the Tevis' backyard. The health of the bride was pledged in water from the Neches River. A record of the Civil ceremony was made and later a Catholic ceremony was performed. Gilbert, among other things, served as coroner in the community.

Among the early settlers in the area were the families of Joseph P. Pulsifer and Thomas B. Huling. Colonel Henry Millard, who fought at San Jacinto and had returned to the settlement about 1836, is said to have named the town and county for Jefferson Beaumont, his brother-in-law in Natchez, Mississippi.

The establishment of the townsite of Beaumont was effected in 1836 by an agreement signed by Nancy Tevis, who owned the greater part of the land upon which the townsite rested, and Messrs. Joseph P. Pulsifer, Thomas B. Huling, and Henry Millard, who pooled their real estate resources with those of the widow. Joseph Grisby, who owned fifty acres intervening in the tract, was also included in the agreement. The agreement is filed in the Jefferson County Courthouse.

The Corporation deeded large tracts of land to "the common good." Nancy donated land for the Courthouse Square, City Hall Square, old Beaumont High School, the Millard School Square, Nancy Tevis Market Square (now occupied by the Police Department), and other things.

The general location of the Tevis' log cabin is believed to have been near the Main Street and Pine Street intersection. In 1974 Tellepsen Construction Company crews in their excavation for the foundation of the new Southwestern Bell Telephone building, uncovered a cypress-curbed well, 75 feet from the Pine and Main intersection. The well was 42 inches square and at 13-foot level the excavators found water. It was from this well Beaumont's first settlers drank the water.

In the Beaumont region there was great need for ferries to cross the Neches River and bayous. In 1839 Nancy Tevis (who had become Mrs. Joseph Hutchinson), put her ferry into operation. She received two cents a head for all cattle that crossed. Old records in the Jefferson County Courthouse show that passengers paid a toll of 25 cents a wheel for carts and carriages, 25 cents for a man and horse, and for a wagon and team, and all persons belonging to the same $6.00.

Nancy died in Beaumont in 1876 at the age of eighty and was buried in the Tevis graveyard two miles south of the Tevis Homestead in Beaumont. Although in 1880, a substantial fence was put around the graveyard, the cemetery no longer exists.

Beaumont which celebrated its centennial in 1936 seems to have forgotten this gifted and generous pioneer woman.

Margaret O'Bryant Thompson

Margaret O'Bryant Thompson (1822-1895)

By Olive Donoho*

Margaret O'Bryant was born October 30, 1822, probably in Georgia. In about 1843 she married Gideon Thompson, son of Jacob Thompson and Mary Estes Thompson, and lived in Perry County, Arkansas. Here four of their children were born: William, Hiram Gideon, Robert, and Mary Ann.

Since Gideon was one of the six children, he expected little help from his parents in either land or money. With his own family increasing, he was attracted to Texas with its fertile land and prairies for raising cattle. In 1852 in a covered wagon and with the barest necessities, Margaret and Gideon brought their three sons and little daughter to Texas.

After a brief stop in San Antonio, the Thompsons settled in Sabinal Canyon, Bexar County, in the late fall of 1852. The first winter the Thompsons spent with John and James Davenport, Lee Sanders, and Henry Robinson in Captain William Ware's cabin. Captain Ware was temporarily in East Texas. The winter was a very cold one and hostile Indians had built a cabin six miles from the Ware Cabin and five miles from Utopia. However, it was not until 1856 that Gideon experienced his first Indian raid.

In the spring of 1853, the Thompsons built their own cabin and moved into it. In 1856 Uvalde County was organized from a western section of Bexar County. The new County was named

---

*Granddaughter

from Juan de Ugalde who had been Governor of Coahuila in 1778. Also in 1856 Camp Sabinal was set up by Captain Albert C. Brackett. In addition, this served as a Ranger Camp. Comanche Indian raids were becoming more common and settlers often needed armed protection.

Until 1875 the Comanche Indians offered stubborn opposition to Anglo-Saxon and Mexican settlements. Preferring bow and arrows to rifles, the Comanches were faster in their shooting than the settlers. Warriors were regarded the most important members of their tribes.

Utopia, so named because of its beautiful location in the Sabinal Canyon, became the Thompsons' residence. Margaret is said to have been the first Anglo-American woman and her children the first Anglo-American children in the area. Six daughters (Frances, Elmina, Milla Jane, Emily Texanna, Lilly, and Margaret) were born in southwest Texas where Gideon farmed and ranched.

In addition to his other duties, Gideon often went to Bandera to get meal, as there was no mill closer. There were motts of live-oak trees, cedar brakes, rocks, cacti, and low bushes along the so-called road. Margaret worried until Gideon returned because unfriendly Indians: Lipans and especially fast-riding Comanches, roamed the area. Once a ball from an Indian's gun went through Gideon's hat.

Margaret knew that Comanches carried off children and women, killed men, shot oxen and cows, and stole horses. She was always alerted, but tried not to alarm her children.

Margaret spun the wool into thread and wove the thread into cloth, which she sometimes dyed from herbs, berries and nuts. Then she cut and sewed the cloth into garments for her family. This was an endless task but she early taught her daughters to help her.

She saw that her family ate well. Game was plentiful. Pecans, berries, and honey from bee-trees could be found in season. Grain, corn, and other vegetables were grown except in drought years. Eggs, butter, and milk were at hand. Bread was baked.

Margaret was religious and, by example and precept, reared her children to be industrious and honorable. Many miles away from civilization and with hostile Indians roaming the land, Margaret had little time for other interests, even if they had been presented.

When Margaret died in Utopia on May 27, 1895, only four of her ten children were left to mourn her: Hiram Gideon and Robert, both ranchers; Elmina, the mother of the writer of this sketch; and Lilly. Two of Margaret's daughters had died before they were a year old and two others, in their twenties. Pioneer life was hard on children. William Thompson, the eldest child, was killed by an Indian. Pioneer life was permeated also with dangers.

Margaret was buried in Waresville Cemetery about a mile from Utopia. Gideon died of pneumonia on Valentine's Day, 1908, and was buried beside his wife. Both graves are marked with old-fashioned monuments.

On Farm to Market Road 187, about a mile from Utopia the Texas State Historical Commission has marked the site of Old Waresville, honored Gideon and Margaret Thompson, and memorialized other early settlers. The monument is inscribed:

> First Non-Military Colony, Uvalde County, Founded 1852 Capt. William Ware, Veteran of Battle of San Jacinto. Ware built first log cabin home (still standing). Other early settlers included Gideon Thompson, whose wife was first Anglo-American woman in Sabinal Canyon.
>
> Colony lost settlers in Indian Raids, 1856-1866. Although the Post Office moved to Utopia in 1883, still here is the Cemetery where Capt. Ware was buried in 1853; first store and Post Office built by Charles Durbon, 1856; Homes of Joel Fenley, John Ware built of native stone, 1870's.

Helen Mary Kirkpatrick Tinnin 1825-1893

By Helen Mary Tinnin*

Helen Mary Kirkpatrick was born in Kentucky in 1825. Her family migrated to Fayetteville, Arkansas, where she met and married Hugh Tinnin, whose wife and child had died, leaving him a widower for the second time. Tinnin, who was a native of Mississippi, had heard glowing reports of the new territory of Texas. He and Helen Mary made plans to migrate there.

John Carr, Tinnin's brother-in-law, had persuaded Tinnin to try his lot in Texas. Carr had come to Texas shortly after the fall of the Alamo. When he had come, he had used the southern route and had been hindered by swollen streams. He advised the Tinnins to take the northern route to avoid such and to evade, as much as possible, attacks by Indians. This the Tinnins did, but since Hugh, in order to help finance his way, stopped off along the way to buy supplies for soldiers quartered at various camps, the trip took the greater part of two years. The family and the many slaves which they brought with them fell ill with malaria fever, too. This delayed their progress. Malaria was an illness foreign to them before they started their trip.

The Tinnins arrived in Texas in 1850. Hugh bought land—about 500 acres of fine bottom land   south of the Colorado River—land which today is completely within the boundaries of Austin. Tinnin had about a two-mile frontage on the river. The old

---

*Granddaughter

crossing where cattle were driven up the Chisholm Trail was on the Tinnin land. This crossing was called Tinnin Ford.

The Tinnin slaves, about one hundred in number, went down the river and cut huge logs which were floated to a natural harbor or cove about five or six blocks from the present Congress Avenue bridge. They built the big house and their own cabins in the area which is now known as Travis Heights.

Hugh and Helen Mary Tinnin held a very enlightened viewpoint on slaves. They bought their slaves only in families, never consenting to breaking up a Negro family; if slaves had to be sold, they saw to it that families were kept together. Because of this, they were rewarded by a great loyalty.

The first sewing machine that was ever bought in Travis County was purchased by the Tinnins. Helen Mary undertook to teach one of the house servants, Old Aunt Rose, how to use it. The old Negro woman then taught other women slaves. All of the clothes worn by the slaves on the plantations were made by the slave women on Helen Mary's "first" machine. Helen Mary also taught the women how to sew by hand. Still in the possession of her grand daughter and namesake, Miss Helen Tinnin, are two of the fine linen sheets made by the slaves.

The flax for these sheets was planted at Helen Mary's direction in the low-lying areas along the river. The sheets were woven on the plantation itself. How well she instructed her slaves is shown by the tiny hems and stitches so beautifully done. The Tinnin machine, with its original needle, is on display at the Austin Library in the Travis County Room. In her own lifetime, Helen Mary kept her linens in a linen press which she had especially made for that purpose from fine black walnut wood floated down the Colorado River.

Hugh and Helen Mary Tinnin had four children. Albert, who was born in 1849, was severely burned while a small child. He was playing on a creek bank near the site where the Negro slave-women were washing. Bothered by red ants coming from an ant hill nearby, the women poured kerosene on the hole and "fired" it. Albert's clothing caught fire. Though Albert lived to early manhood, his death was largely attributable to the severe burns he sustained at this time.

The next child, a daughter named Cleopatra, was born in 1852. She soon acquired a nickname, given to her by one of the small slave-boys. The slave children had been playing in Helen

Mary's fine vegetable garden that had a profusion of potatoes, turnips, and onions. The children pulled some of these and made them into dolls to play with. When their master discovered it, he told them that this was food and that they must not destroy it by pulling it to make dolls. He asked who had done the deed. With the whites of their eyes showing large, each pointed to the next. Finally the little one on the end (for they were more or less lined up) lisped the name of the "culprit"—"Miss Clippy," who, or course, was innocent. Hugh Tinnin was amused at the saving attempt made by the little child. He "let them off" with a mild reprimand, but Cleopatra never lived down her new name, "Clippy."

The third child was a son, Pinckney, who was born in 1854. Pinckney developed some illness, probably diabetes, that necessitated the amputation of one of his legs. This handicap prevented him from working actively on the farm. The youngest son, Madison, was born in 1857. Though a delicate child, he grew to be a fine, able-bodied man.

The Tinnin plantation, because of its strategic location, could not but figure in the greater life of the area. At Tinnin Ford, the longhorned cattle being driven by Texas cattlemen were herded across the Colorado. Often some of the cattle would fall by the wayside, as it were, and "get down." The Blocker family, one of the early ranching families of the area, would give the unfortunate animals to the Tinnins. Hugh and his sons would care for the animals and nurse them back to health. On the next cattle drive the Blockers would buy them back to drive north to market. One old cow, the story goes, fell by the wayside seven times. She, however, did finally make it to market.

Because the plantaion bordered on the river, the table of Hugh Tinnin never lacked for a variety of fresh fish. The marshes were full of game-birds, too, and the woods provided many kinds of game: venison, wild turkey, quail, doves, and the like. The slaves kept the smokehouse filled, too, with beef and pork.

One of the best-remembered stories of Helen Mary is that of her love for growing things. Her vegetable garden, for instance, was her especial pride. Friends often brought gifts of fruit. Her children remembered that when she was old, she would take a stick and walk over the grounds pointing out places where she wanted the peach and plum seeds and pecans to be planted. As a result, the fields surrounding the Tinnin home were filled later with blossom fruit trees and nut trees, some of which were living as late as the 1930's when W.P.A. crews, clearing the roadways, mercilessly chopped them down.

The Tinnins grew fine cotton in the rich Colorado bottom. With the help of his slaves, Hugh ran his farm very successfully. With emancipation, he lost many of his slaves though he told them they could stay and work on shares if they wished. Neither master nor slave had principal to invest so most of the slaves could not avail themselves of the offer. A great many left, thinking that the North would guarantee them food and money.

Helen Mary and Hugh made a trip to Burleson County to look after some property that they held there. Suddenly, Hugh fell ill, died, and had to be buried there. Helen Mary sadly returned to Austin. After Hugh's death, a son by his first wife, came to Texas to claim his portion of the estate. A general division was made to all the surviving children; thus a very large plantation was broken into many parts. The last owner of any of the Tinnin property was Miss Helen Mary Tinnin. Helen Mary, Hugh's wife, was pleased to find, even in this period of sadness, that her husband had left his business affairs in good shape. He had been a good manager.

The Tinnin children received their educations in private schools, one such being Johnson Institute, housed in a two-story building erected in 1852 by slaves, who gathered the stones from Bear Creek near Friday Mountain. The teacher, Professor Johnson, was such an excellent teacher that he attracted pupils from all over the state. The Moody children from Galveston were educated there. When Johnson died, the school closed. An interesting foot-note as to the origin of the name Friday Mountain might be added here. That name was given to the mountain because every Friday Professor Johnson would take the students on a camping trip there. Food would be loaded on horses and the students would walk out to "Friday" Mountain.

During the years that the Tinnins lived, they remembered no Indian attacks around Austin except an early attack on the Hornsby party near Hornsby's Bend, but they often plowed their fields and found arrow heads and other Indian artifacts scattered over the land. They found many evidences of Indians on land where the School for the Deaf now stands.

Helen Mary's children grew up and married. Pinckney married Miss Effie Littlepage, Cleopatra married Henry Roberts, and Madison married Miss Elizabeth Willoughby, who was from Ft. Worth. The Madison Tinnins moved for a while to Brady, Texas, but returned to the home place in Austin. Helen Mary deeply loved her children and the love was reciprocated by all of them. Her daughter-in-law, Elizabeth, once said that no woman ever had a kinder or more thoughtful mother-in-law than she did in Helen Mary. Helen Mary Tinnin was well-liked by her neighbors and by her slaves, too.

Members of her family remember Helen Mary as a nice-looking woman of average height, a wonderful cook, and story-teller. She was deeply attached to Elizabeth, her daughter-in-law, and to all her grand-children, especially her namesake, Helen Mary, Madison's daughter.

Helen Mary Tinnin always regarded herself as lacking in business knowledge. She modestly actually believed it! And yet, she assumed the management of the big plantation after her husband's death and ran it quite successfully, as her children were proud to point out to her.

On June 24, 1893, at the age of sixty-eight years, Helen Mary Tinnin died. She had lived in Texas for forty-three of those years. The Tinnins had come to Texas in the difficult years after its independence; they had, through fortitude and hard work, seen the state suffer but survive through the Civil War years and the harsh era of Reconstruction. They had shared in two of the most prominent aspects of early Texas life—the period of cotton supremacy on the plantation and the era of the big cattle drives up the Chisholm Trail. Theirs was an integral part of both.

Helen Mary Kirkpatrick Tinnin was laid to rest in the Oakwood Cemetery at Austin in the Tinnin family plot, land not over a mile or so from the rich river bottom where she had spent her years in her adopted state of Texas.

Elise Amalie Tvede
Waerenskjold
(1815-1895)

By W. A. Flachmeier*

Among the Norwegian immigrants who began coming to Texas in 1845 was an outstanding woman by the name of Elise Amalie Tvede. When she arrived in New Orleans she continued on the route the first immigrants had taken: up the Mississippi and Red Rivers to Natchitoches and overland to the settlements in Henderson, Van Zandt and Kaufman Counties via Nacogdoches. In Four Mile Prairie, on the Van Zandt-Kaufman County line, she bought a square mile of land.

The settlements centering in Brownsboro and Four Mile Prairie were established by Johan Reinert Reiersen, a Norwegian who was interested in providing new homes for his poverty-stricken countrymen. To promote his venture he and his brother Christian had begun to publish the magazine *Norge og America (Norway and America)* and they appointed Elise Amalie Tvede editor in Norway.

A woman editor was an unheard of thing at this time; nevertheless, they did it because they had known Elise since childhood. She, the only daughter of Pastor Nicolai Tvede and his wife Johanne Meldahl Tvede, was born on February 19, 1815. As a daughter of a socially prominent family she had received a liberal education including English, French, and German as well as music and painting. Like her father she had been touched by the current

---

* Pastor and author of *Lutherans of Texas in Confluence.*

Elise Amalie Tvede Waerenskjold

rationalism and also had a real concern for the poor. At the age of nineteen she showed that she would not be bound in her activities by the limitations customarily imposed on her sex, by starting a craft school for girls in the face of opposition. This school, incidentally, long outlived its founder.

Unprecedented for a woman was Elise's writing of articles and a popular pamphlet for the temperance movement. She had observed what alcohol did to the lives and homes of the small farmers who were turning their potato crop into liquor as a more profitable way of selling it than hauling it to market. The problem was that they did not take enough of it to market. The temperance movement, in Lillesand at least, permitted moderate use of alcohol in punch but demanded total abstinence from such strong drinks as brandy, toddy, and grog.

In 1839 Elise had married Sven Foyn, a struggling young sea captain who later came to be an economic giant from his invention of the harpoon cannon for use in whaling. After three years of marriage, because of incompatibility, Elise and Sven agreed on a friendly separation. In consequence of this separation, and probably because her parents had died without leaving a son, she resumed her maiden name. Elise was just the person they needed as champion of an unpopular cause: independent, compassionate, and free. The Reiersens appointed her editor.

Then, in 1847, something happened with which the Reiersens had not reckoned: their editor demonstrated her independence once again by joining a group of emigrants from Norway. Undoubtedly relatives and friends wondered how this thirty-two-year-old "delicately trained lady" would adjust to the rugged life of a pioneer woman. Rather soon after her arrival in Texas she married a cultured young man whom she met on the voyage, Wilhelm Waerenskjold.

The young couple went into cattle and sheep raising business in as big a way as they could. Before long, Wilhelm and two partners set up a lumber and flour mill. There is evidence that Wilhelm also went into contracting. He was respected in the community, having been appointed to a small office in the area of law enforcement. In the course of time three sons were born: Otto, Niels and Thorwald.

The Waerenskjold home came to be something of a community center. For newcomers it doubled as welcome wagon and hospice. Estelle Nelson commented: "Elise became known as the little mother of Norse hospitality whether the stranger was a Norwegian or just a plain Texas with the bark on."

The young couple had a good start and a promising future, but on the Texas skies dark clouds were gathering. Abolition and secession were centers of fierce arguments. Elise wrote:

> I am convinced that slavery will be abolished by gentle means or by force because I believe that institutions founded on injustice cannot survive. . . . We emigrants, to be sure, can do nothing to abolish slavery. . . . We are too few and would only bring on hatred and persecution if we tried.

Time soon proved her right: outspoken unionists were often hounded unmercifully when Texas had seceded. The war brought untold hardships and calamities to thousands of families throughout the state. The Waerenskjolds also suffered disruption of all communications not only with the northern settlements but also with Norway and incurred economic losses. It was the one time when Elise regretted living in Texas. William Waerenskjold was in the Confederate Army but never in combat.

For Elise the greatest loss came after the end of the conflict. On February 2, 1866, she wrote: "It has pleased the Lord to take from us the dearest thing we possessed on this earth, our most beloved child Thorwald." On November 17 of the same year her husband was killed by a man in the community for an unknown reason, possibly because of a disagreement on the slavery issue. The widow accepted her losses with Christian resignation and continued to serve her home and community.

For twenty-nine years Elise carried on as a widow. There were good days and bad days, fair weather and foul, ups and downs. Once she wrote that doctors, and especially lawyers, made her poor. There were times when she was pressed by debtors. Once they pressed so hard that she contacted her former husband, Sven Foyn, in Norway about her problems and could then report that he had been "so extremely kind as to send $400." Again she wrote of debts having been paid. M. T. Jensen, pastor of Four Mile Church, summed up her life in the words:

> This lady of the aristocracy became a lady-jack-of-all-trades in her adopted country: She was a recognized authority on land, cattle, grain insects, prices, bankers, orchards, cotton, animals wild and domestic, freed slaves, and weary willies! . . . She learned to cope with grasshoppers, with blizzards, droughts, and floods, wind and weather of all kinds; such as tornadoes, thunder, lightning, hail, snow, ice and sleet.

Her letters indicate that she had trouble with borrowing, paying and collecting; that she milked her cows and fed her cattle when no help was available. When she had trouble making ends meet, she taught school, sold books and magazines and peddled seeds.

As she grew older and her sons married, she enjoyed and helped her grandchildren, turned over more and more of the management to her sons and eventually lived with Otto in Hamilton.

Then she wrote, "Things are well with me now—yes, much better than I deserve and cannot thank God enough who arranges everything so well for me." When she was seventy-nine, she was still busy, selling silverware from house to house. According to one of her letters, she read and wrote in the evenings and sewed during the day. Jensen wrote: "One marvels that she could leave so much and be content with so little in Texas." Once she wrote: "I have always been fortunate enough to have good friends wherever I have been, and that is a great blessing." Another reason for her contentment was, as she put it, she had never been fond of luxury. Her interests were numerous: her garden, books, her relatives, history, her church, and her faith as witness a statement she made in a letter in 1893 to the effect that she was not afraid to die because there was a Friend who carries us over into a better home where there is no death or separation. She lived until 1895.

Scanning Elise's letters that have been collected in the book, *The Lady With A Pen*, one might ask: what became of her early ambitions, her interest in the liberation of women, temperance, education and the welfare of the poor? One sign of her continuing interest in the status of women are her comments on the attitudes of Norwegian writers. A more meaningful sign of her conviction was that she cited Jesus' "giving women their natural and rightful place at the side of men as proof of the superiority of the Christian faith." Possibly she did not promote feminism in Texas because she saw that pioneer women, as partners of their husbands, had all they could do and that customary division of labor was desirable. As a widow she did not hesitate to tackle anything that needed to be done. Her support of temperance was most noticeable in her joy at Wilhelm's leadership in a local temperance society and approval of the service in that area by evangelist Elling Eielsen.

Her constant interest in education was obvious not only in the teaching she did but also in the remark, especially when men of the community like other pioneers of Texas seemed apathetic toward the building of a school, she wrote

> God only knows how our husbands can be so indifferent toward this project that is so very important to our children. . . . In a society where spirit is lacking nothing can thrive or prosper.

These words remind us of the famous statement of President Lamar: "A cultivated mind is the guardian genius of democracy." Elise's organization of a reading club illustrates this same interest. Her appreciation of Christian education may be surmised from her becoming the first lady Norwegian-American Sunday School teacher in Texas.

The social concern Elise manifested when she promoted emigration of impoverished Norwegian families became evident again in her attitude toward slaves. While she realized that many slaves were treated rather well, she contended that "The loss of liberty cannot be replaced by anything." She seems to have felt the anguish of slaves who were separated from mate or children by sale and their hopelessness with regard to their future or that of their children as well as their frustration when they were free but lacked important resources. She sympathized as well with the landholders who had sustained enormous losses through emancipation.

Soon after coming to Texas Elise sang its praises. While her enthusiasm waned somewhat during the war years, she became an advocate again and again when peace had been restored. In addition to the generally balmy days of Texas she appreciated the American political system saying:

> One cannot praise too highly that real freedom and equality which exists here and make themselves felt in numerous ways, not only in social relationships, but where the poor are treated with equal politeness as the rich, the laborer like the official. . . . When public officials are chosen by the people, and only for a certain number of years, they will not be tempted to be overbearing. . . . I have lived here 33 years . . . I am well satisfied with Texas and Texans. . . .

She was interested in the story of the settlements but never lost her interest in Norway and the desire that her new friends might get to know about it.

In one letter in praise of Texas she called attention to one problem area: "It has been a serious drawback for the Norwegians of Texas that most of the time they lacked a Norwegian Lutheran pastor." In elucidation of that remark she wrote:

It is sad to be without divine services and religious instruction, especially for the younger generation. . . . I cannot tell how much we wish we might again get someone who could instil love and respect for Christian teachings in the young people. . . . The life we live here is not a very spiritual one. We think far too much of earthly things and lack all concrete reminders of God's heavenly kingdom.

She and her husband did their best to fill the vacuum, conducting devotions, promoting construction of a place of worhip, securing necessary pledges and contacting potential pastors. Her personal influence especially on young pastors is difficult to assay. Elise lived to see the steady development of Lutheran congregations in North Central Texas.

Elise Tvede Waerenskjold has been called the "Lady with the Pen." Even though she did not get to complete a history of the early Norwegian settlements in Texas, most of what we know about them stems from her letters—with a hundred details that are not found in history books. Dr. Theodore Blegen, the leading historian of Norwegian Americans, said of her in the foreword to the collection of her letters:

This gifted, scholarly, kind, brave and noble woman, a devotee of the pen, a woman ahead of her time . . . has a secure if modest place in the pioneer history of Texas as indeed in the larger saga of Norwegian immigration to America. . . . Her interest in and affection for Texas were never ending, as was her concern for the settlements she helped build and whose history she recorded.

Isaac Johnson Webb and Kerenhappuch Sophronia Buie Webb

Kerenhappuch Sophronia Buie Webb (1842-1921)

By Aline Law*

Kerenhappuch Sophronia Buie was born in Tipton County, Tennessee, on January 16, 1842, the third child of Kerenhappuch Tanner of Virginia and Stacey Buie of North Carolina. In the family, her father was always referred to as "Stacey Buie, the Scotsman." Sophronia, as well as her mother, was named for Kerenhappuch Norman Turner, an ancestress, who during the American Revolution at the age of eighty rode horseback from Maryland to Guilford Courthouse, North Carolina, to nurse a wounded grandson back to health.

The Buies were restless people moving ever southwestward where the land looked fairer. Stacey Buie died about the time the family moved to Arkansas. His two elder sons, W. L. and John W., were Confederate soldiers and died in Federal Military Hospitals. This left only Jimmie, aged 13, his mother, two sisters, and one servant to manage the property. To make things more difficult, renegades from both armies took tools, animals, and household valuables, destroyed crops, and stole food. After the Civil War, it was worse. At times the family had to hide in swamps until raids were over.

In the face of such a desperate situation, Sophronia persuaded her mother to move to Texas where some of their friends and neighbors had already gone. She assumed leadership and

---

* Cousin

was manager of long, troublesome migrations through East and Central Texas.

By September 28, 1867, the family had arrived in Falls County, Texas, and Sophronia wrote a long account of their ordeal to her uncle and aunt, the Tanners, in Arkansas:

Dear Uncle & Aunt

I write to you to inform you that we are now camped in some old vacant houses about a mile from Mr. Johnson Bulls. . . . We arrived at Bulls on the 20 of August. When we got there Ma was sick. She had had the bilious fever. Mr. Bulls family received us very kindly. They invited us all in the house and gave us supper. . . .

Ma stayed in the house but the rest of us stayed at the wagon & next day we drove the wagon not far from the house under two large pecan trees and close to the tank. A tank is the creek dammed up to hold water for the neighborhood people and stock. . . . Mrs. Bulls furnished us with milk and meal and sometimes butter and did not charge us anything. I helped them milk and churn sometimes.

Mr. Bulls family are all sick, first one & then another with chills. They invited us to go back to the house so we drove the wagon back to the house and stayed there until we got well. . . .

Before we got sick Jimmey helped a man make molasses 2 days & got 2 gallons of molasses. I sold 10 lbs of tobacco at a stower (store), & got goods for it. We sold it at 75 cts a lb., it was as much as they would give for it, but I got goods as cheap as they was back in Ark. before the war. . . .

We started for Bell Co. as soon as we was able to travel. We liked it verry well until we crost the Leon River & passed through Belton. . . . We did not like it at all, so we went 7 miles toward Auston (Austin) to the Sulpher Springs on the Salar (Salado) River. We thought that perhaps the water would help us but it made us all sick except Ma & it helped her. . . . The sulpher water had sal & salts & soda; it made Mag & Jimmey sick at the stomack & it made me verry weak.

I had the oxen to attend to for the ticks had come on them so bad while we were at Mr. Bulls that they got screw worms in them, we cured them.

While Jimmey was sick Mag and I went to a mill a mile from the springs to get some meal but they did not have any meal on hand but had flour at 6½ ct to 7½ cts a lb. We got 50 cts worth at 6½ cts. We then went to a mill that was 3 miles off . . . they had no meal then but said that they would take tobacco & give us a bushel of meal for a lb. for tobacco . . . we ingaged 4 bushels.

We bought a chair without any bottom from a chair maker and gave him 1½ lb of tobacco & we bought some beef from a man that was camped at the Springs & paid part in tobacco, the hind quarter at 3 cents. a lb.

The reason that we did not like out there, it was hilley & verry rocky and poor range & the people was mostly northerners & abolishinors. The water was limey. the river and the spring water both. . . . We could

272

not hear of any house or place that we could rent but several wanted to sell at $5 to $6 per acre....

When we got to Belton, I tried to sell some tobacco for bacon but they would not take it, because they said it did not have enough lickerish in it. I then bought 10 lbs of midlin at 12½ cts lb ... we stopped where they was making molasses & got 1 gallon for one lb of tobacco.

We got back here on the 25 inst. We will have to stay in these houses until we can get a place to rent. Jimmey can get plenty of work to do, one wants him to help him pull corn & 2 others want him to pick cotton ... they give 75 cents a hundred & will pay in corn or such things as we need. I think I can get a small school here, some wants me to teach.

Corn is 50 cts per bushel. People can take up as many cows to milk as they want to.... We want to take up some when we can. Horses is from $25 to $50.... A large beef is from $10 to $15. This is verry rich country and fine crops made. Corn will average from 45 bushels to 75 bushels per acre and there is a fine range but seldom any preaching, no school here at present. It has been sicklier here this year than was ever known so we are told, it is thought to be on account of so much rain and the east wind. I do hope you all have had good health this year.

I will now tell you something about our trip out here.... We had a very hard time of it, so much rain & mud we all were sick. Mag had a hard spell of the chills and Ma was sick several times and so was I & Jimmey.

Our brindle ox kept giving out, so we could not travel but 5 or 6 miles a day and then we would have to rest him a day every once awhile. At last he got down at Hender (Henderson) in Rusk Co. & we had to leave him. A negro gave us 50 cts for him, so as to get his hide.

We then put the black ox (Buck is his name) in the lead by cutting the yoke off short & putting ropes each side of him, we then went on verry slowly. Some wagoner wanted to swap me a yoke of oxen for Meta but I would not do it....

When we got to Cherokee Co. there Buck began to lay down in the wagon, though by resting him we went on slowly....

An old gentleman by the name of DeLong came along loaded with lumber, he said if we could keep up with him he would haul the most of our load for us out into Limestone Co. & not charge us anything, but he had a mule team & we knew that we could not keep up with him, so he bought 25 cts of tobacco & then gave Ma a dollar to pay her ferrying across the Trinity River....

This side of Palestine at a Creek ... some ox wagons ... from the same neighborhood of this old gentleman & one that was carrying lumber to Waco came on ... and a Negro was driving one of the wagons ... behind the white men & his oxen wanted to go in the shade & they run against our wagon & he then turned them and broke the axelrod of his wagon so he had ... to make a new one & it was Sunday. The white men came back to help him & they told us if we could come on the next morning that they would take our load & carry it for nothing.

The next morning we got up to start early and when Jimmey went
to drive Buck up he run into a quick sand place & we could not get him
out. . . . When the negro came after his wagon, he took a yoke of his
oxen and pulled him out by the horns.

Buck could not then get up by help, so Jimmey took the one yoke
in and went on . . .

Mag and I went back after Buck & a man helped him up for us. We
then led him on . . . he would lay down for sometime but we would whip
him up then lead him some piece. We got to the Trinity River bottom
that night & camped. . . .

The rain made the bottom verry bad. The old gentleman told us
that he did not want to see us walking any more. if we could not ride in
our wagon to get on his so Mag got on his & me in ours and J (Jimmey)
got Meta to go through the bottom. . . .

I had to get down and put Ma on Meta & pull off my shoes &
stockings & walk so as to show Jimmey the bad places. . . .

A negro loaned us an old ox he had. We went on ahead of the
wagon that had our load for their wagons stauled. We . . . had some
awful sand to go over & we passed by a place where there was boggy
places that they call salt spews. . . . We then went on to Mr. Jim Lunyes
& stopped. They seemed to be very glad to see us . . .

The negroes came on then & got their ox . . . we was over all the
sand and in the prairies. . . . We stayed there 2 days until the wagons
came along. Mr. Lunyes gave us a midlin of meat & 4 water melons . . .
they had a great many. Becky Lunyes is a very pretty girl.

Those men . . . put all of our things in one wagon & went on. It
rained verry hard so that we could not travel as fast as they did. The
neighborhood is called Horn Hill. Mr. Lamsacus was the old gentleman's name & the two young men that was going to Waco was named
Bullock & Johnson.

We stayed at Mr. Lamascus awhile & we then went to Mr. Johnson's. I went to church with his wife and daughter, but no preaching. We
then went home with a young lady & then went to a singing. I got acquainted with several gentlemen. They was verry galent (gallant). Mr.
DeLong loaned me a verry nice paceing pony to ride. They wanted us
to stay there. It is verry pretty country & rich, & the people live verry
well & they have good school there. When we left Mr. DeLong gave us
a bag of gritting corn. We then come on verry well.

We are living in Dog Town near Bull Tank on Power creek, but the
town is only 2 stower (store) & the right name of it is Jena. We are in
sight of one of the stowers. Mr. Bulls older daughter is married to a Mr.
Anderson. Mr. Robert Bull & Mr. Stindny have been gone some time
with a drove of beef cattle, they carried them to Kansas so they have
heard & Mr. John Bull started with a drove last week to new orleans.

Mag and I was invited to a party before we went to Bell Co. but it
rained & no ladys went. We sold our tobacco & paid our expenses
sometimes. We only sold a few lbs for a dollar a lb. 75 & 50 cts was all
we could get for it, they would say that it did not have lickish enough in
it & it was not prized hard enough & then it was in such ugley shapes.
We only have 4$ of money & some tobacco yet. I had to spend one

dollar yesterday for medicin at the stower. There is verry nice people in this neighborhood.

I do not know what to tell you about coming, if it is a cold rainy fall & winter it will be dreadfull & if you come in the spring & corre the way we came you will have water but not much grazing & if you come the upper rout you will have to have a barrel to hall water & you must not try to drive your cows but work some in your wagon & start with a strong wagon & team. Mr. Bull said that he knew no one for to ship anything to.

You must all except (accept) all of our love and direct your letters to Jena, Falls Co. Your niece

Sophronia Buie

(A postscript in front of letter)

You must please send Mrs. Ramsour and Mrs. Wimbleys letters to them. You must be shure to bring some herbs out of the garden & please bring some white peonys, for all of our shrubrey died before we got here, and I have not seen an arbor vita anywhere out here. Bring one or some seed if you can come. I think this country would suit Alick (Alexander David Tanner, called Alec, her cousin), it is an easier country to live in than Ark.

Kerenhappuch Tanner Buie, Sophronia's mother, was not to enjoy the fine, rich country of Texas for long. In a few months after their arrival in Falls County, she died at the age of fifty-seven, trying for the fourth time to make a home in a land that was new to her.

On September 8, 1868, Sophronia was married in Cameron, Milam County, Texas, to Isaac Johnson Webb. Isaac had come from Tennessee to Texas in 1851. He had served in the 2nd Regiment of Sibley's Brigade, Texas Mounted Volunteers, Confederate Cavalry for four years. Their first child, Nettie, was born June 2, 1869, in Cameron.

Isaac was a part of the restless after-the-war movement and moved his family to Bee County where he planned to operate a goat ranch. Jimmie objected strenuously to Sophronia being taken to a remote and isolated situation. Margaret, however, went to live with the Webbs.

Four other children were born to the Webbs at Beeville: Francis (1873); Nonie (1876); Asa (1879) and Lillie (1880). In 1882 the Webbs moved farther west to Dimmitt County, living part of their time in Carrizo Springs. Here their last child, Stacey, was born in 1884.

Margaret, Sophronia's beloved and faithful sister, died and was buried in Carrizo Springs Cemetery on February 13, 1885.

Sophronia was a typical pioneer woman who moved

wherever her husband wished. She faithfully put all family items in the Family Bible. Her house was opened to her children's friends. Her daughter, Stacey, remembers her mother as always being busy . . . and always making clothes for the children. Sophronia's grandchildren have vivid memories of her producing cookies and milk for them magically any time of day they came.

Isaac died in September, 1913, and Sophronia received a Confederate pension as the widow of a soldier. She had a flower garden in front of her house. Every afternoon when she had a visitor, Sophronia put on a white dress with a black jacket or a black dress with a white jacket and lace mitts.

While on a visit to friends in the Bermuda community near Carrizo Springs, Sophronia Buie Webb died suddenly on May 14, 1921. Her life was characteristic of the sturdiness and of the fortitude possessed by all who struggle through such vicissitudes as she did to earn the coveted title "Texan."

Louise Klinglehoefer Wehmeyer (1834-1903)

Compiled from Esther Mueller's Notes *

A two-room house, 36 x 18 feet, built of logs, adobe and lime-stone once stood facing south near the center of the east one hundred block of Main Street, Fredericksburg, Texas. Here Louise Klinglehoefer came to be married to Conrad Wehmeyer in a double wedding ceremony with her sister Elizabeth and Herman Hitzfeld on December 3, 1851. In the presence of friends and relatives Pastor Dangers gave them God's blessing and Conrad placed on Louise's finger a ring hammered out of a piece of gold.

Louise was born in Eibelshausen, Nassau, Germany, January 9, 1834, the oldest daughter of Johann Jost and Elizabeth Weil Klinglehoefer. Her mother died when Henriette was a baby. Louise's face always lighted with tender happiness at the mention of her mother and their home in Eibelshausen. Now, at age seventeen, she had spent six exciting and strenuous years in Texas.

Among colonists seeking freedom in Texas under the auspices of Der Adelsverein, and embarking on the brig *Johann Dethardt* at Bremen, Germany, September 1845 were her father Johann Jost Klinglehoefer, her step-mother Elizabeth Heiland Klinglehoefer and the children: August, Louise, Elizabeth, and Henriette. They reached Galveston in the cold, wet Texas winter of 1845-46. Louise and her family experienced delay, deprivation, hunger and sickness. She helped care for the younger children on

---

* Esther, a granddaughter

Louise Klinglehoefer Wehmeyer

Home and Bakery of Louise Klinglehoefer Wehmeyer

an overland trek which, interrupted many times, ended at Fredericksburg in the early spring of 1847. Louise's father received a town lot where they lived in a tent until a house was built. They had little food and less money, but they worked—building, hunting food, hiring out to make money. Louise and her sisters walked across town to the abandoned over-night camps of the U.S. soldiers to gather the grains of corn wasted where horses had been fed. At home the corn was washed, ground with stones and cooked for food.

Louise had brought from Germany a five-year attendance certificate at the elementary school in Eibelshausen dated September 15, 1845. Whether she attended school in Fredericksburg is not known. A letter that she wrote shows concise, correct, fluent expression in a neat, legible handwriting.

Moved by the family's desperate need for food and money, August, Louise and Henriette took an eighty-five mile trip on foot and by ox team to San Antonio for work. They took just enough food to last the journey. Louise, in the home of a kindly, well-to-do family, cared for younger children and helped with chores in return for meals, lodging and a small salary that she sent her parents; she wished that they could share her good food, too. She learned to speak the English language, observe American customs and sew pretty dresses. She returned to Fredericksburg at seventeen—small of frame with hazel eyes, smooth brown hair and by nature high-spirited, energetic and generous.

Conrad Wehmeyer often visited at the Klinglehoefer home. Older than Louise, he had been born February 16, 1816, in Huttenhausen, Westphalia, Germany. Seeking political freedom, he arrived at Fredericksburg with the first settlers. He was successful in business and in 1851 built a combination store and house on town lot 172. It consisted of one-half acre of land received from Der Adelsverein. Here Louise was married, lived the rest of her life and died. In San Antonio, Conrad bought her a set of blue and white dishes for twenty-five dollars; two plates, two cups and saucers, sugar bowl and teapot. Writing a brother in Germany for items to stock the store, he added, "Please enclose some things for my wife." Another quote: "In housekeeping she has accomplished a great deal and can cope with anybody and excel . . . I am living with her happy and content."

So together, Louise, young and active, and Conrad, gentle and skilled, worked to make their home. The house had a sloping roof, and attic, front double doors of cypress, and oak floors. Louise saw the house changed many times—logs and adobe were replaced by white-washed limestone walls, bedrooms were added, a kitchen with a fireplace for cooking; later a cookstove and a cellar for storing cured meats and products of the garden and orchard, and even ripening cheese and Louise's dried noodles. Furniture was made by local cabinet makers and was acquired as came the need and means.

The half-acre yard, where she was ever active, changed, too. A cedar-post fence and flagstone porch floor improved the front. Neighbors lived on lots to both sides. After the post oaks were cleared in back, there were a well, pens for cows, hogs, chickens; also a grape arbor, orchard, garden and cornfield, and later a two-roomed house for Louise's widowed sister.

Louise welcomed Conrad's plan to operate a bakery—a skill he had learned in Germany. The front sales room opened into the kitchen behind which were built the bakery and oven. The bakery contained barrels of flour, a warming closet for yeast and rising dough, a spice cupboard and a wide, six-foot wooden trough for mixing dough. Opening into the back wall was the door to the dome-shaped, adobe oven that extended outside, sheltered by a roof and built on a limestone foundation. Out of the front end rose a chimney, so constructed that smoke from the fire built inside to heat the oven surfaces was drawn upward instead of blackening the interior. In the bakery Louise contacted many different people who came from near and far—the soldiers from Fort Martin Scott and even Indians who liked the sweet foods, and not having money, gave trinkets in exchange.

The yard, house and bakery partially testify to Louise's daily and seasonal tasks. In twenty-two years she brought nine children into the world. In order of age, they were: August, Pauline, Sidonie, Alwine, Robert, Elise, Adolph, Bertha, and Emma. Pauline and Robert died in infancy.

Louise taught the older children to care for the younger ones. In that she expected faithfulness in assigned chores and responsibilities, she was considered strict. When her pressured spirits gave way to a quick temper, the understanding Conrad responded gently to calm the family atmosphere. Louise, remembering the San Antonio girls unable to iron their own dresses, taught her daughters to iron well and to perfect all household skills.

The children attended the schools of early Fredericksburg: church schools, elementary schools and after it opened, "the college." They learned both English and German. Louise made their assignment preparation a part of home routine. August and Adolph took business courses after they left home. Elise, with her mother's love of sewing, apprenticed as a seamstress. Bertha attended a crafts class at the Catholic school; there is still a framed hair wreath which she made and which hung in Louise's home. Adolph, for a hobby, studied drawing at which he was excellent. Alwine's particular skill was cooking. Louise encouraged and enjoyed the children's progress.

Conrad and Louise, after first belonging to Verein's Kirche, later joined Zion Lutheran Church where the entire family attended regularly and participated in its rites and activities. After her child's baptism, confirmation or wedding, Louise would serve a meal, inviting guests to celebrate the occasion. Sunday started a special day. Sidonie recalled how on Sunday morning with breakfast, Louise would serve slices of Conrad's unsurpassed pound cake.

At night the family gathered in one room—studying, spinning, knitting or patching. There was conversation or Conrad read aloud to them or they sang favorite songs and as Louise worked, she listened or joined in.

On their Christmas tree, she hung Conrad's pretty, iced cookies among the other decorations. She made rag dolls for the younger children and each child received a gift. Elise recalled a December when a new baker brought factory-baked cookies into town. Conrad's cookies did not sell. Louise gave no gifts that year.

Louise always celebrated her father's birthday July 11. The family walked to his house, taking a handcart filled with delicacies. Relatives and friends joined them to spend a happy day.

In crisis situations, Louise exhibited great presence of mind. Once, in the bakery an impudent soldier from Fort Martin Scott helped himself to cookies, refusing to pay. Conrad evicted him. The soldier, seeing an axe near the door, raised and aimed it at Conrad's head. Louise slammed the door between them just as the axe came down to splinter the wood.

Louise felt an intense sympathy for people. A granddaughter remembered being sent by Louise to the Pastor with money for the needy. During an electrical storm, the neighbor's children called Louise for help. Their mother had been struck down by lightning. Louise worked with her until consciousness returned. A sick Indian came to town for medication. Hot-headed men of the village, remembering Indian atrocities, overpowered him and headed for a "hanging tree." Outraged, Louise walked into the street pleading for the Indian's release. She was disregarded, but she had tried to have right prevail.

Both Louise's husband and father, who had sworn allegiance to the United States government, refused during the Civil War to join the Confederacy. However, her brother August enlisted with the South. He was reported missing and never returned. A group of outlaws belonging to neither the Union nor the Confederacy searched out Fredericksburg men for hanging. When Conrad's name appeared on their list, Louise, with the help of friends, hid him in their attic. For weeks she took care of the bakery and acted as if everything were as usual.

Louise saw her children leave home as they matured. In their adult needs she was, as ever, counselor or helper. August and Adolph worked and lived in Quincy, Illinois. Sidonie was married to Edward Maier and after his death to August Sembritzkey. Alwine married August Weber; Elise, Richard Tatsch; August married Emma Grumm, and Adolph, Helen Scheidt. After her death he married Wilhelmine Bruening. Bertha married William Kiehne; and Emma, William Mueller. Louise and Conrad had twenty-four grandchildren; six died in infancy. The grandchildren were her joy and concern, recipients of her generosity. She made rag dolls and sewed clothes for them.

After Conrad discontinued the bakery in the mid 1880's, Louise opened a millinery store in the sales room. Making pretty attire had always been her especial interest. August sent a St. Louis salesman to her with ladies' hats. In Fredericksburg these did not sell readily, but she used the veils, flowers and ribbons from them to re-decorate hats belonging to local ladies. To the needy, she gave yard goods from her store.

Conrad died October 31, 1898. Louise survived him for nearly five years, dying on April 25, 1903. As her remains were carried through the front double doors of her home, her older grandchildren, dressed in white, followed, walking in the funeral procession to the city cemetery. In her church is a marble baptismal font which was given as a memorial to her—a place to bring children to their God.

A hundred years after Louise was born, her youngest daughter, Emma Mueller, expressed a deep desire to leave Louise's grandchildren a word portrait of her that would endear her to them, even as Louise's own children remembered her. Could Louise comment, she might say, "No, rather bring up my grandchildren so that they will see me with our Savior in Eternity."

Captain W. F. Whitehead and Mary Burleson Whitehead

Mary Burleson Whitehead (1843-1911)

By Mary Wilson Russell*

Mary Burleson was born in 1843 in Marion, Alabama, the daughter of Bennett Burleson of Welsh stock, who had come to North Carolina in 1742, and of Matilda Lowery. Bennett settled his debts in the Burleson General Store and left with a wagon train for Texas to take up land. Wandering around Texas for a while, the Burlesons finally settled in Denton, Texas. Mr. Burleson died there in 1864.

When the Civil War broke out, Mary married a Mr. William-son, a Union sympathizer, who left his wife and baby to fight against the South. He failed to return home from the War and later it was learned that he had been killed in line of duty.

The Burlesons had fought for the ideals and principles of the South. The young widow met Captain William Franklin White-head, they fell in love, and were married on March 2, 1868. They settled in Sanger, Denton County, where Mary was an active Baptist and true to that religion until her death.

The Whiteheads had six children: Bennett, Eugene, Modena, Lucy, Alice, and Maude. Lucy married a lawyer, A. E. Wilson, and became my mother. All of the Whitehead children were well educated, four graduating from college.

William Franklin Whitehead, of English descent, was Capt. of Company F, Bryant's Battalion, 3rd Arkansas Infantry, Regiment

---

* Granddaughter

285

of the Cherokees, prior to coming to Texas. After the Civil War there was great disorder in Denton County. There were train robberies, bank robberies, and stage coach holdups. Most men wore guns to help suppress the outlaws. Captain Whitehead was appointed to the Terry Texas Rangers by the sheriff, a Mr. Egan, of Denton County. Sam Bass, one of the robbers, used Denton as one of his hideouts. In 1877 and 1878, Bass and his band of outlaws robbed two stages and four trains in North Central Texas.

One day Captain Whitehead was away from his home on duty. Mary was at home by herself, caring for the baby and the farm. Late that Sunday afternoon, there was a knock on the kitchen door. As Mary opened it, a man with a gun pointed it at her head. Pushing by her and closing the door, the man still pointing the gun at her, said: "Mrs. Whitehead, I know you and the child are alone. I have been watching the house for quite a spell and know that the Captain is hunting me. I do not want to hurt you but I am so hungry that I want you to cook me some supper. Then I shall leave quietly and vanish into the night."

Mary recognized Sam Bass and knew he was desperate, so she cooked him some side meat, eggs, biscuits, and coffee.

Bass was very hungry since he had not eaten since the day before. He kept the gun in one hand, and ate with the other, watching her all the time.

After he had eaten all the food, he got up hurriedly, thanked her for a nice supper, and placed a $10.00 bill on the table. He left after telling her not to leave the house as he would be watching it. She followed Bass's orders for twenty minutes; then Captain Whitehead suddenly returned home.

Mary was so scared that she could hardly tell her husband what had happened. She emphasized that Sam Bass had left $10.00 to pay her for her trouble.

Captain Whitehead, angry and scared, went out to tell the other men. The posse hunted the outlaw unsuccessfully as he had slipped away from them in the night.

The Whitehead's Farm was on Clear Creek bottom and their nearest neighbor lived about four miles away. Sam Bass was killed the next day at Round Rock, Texas, where he attempted to rob the local bank.

Although Mary often told the story of her encounter with Sam Bass, she never mentioned what she did with the $10.00.

Captain Whitehead and his family soon left Sanger and moved to Brownwood where he put in a cotton gin, the first gin in that part of the country. He sold this shortly, though, and became a contractor and carpenter.

Both Captain and Mrs. Whitehead are buried in Brownwood, Texas. Mary died April 7, 1911, and the Captain on June 16, 1916.

Lela Jackson with her grandmother's quilt and her father's violin

Rachel Whitfield
(1814-1908)

By Lela Jackson *

In 1852 Rachel Whitfield and her six children came from the auction block in Arkansas, Missouri, to live in Williamson County, Texas, as slaves of Washington McLaughlin. Rachel's husband, Jim Whitfield, did not come with them because Mr. Whitfield, his master, had sold him to another slave owner. None of them ever knew to whom he had been sold and he never knew what became of his family.

Jim and Rachel had six children: Allen, Silla, Demmie, Ella, Myriah, and Lucy. Now thirty-eight-year-old Rachel was left to rear them alone. Fortunately, Rachel still had her children. Often Negro families were separated like cows from calves. An old colored woman would sit to one side of the slave auction block and into her care the young children were given, wailing, hollering and weeping.

Slowly Rachel and the children made their way, sometime by foot and sometime by ox cart toward Texas as slaves of the McLaughlin family. Their name was no longer Whitfield but McLaughlin.

The land across which they traveled was uncharted. In places they followed trails, stopping here and there somewhere else, always fording streams and circling swamps or deep forests. Eventually by 1853 Mr. McLaughlin forded a stream and sud-

---

* A granddaughter, interviewed by Stacy Mikulencah Labaj

denly found the land he sought: level land as far as eye could see with deep, rich soil. So it was here that McLaughlin, his family, and his slaves settled on the north bank of the San Gabriel River just below where Willis Creek emptied into it and where Sore Finger Creek flowed into Willis Creek. There they stayed until the time of freedom.

The slaves cleared the land by cutting thick brush and mesquite, elm, oak, black walnut, and other tall trees. They built cabins and broke the land for cultivation. Mr. McLaughlin was not even-tempered and, at times, whipped the slaves. However, he would give them passes to go where they wanted to go. A signed pass had to be shown on entering another owner's property or the slave would be caught and whipped.

Just before the Civil War early one morning a long double row of mounted horses approached the plantation. The riders were all soldiers. They rode directly to the main cabin where the master stood waiting. The leader asked for feed for their horses. The soldiers took what they wanted for their hundred horses and rode on south toward New Orleans.

Rumors spread among the slaves that they might be free people. The slaves could hardly believe this until one of them happened to hear the master read "Proclamation of Freedom." Mr. McLaughlin did not share this knowledge with his people for some days.

Then one evening he gave orders for everybody to be at the main house early in the morning. So with the dew heavy on the ground, all the slaves stood straight in fear, waiting for the master to come out. He came, standing straight and angry and in a hard voice said:

> You are now free people. You are as free as I am. You can go anywhere you want to. You can stay here if you wish, but I don't need you. I can do without you.

The slaves stood in shock, fearing to move or to whisper. They stood frozen. Emmaline, the cook, was the first to move; she turned and went straight to the kitchen to prepare the McLaughlin's breakfast as usual. After the master and his family had finished eating, he stepped out and told everyone to go. He did not let them cook their breakfast or do anything. He ordered them to go, and he gave them nothing after all their years of slavery for him.

Rachel, her children, and others quietly slipped away along the Gabriel River to where Willis Creek emptied and followed the creek, finding good hiding places. They did not know who might harm them. They were stunned, afraid, and lost—not knowing, as yet, what the word "freedom" meant. In the cover of thick underbrush and large trees, they stealthily crept that first day to shelter themselves, studying what to do and watchful of any strange noise.

It was here Rachel's son, Allen (now twenty-four years old) met Adelaide Coleman, who in the spring of 1865 became his wife. In the meanwhile he helped his mother settle along Willis Creek in a log cabin. She was energetic, planned well, and was a good cook. She had an old cracked pitcher, a flat wooden pail with a metal rim and lid, a basket, a wash kettle, and a big, long and deep iron baking or roasting vessel with a lid, and several flat irons.

She and her daughters made hominy, "chitlings," and ash cakes; roasted eggs, sweet potatoes, and cushaw; boiled cabbage, beans, turnips, collards, okra and ham hock, and made corn bread and biscuit. From the river bottom they picked wild plums and berries and made preserves. They had molasses.

When one of the Whitfields found a cow and a calf in the bottom belonging to Mr. Young, she would ask him if the cow could be milked and the calf raised for him. In this way the family had milk, clabber, butter, and cream. These dairy products were kept fresh in a bucket that was lowered into the well.

Rachel and her family picked cotton through January and February. What was left in March was their for the taking. In years of drought, they went where fields were less dry. They also picked vegetables for land owners and gathered prairie chicken eggs in a foot tub. They trapped birds, doves, quail, squirrels, and possums. They had several hogs. There were pecans and black walnuts for eating since fences were few. When a pecan tree was planted, it was often named for its planter.

Rachel and her children traded their chickens, eggs, and butter for cloth, pins, needles, stockings, combs, and brushes from a peddler. For instance, a dozen eggs would be traded for a yard of calico.

She and her daughters ironed all the family's clothes and twice a week ironed for white people. There was a fire log in the yard and the flat irons would be placed standing up before the fire

291

to absorb its heat. Often the iron would be cleaned by running it over the dirt. With big ironing pads the women lifted the hot irons, which on warm days, they used out of doors and on cold days in the house.

Rachel sang as she sewed and made quilts. "Georgia Leaf" was the pattern she used during slavery times. After Emancipation, the common patterns were: "Pineapple," "Snow Ball," "Jack Bean Leaf," "Monkey Wrench," "Running Rose" and "Nine Patch," which was the beginner's quilt pattern. Rachel lined her quilts with ten-cent Bull Durham tobacco sacks, bleached and ripped open. She often reminded the men to save the sacks for her.

Allen, his wife, and children lived on Sore Finger Creek. He was industrious: building fences, working for white war widows in the area, farming, hauling cotton to Taylor and lumber from Austin, playing Civil War songs, hymns and dance music on his violin, and raising horses. He was a good son to his mother.

Pastoral days were the big thing—the high point in their lives. These were the Sundays when a preacher held worship service with them. People from miles around attended each other's Pastoral Services. They came in wagons, some oxen drawn. Those who did not have reading skill took full part in the devotional, for the leader "lined" out the words. The old people were drawn to the slave-day songs such as

I couldn't hear nobody pray
'Way down yonder all by myself
I couldn't hear nobody pray.

Rachel and her daughter, Demmie, always were called upon to lay out the dead. They prepared the body and then laid it on boards or a door resting on chairs. The coffins were made of cedar or of pine and always were stained dark brown. The cedar was plentiful locally while the pine came from Bastrop County. The coffins were made wider at the shoulder, tapering toward the feet.

For amusement Rachel and her family enjoyed baptizings in Willis Creek, preachings, dances, sing-songs, and camp meetings. These meetings were generally held during July and August in a brush arbor. When bad weather threatened, wagon sheets were stretched over the arbor. If no preacher was available, some man or woman conducted the service. Favorite songs were: "Oh, John, Preachin' in the Wilderness," "Must Jesus Bear the Cross Alone?", and "Oh, Mary, Don't You Weep No More."

All of Rachel's children except Myriah married and had families respected in their communities. They had a good relationship with both their white and colored neighbors.

Rachel died in 1908 and is buried in the Taylor Cemetery. Although she was 93 years old, she could still thread a needle without the aid of glasses, and she walked standing straight and without using a cane.

Rebecca Raworth Williams, Dan Williams (a son) and Thomas Barlow Williams (her husband)

Rebecca Raworth Williams (1850-1927)

By Jean Lockwood Williams*

Rebecca Raworth was born in Nottingham, England, on February 27, 1850, the eldest daughter of Mary Barker and George Raworth. Mary Barker was an unusual woman for the times: she had been educated at the Sorbonne as a physician but not licensed to practice because she was a woman; had been a riding companion of Lord Byron; and had sung at the Court of Queen Victoria.

Rebecca's father, George Raworth, decided in 1851 to migrate to the United States where his wife's brother had already gone. The family, after a stormy voyage on *The Albert Galitan*, reached New York. Traveling westward to Princeton, Illinois, George secured 640 acres of land. The family had many unhappy experiences: their stock was killed by unfriendly neighbors who put tacks in the feed; George was almost hanged by a group of men who did not like his views regarding Southern States' Rights; and no help could be secured to assist the family in binding the wheat harvest.

George sold his land. First, he moved his family to Clinton, Iowa; second, to Lehighton, Pennsylvania; and third, to Mauch Chunk in 1879. Rebecca grew up in a family of uncles, aunts, cousins, and two younger sisters. She helped her parents in their work and was active in the Methodist Church.

---

* Wife of Rebecca and Thomas Williams' son, Dan

On September 7, 1871, Rebecca married Thomas Arnold Barlow Williams. Thomas, when sixteen years old, had joined the Union Army and was present at Gettysburg, Manassas, and Appomattox. Leaving the Army, he learned to manufacture shoes in St. Louis.

After their marriage, the young couple moved to Philadelphia where Thomas worked for a Quaker shoemaker. On September 7, 1872, Mary was born and on July 5, 1874, Sallie was born. The sisters were followed on November 3, 1876, by a brother, Charles Sumner. The family had the opportunity to attend the Federal Centennial Celebration in Philadelphia.

Thomas was always restless and now tired of the East decided to go to Texas, a State that gave promise of agricultural plenty. He went ahead while Rebecca and the children went to Mauch Chunk, Pennsylvania, to await the birth of her fourth child, Thomas Edward Williams, on May 17, 1879. When Edward was six weeks old, Rebecca and her four children, the eldest being seven years old, left for Brenham, Texas.

Rebecca and the four little children had to change trains in Missouri where they were put on a small platform and told to wait for a train going south. A signal was placed so the train would stop. All night the little group huddled on the platform while coyotes howled seemingly near enough to pounce on them. The next day the southbound train picked them up.

In Brenham, Mary, the eldest daughter, went to school and was the proud possessor of a beautiful doll house her father had built for her and her mother had furnished with small dolls, decorations, and furniture. When nine years old, Mary died of diphtheria. The Williams were regarded by their neighbors as "damn Yankees." Only Mary's teacher came to see her. When the teacher came, for the first time Rebecca cried, knowing that she had a friend.

Thomas heard of the wonderful wheat crops in the Panhandle of Texas. After two unhappy years in Brenham, the family moved to Vernon, Texas, where they "lived out" a section of land, 640 acres. Thomas worked hard and had many men working for him. One farmer, fleeing a bad venture, stopped for water and asked for work.

Rebecca took the family in and fed them. Thomas offered the man a year's work if he would help him "live out" another section of land that he was working. It was understood that the man would be paid when the crop came in. The man fulfilled his contract, took his pay, and moved farther into the Panhandle. He later "struck it rich" when oil was found on the new land on which he had settled.

Thomas sold his land for a good price. This time he wanted to move father west and form a new county. Rebecca, tired of moving, did not sign the deed of sale. Later the first Waggoner oil well was discovered on the Thomas and Rebecca Williams' homesite.

The land farther west looked promising. It was below the caprock and at times had adequate rainfall. Several good years of wheat crops ensued. The land attracted other settlers. In 1884 there were enough settlers to be organized into a County. Cowboys took petitions around and it was rumored that some faithful horses' names appeared on the list. Thus Childress County came into being in 1884.

In the early days, there was no lumber in Childress to build houses; so dugouts were made in the Canyon's walls. As lumber was hauled in by wagons, sheds were built on the Canyon's floor adjacent to the dugout. In her dugout home, Rebecca Williams founded the Methodist Church of Childress which still bears her name.

On May 18, 1883, Rebecca gave birth to twins. The boy died and the surviving twin was named Ophelia Raworth Williams.

From her first days on the West Texas Frontier, Rebecca had used the medical knowledge derived from her mother, to help her family and her neighbors. She delivered babies, nursed the sick, and helped lay out the dead. On the Frontier there were few doctors and most of these were travelling doctors on horseback.

Once Thomas took some medicine by mistake which made him somnolent and probably would have killed him. Rebecca had two of their children, one on each side, support their father and keep him walking. She followed with a coffee pot in one hand and a cup in the other to keep him from "dozing off." He recovered.

Accidents befell the children but Rebecca was able to handle these with competence. Much later one of Rebecca's granddaughters wrote: "She is a pillar in the Church and an angel in the Community."

In 1890 when the Williams were expecting twins, Rebecca insisted that a house must be built for the babies to be born in. Crops had been good, harvest machinery had helped to produce more wheat, so Thomas hauled lumber and built the house. On October 17, 1890, Daniel Mortimer and David Reichard Williams, very healthy and lively, were born. They were followed two and a half years later by George Raworth Williams, born on February 2, 1893.

In the late 1890's the Fort Worth and Denver Railroad decided not to go through Childress which was on high ground but chose a flat bed roadway some miles away. The Railroad offered the settlers of Childress land near the railroad if they would move their homes. Many people moved. Thomas kept his farm but, after several years of drought had made the wheat harvest unprofitable, he opened a shop for manufacturing boots.

Some of the boots were plain but many were fancy enough to catch the eyes of the farmers and cowboys. Boots were made to order. The business flourished.

Moving into the new town in 1898, Thomas became City Judge, a leader in the Masons, and an honorary member of the Civil War Veterans. Rebecca continued her medical and church work and became a member of the Eastern Star.

Several doctors located offices in Childress and urged Rebecca to make application for a physician's license. At that time a full college course was not required. Only an examination successfully passed and statements from several physicians regarding the applicant's competence were all that were required for licensing. Rebecca preferred to remain a volunteer.

The Williams' second son, Edward, enlisted for service in the Spanish American War. The other boys helped with the sheep that the family kept for meat, wool, and sale. It is said to have been so cold in Childress some winters that the sheep would freeze to the ground. They could not get up until Rebecca, riding side-saddle, would go out with kettles of hot water to thaw their wool.

Once when Sumner and Edward, aged nine and seven, were minding the sheep some distance from home, they fell asleep. It was dark when they awoke and they did not know the way home. They turned the horse loose and he guided them home.

Even during the hard years on the farm, Rebecca fed her family well. The family took their wheat to be ground and enjoyed whole wheat bread and muffins. Chickens, sheep, and cattle gave meat. There were always eggs and milk. A garden, ever in cultivation, gave bountiful vegetables. Cookie jars were always filled;

so the children and their playmates could come indoors for a snack.

While Rebecca cooked, sewed, and did her housework, her three young sons sometimes played in the yard with their friends. The boys not infrequently got into fights. Rebecca maintained discipline with the boys by a rap on the window pane with her thimble which brought her sons into the house.

The boys had chores among which were feeding the horse, dog, cat, and pet prairie dog; and bringing in wood for heating and cooking. Like other children, the boys would forget their duties or leave the work for one of the other boys.

While the family lived on the farm, water had to be hauled during the drought years. When it was often unbearbly hot, Rebecca kept the doors closed and locked. One morning she opened the door for some fresh air and fell asleep. She was aroused by Indians standing at the foot of her bed and saying: "Give water!" She jumped off of her bed. The Indians had taken the feathers from the clock that had been used to oil the clock. She had accumulated many old clothes and rags to plait into carpets. The Indians took them all. After getting water, they left.

Sometimes Quanah Parker, Indian Chief from Quanah, Oklahoma, thirty miles away, and a large group of his tribe would come to Childress. Some of the Indians drank too much "fire water" and became unruly enough to scare the women and children. No real damage was done. Incidents of Indian raids were not so far in the past as to prevent the settlers from being uneasy and cautious.

Accidents and dramatic episodes, which happened to the children, invariably found Rebecca steady and ready to cope with the situation. David, always interested in mechanical things, on one July 4th, "rigged up" a can with some caps to make a big bang. The can exploded and blew off the ends of his right thumb and index finger. Rebecca's first aid was so successful that David was able to become a draftsman and pattern-maker at the Fort Worth-Denver Railroad Shop and still later a successful engineer and architect.

The other twin, Daniel, while helping to break a young colt, was thrown from it. His arm was so badly broken that the bones protruded from the flesh. His father took him on horseback into town where Dr. Christler set the bone. Rebecca did not have the instruments and antiseptics for such a task. She knew her limitations.

Edward, returning from the Spanish-American War, took up land and had almost "lived it out" when he decided to go to Clarendon College. Rebecca and the other children would go to his place on weekends; so that he would not lose the land. Some men were reported living in Edward's house when the Williams were not there. On one weekend trip to the farm, the family was settling down for the night when the men appeared with guns, shooting into the air; ordering them to come out; and shouting that this was their place. Rebecca came out with her lamp and said in a firm, quiet voice: "That will be enough!" The men left and never bothered them again. Edward later sold the farm to pay for his education for the ministry.

Rebecca was ambitous for her children. The two girls early married good men. Sumner became a lawyer; Edward, a Methodist minister; Daniel, a lawyer and writer; David, an engineer and architect; and Raworth, a surgeon and a polo player in his leisure.

Thomas and Rebecca lived out their lives in the new house that they had built after the sale of the farm. Until well into their 70's they were active in their community. Thomas lived to be 79 and Rebecca to be 77 years old. During their last years, their youngest daughter, Ophelia, and her husband lived with Thomas and Rebecca and cared for them.

The dreams of great prosperity from growing wheat were partially fulfilled. However, it took irrigation from artesian wells and conservation of rainfall to make wheat growing profitable.

Adina De Zavala
(1861-1955)

By Virginia H. Taylor*

Adina De Zavala was the granddaughter of the illustrious Texas patriot Lorenzo De Zavala. By his career she was imbued with an abiding interest in the history of her native state, and it became her lasting wish to preserve not only the spirit but the physical evidence of the historical drama in which he participated.

As well as a devoted Texan, Lorenzo De Zavala was a man of superior talent, culture, and achievement. He was born near Merida in the province of Yucatan on October 3, 1789. He represented Yucatan in the Spanish Cortes in Madrid; he was a member of the Mexican Constituent Congress and the first to sign the federal constitution of Mexico in 1824, a senator from 1824 to 1826, and governor of the state of Mexico in 1827 and 1832.

On March 12, 1829, he received an empresario contract from the state of Coahuila and Texas, then made a tour of the United States. He was Vicente Guerrero's Minister of the Treasury but was deposed by the Centralist party. In 1833 he became a member of the Chamber of Deputies and was appointed Santa Anna's Minister to France in October of that same year.

When Santa Anna adopted a centralist policy in 1835 he resigned and went to Texas to fulfill his empresario contract but fled to the United States when Santa Anna ordered his arrest. He soon returned to take part in the Texas Revolution. He represented the

*Spanish Archivist, General Land Office of Texas

Adina de Zavala

Harrisburg delegation at the Consultation, signed the Declaration of Independence, and was elected vice-president of the ad interim government of the Republic of Texas. Little wonder then that Adina, even as a child, was acutely aware of her heritage, that in later years its pervasive influence intensified her interest in every facet of early Texas history.

At an undetermined date Lorenzo De Zavala married Teresa Correa by whom he had three children: Lorenzo, Jr., Manuela, and a daughter who died in infancy. After the death of his wife he married Emily West in New York City in 1831. They had three children: Augustine, Emily, and Ricardo. On his return to Texas in 1835, De Zavala bought the Harris and Carpenter league on Buffalo Bayou, just east of Lynchburg and the San Jacinto battlefield, and made his home there.

As a Mexican citizen De Zavala was entitled to receive a head-right of one league of land. He wrote Stephen F. Austin on November 30, 1835, saying that he would like to have the league promised for his family located on the tracts across the Bayou, just below him; they were near Dr. Patrick who wanted them but he already had his league. Austin wrote the following note on the bottom of the letter and sent it to Gail Borden:

> Zavala wants his land on buffaloe bayou opposite where he lives— below Earle's, between him and the irish widow woman—he ought to have it there—Patrick also wants this piece—by the old law a native Mexican has the preference—attend to it.
> S. F. Austin.

It happened that the three leagues granted to Dr. George M. Patrick, Nicholas Clopper, and James Lindsay in 1828 were later forfeited for failure to build a factory, the condition on which the grant had been made. It also happened that the Consultation had ordered the colony land offices closed on November 13, 1835, and suspended the granting of land. So both De Zavala and Dr. Patrick failed to obtain land from the Mexican government. Both, however, would be entitled to a head-right of one league and labor from the Republic of Texas as soon as the new government was established. But De Zavala died on November 15, 1836, and Dr. Patrick, who was appointed the Harris County surveyor obtained the designated tracts in 1838, selling them immediately for $15,000.

Ultimately, the heirs of Lorenzo De Zavala applied for and were granted his headright of one league and labor in Lamar and Parker counties. This land too was lost to another claimant when the administrator of the De Zavala estate filed suit for recovery in 1880. The only land received from either government by the De Zavalas was a single man's headright of one-third league granted to Lorenzo, Jr., by the Land Board of Harrisburg County in 1838 and finally patented to him on July 3, 1860.

The family of Lorenzo, Sr., joined him in Texas in December, 1835. After his death they continued to live at their home on Zavala Point. Emily West De Zavala married Henry M. Fock previous to 1841, and he became administrator of the estate, replacing Lorenzo, Jr., who had been absent for a period of twelve months.

After attending St. Mary's College in Galveston, Augustine married Julia Tyrrell in New York City on March 17, 1860. He then returned to Texas and built a cottage near the home of his mother. Adina was born there November 28, 1861. She was the first of six children: those following were Florence, Mary, Zita, Thomas J., and Augustine. Their father became the owner and captain of a river boat during the Civil War. He was a blockade runner and later did coast guard duty. The coastal dampness caused him to suffer from rheumatism by which he was completely incapacitated at the end of the war.

The De Zavala family then moved to Galveston, leaving the house on the Point in care of servants. The cottage that Augustine built was placed on a barge and towed to a site on East Broadway across from St. Mary's College.

Adina was a child during that period of postwar uncertainties. Her early playmates were the children of the family slaves who refused to leave when the war ended. She was at first taught by her mother, then by a private tutor. She was precocious; she read avidly—"I cannot remember when I could not read," she has said. Her favorite stories concerned history. She and her sisters dramatized historical occasions and produced plays based on historical events. At an early age the children entered school in Galveston. Adina and her sisters attended the Ursuline Academy, the brothers, St. Mary's College. When their father could no longer endure the damp climate he moved his family to San Antonio, to a ranch home on Fredericksburg Road, twelve miles north of San

Fernando Cathedral. Adina remained in school but joined them later in 1873.

At the age of seventeen she continued her education at Sam Houston Normal Institute, taking courses in algebra, physiology, Latin, physics, and astrology. Soon afterward she enrolled in a school of music at Chillicothe, Missouri.

About 1884, "Miss Adina" began teaching school at Terrell, Texas. She returned to San Antonio in 1886 to take a position as a classroom teacher at the David G. Burnet School, later transferring to the De Zavala School.

At that time she had developed strong convictions concerning the preservation of the landmarks and relics of Texas history. She wanted to make it possible to view history as well as to read or commemorate it and dedicated herself to that purpose.

In 1889, she organized a group of San Antonio women who began the work of keeping San Antonio history alive. In 1882, this group affiliated with the newly organized Daughters of the Republic of Texas and was called the De Zavala Chapter. The chapter first turned its attention to Ben Milam, who was killed in San Antonio on December 7, 1835. A monument was placed on his grave in Milam Square, and services were held there on March 6, a date observed each year since as Texas Heroes Day. It was one of Miss Adina's favorite memorials. In 1902 the chapter succeeded in naming elementary schools for Texas heroes; hitherto they had been designated by numbers.

One of the earliest relics sought by the De Zavala Chapter was the "Little Treasury of the Republic of Texas," as Miss Adina called it. It was a wooden chest about five feet long, three feet wide, and two feet deep, constructed of wide planks, and used as a safe for money, papers and valuables at Washington-on-the-Brazos in 1842. The chest was the property of Asa Brigham, then Treasurer of the Republic of Texas, and his office was the front room of the double log cabin in which the Brigham family lived.

In 1904, this chest was in the hands of W. J. Cloud of Junction, Texas, whose father John Wirtz Cloud had married secondly the sister of Asa Brigham's second wife. Through Judge Clarence Martin of Fredericksburg the chest was located, and though W. J. Cloud, a true Texas hero himself, was not anxious to part with it, he agreed to send it to the De Zavala Chapter to be preserved in the Alamo.

Years later when a great-grandson of John Wirtz Cloud was writing a history of the Cloud family, he learned of the existence of the chest and decided he would like to see it. Eventually, in his search, he was directed to Miss Adina who was then ninety-three years old, very frail, and almost blind. But she distinctly remembered the chest and the correspondence concerning it. She said it was exhibited at the Alamo for many years but some time ago had been sent to the University Archives at the Eugene C. Barker Center in Austin. The chest was found at the Archives, unmarked, and has since been returned to the Alamo with an engraved plaque indicating its origin, history, and donor.

When Miss Adina was elected a member of the State Executive Committee of the DRT in 1902, she proposed that the state organization undertake to save the neglected missions from falling into ruin. The De Zavala Chapter was then the custodian of the Alamo Chapel which had been purchased by the State, but the remaining property, the original mission grounds and walls, was owned by the firm of Hugo-Schmeltzer and had been converted into a business establishment, a large wholesale grocery which completely overshadowed the historic shrine. The securing of the grounds therefore became a major project of the DRT.

Miss Adina soon learned, quite by chance, that an eastern hotel syndicate had offered $75,000 for the site. As the Daughters had an option on the property which would soon expire, she immediately sought financial assistance. It was obtained from Miss Clara Driscoll of San Antonio, who had just returned from travels abroad, had become a member of the Zavala Chapter, and had publicly expressed her concern over the plight of the Alamo. She advanced $500 for a thirty-day option and at the end of thirty days paid $3,478.25 of the $4,500 balance required to extend the option until February 10, 1904, the remainder being provided by the DRT.

The initial down payment was to be $25,000, and by February, 1904, the DRT had been able to raise only a little over $7,000. Miss Driscoll herself assumed the obligation to pay $50,000 in yearly installments of $10,000 at six per cent interest. The DRT then appealed to the State for funds to repay Miss Driscoll, and on January 26, 1905, the State Legislature appropriated $65,000 for the purchase of the Alamo grounds. In the meantime the DRT had raised $10,000 to cover the balance of the purchase price.

At that point all progress ceased. The project developed by degrees into a statewide controversy which has since been called "The Second Battle of the Alamo." It tore the state organization apart and left Texans divided into two hostile camps, the Driscollites and the Zavalans. Once the grounds had been secured, the Driscollites wished to clear them completely and park the area while the Zavalans wished to preserve all original walls insofar as possible and restore the old convent to serve as a museum. The battle was fought in the newspapers, the courts, and every DRT chapter in the State. At the end, five years later, the adjoining grounds, the Chapel, and one of the old walls remained intact, the convent was not restored, and the custodianship of the Alamo passed, unjustly, into the hands of Miss Adina's opponents.

In 1912, Miss Adina found two new organizations: The Daughters and Sons of the Heroes and Pioneers of the Republic of Texas and the Texas Historical and Landmarks Society. The purpose of the latter was to preserve historical buildings, battlefields, sites, roads, mementos, manuscripts, paintings, and sculpture pertaining to the history of Texas. Miss Adina was the leader of the group, the state president, and usually the *de facto* president. She was a member of countless other historical societies, one, the Texas State Historical Association, of which she charter member, on the Executive Committee for many years, and elected a life member in 1945. She was appointed to the Texas Historical Board by Governor Pat Neff in 1923, took an active part in San Antonio's Bicentennial celebration in 1831, and served on the Committee that designed the bicentennial medal. She was awarded a citation by the San Antonio Conservation Society on March 2, 1931, for years of diligent service in marking historical locations, and in 1936 was a member of the State Centennial Committee.

She was also a member of the Barnard E. Bee Chapter of the United Daughters of the Confederacy, the Texas Womans Press Association, the Gibbons Literary Club, the Scientific Society of San Antonio, the San Antonio Council of Presidents, the City Federation, the Society of Arts and Letters, the Historical and Scientific Society of Alpine, the Womans Club, the Philosophical Society, the Descendants of the Signers of the Declaration of Independence, the Witte Museum Art League, the Texas Folklore Society, the American Historical Association, the Old Trail Drivers

Association, the San Antonio Womens League for Betterment of the Life of Women, the Womans Parliament, the Peoples Conservation and Garden Commission, and the San Antonio Historical Association.

Privately and through these organizations Miss Adina pursued her cherished ideals until her death on March 1, 1955. She was buried in St. Mary's Cemetery in San Antonio. Today the fruits of her labor are to be seen, touched, and revered, as she wished them to be.

Index

47; immigrant settlement at, 103. *See also* Groce, Jared (Brazos Crossing of)

Breeding, David: school on land of, 124

Bremond, Eugene: S. Dickinson and, 78

Bremond Mercantile Company (Austin): C. Palm with, 200

Brenham, Texas: T. Williams family in, 296

Brigham, Asa: and papers of the Republic of Texas, 305

Briscoe, Andrew: marriage performed by, 107

Brooks, A. M.: Bastrop home of, ment., 68

Brown, John Henry: on S. Braches, 42

Brownsville, Texas: Cortinas rumored to have taken, 148

Brownwood, Texas: first cotton gin at, 287

Bruno, John: S. Dickinson and, 75

Bruno, Sarah Nash: S. Dickinson and, 75

Brushy Creek: Swenson family settles on, 199

Bryan, Texas: early settlers at, 45, 46, 48

Buffalo Bayou (Harris Co.): immigrants to Harrisburg via, 101; bears hunted along, 170; L. De Zavala home on, 303

Burleson, Rufus: Houston revival of, 76

Burleson County: Czech immigrants in, 151–155; H. Tinnin property in, ment., 261

Burnam, Bennett: 126

Burnam, Jesse: land grant of, 121, 123

Burnam, Minerva: 125

Burnam, Nancy Cummins Ross: 126

Burnam, Temperance: 121

Burnam, William: 124

Burnam's Crossing (Colorado River): ferry established at, 121, 126; J. Burnam home at, 124; J. Fannin at, 125

Burnet, David G.: authorizes Galveston Artillery Co., 68; provisional government under, 104–105

Burnet County: C. Dorbandts in, 79–82; Indians in, a menace to settlers, 81

Butterfield, Jack: on M. Gentilz, 88

C

Caldwell, Matthew: defeats Woll at Salado Creek, 126

Caldwell, Texas: early settlers in, 33; E. Raven family in, 203

Caldwell County: A. Dickinson land grant in, 73

Calvillo Delgado, Maria del Carmen: a maverick ranch woman, 54

Cameron, William: 31

Cameron, Texas: E. Raven family in, 204

Campbell, Thomas Jefferson: marriage of, 204

Camp Sabinal (Uvalde County): established, 256

Canary Islanders: San Fernando de Bexar homesites shown in plan, 50; journey to Texas, described, 51–52; annual mass said for, 57

Candelaria, Madame: 53

Cangelosi, Angela Salvaggio: children of, 43, 45, 48; essay about, 43–48; photograph of, 44

Cangelosi, Giovanne (John): wife of, essay about, 43–48

Cangelosi, Joseph: 43

Cangelosi, Lena La Barbera: 47

Dubuis, Bishop: and Sisters of the Holy Cross, 136

Dubuis, Claude: marriage performed by, 87

Durbon, Charles: 257

E

Eadens, Mary: 177

Eagleton, David W.: F. Darden's poems published by, 63

Eaton, Benjamin: 177

Eaton, Mary (Polly): 175, 176

Eaton, Richard: 175

Ebro (ship): immigrants to Texas on, 85

education: early Texas, M. and T. Allis and, 19–22; early female seminaries, 209–213

Eielsen, Elling: 267

Eisenlohr, Edward: uncle of, 143

Eldora (brig): Texas immigrants on, 59

Elkhart, Texas: Protestant church at, 175

elm trees: roots of, and clearing of land, 152; absorb and pollute water, 153

English, the: Indian dread of, 245, 247

Engstrand, C. A.: 200

Erhard, Agnes: 160

Ericson, Carolyn Reeves: essay by, 135–139

Esparza, Anna Salazar de: children of, 219, 222; essay about, 219–222

Esparza, Enrique: remembers Alamo siege, 219, 221; photograph of, 220

Esparza, Francisco: at the Alamo, 221

Esparza, Gertrudis Hernandez: 222

Esparza, Gregorio: at the Alamo, 219, 221

Europe: cholera to America from, 124

Evers, Charles W.: 77

F

Falls County: early immigrants in, 272, 274–275

Fannin, James W.: at Goliad Massacre, 75, 105; horse of, 125; raises army for Matamoros, 125; Travis sends for, 193–194

Fayette County: first well and brick chimney in, 123; first school in, 124; early settlers of, 223

Fenley, Joel: 257

Flachmeier, Jeanette Hastedt: essay by, 59–64, 101–107

Flachmeier, W. A.: essay by, 263–269

floods: Brazos River, 47

Flores, Francisco: 56

Flores, Maria Josefa Montes: 56

Fock, Henry M.: 304

Ford, John S.: on H. Alsbury, 195

Forsgard, G. A.: 198

Fort Bend County: S. M. Swenson plantation in, 197, 198

Fort Brown: Protestant church at, 175

Fort Croghan: C. Dorbandts at, ment., 79

Fort Martin Scott: trades at Fredericksburg bakery, 280, 281

Fort Parker: Protestant church at, 175

Fort Sill, Indian Territory: C. Dorbandts at, ment., 79

Fort Worth and Denver Railroad: Childress moves to, 298

Four Mile Prairie: Norwegian settlement in, 263

Fox-Genovese, Elizabeth: on challenge of women's history, x

Foyn, Sven: 265, 266

France: and H. Castro's colony, 85

Gonzales, Texas: M. and T. Allis buried at, 22; Comanche relations with, 39; and the Runaway Scrape, 40–41; A. and S. Dickinson at, 71, 73; immigrant route to, 73; cannon at, and Texas Revolution, 74, 124–125; hears of fall of Alamo, 75; Gen. Woll marches for, 126

Gonzales College (Gonzales): M. and T. Allis at, 18, 20

Gonzales County: B. McClures settle in, 39; F. Littlefield plantation in, 164

Goodwin, Catherine Meranda: essay by, 83–88

Grace, Capt. Byrd: 91

Grace, John W.: 91

Grace, Martin: 91

Grace, Dr. Willougby: 92

Gracy, David B., II: essay by, 163–167

Granger, Gen. Gordon: announces emancipation of slaves, 69

Graves, Rev. Harry Lee: and Live Oak Female Seminary, 210

Gray, George E.: 92, 93

Gray, Harriet Newell: essay about, 89–94; photograph with grandchildren, 90; brothers of, 91; grandchildren of, 93–94

Gray, Laura: 92

Gray, Stephen Alfred: and the cotton gin, 92; essay about wife of, 89–94

Greenhill, Joe: grandmother of, essay about, 229–232

Greenwood, Franklin J.: 239

Greenwood, Henry B.: 239

Greenwood, Mary Montgomery: 239

Greenwood, Dr. Thomas B.: 241–242

Griffith, John Maynard: marries A. Dickinson, 76–77

Griffith, Joshua: 76

Grimes County: Texas' first Protestant church meets in, 175

Grimes Prairie: settlers on, and the Runaway Scrape, 239; F. Greenwood home on, 240–241

Grisby, Joseph: and establishment of Beaumont, 252

Groce, Jared (Brazos Crossing of): laid out, 23; and the Runaway Scrape, 25, 26

Guadalupe River: immigrants transported to, 39; F. Littlefield plantation on, 164; A. Perez grant on, 193

Guerrero, Vicente: L. De Zavala and, 301

H

Hallett, John: 95; land grant of, 97

Hallett, Margaret: essay about, 95–100; grave of, marker at, 96 (photograph), 100; children of, 97; as honorary Tonkawa, 99

Hallettsville, Texas: naming of, 95; elected county seat, 99

Hallettsville Herald: Indian incident reported in, 39–40

Hamilton, James: H. Castro and, 83, 85

Handbook of Texas: coverage of women in, ix, xvi

Hannig, Frank: land of, 77

Hannig, Joseph W.: S. Dickinson marries, 77–78

harpoon cannon, the: invention of, 265

Harrisburg, Texas: immigrants to Houston via, 60; Revolutionary government moves to, 75; early immigrants at, 101

Harrisburg County: L. De Zavala land grant in, 304

Harris, Dilue Rose: essay about,

101–107; photograph of, 102; children of, 107; "Reminiscences" of, 107

Harris, Ira A.: wife and children of, 107

Harris County: W. Lockwood estate in, 169–170

Havana, Cuba: Canary Islanders travel via, 51

Head, William J. E.: at San Jacinto, ment., 97

Heffter, H. A.: 205

Heffter, Mary L.: 205

Heffter, Rudolph: 205

Hemphill, John: and Live Oak Female Seminary, 210

Henderson, J. Pinckney: as first governor of Texas, ment., 145; and A. Sterne, 235

Henderson, Mrs. Thomas Stahworth: 209

Henderson County: early settlements in, ment., 263

Henninger, John: marriage of, 109

Henninger, Magdalena Hornberger: photograph of, 108; essay about, 109–112; children of, 109, 110, 112

Henrie, Arthur: 250

Henry, Mary: 107

Hensen, David: 103

Herrera, Gov. (Nuevo Leon): character of, Z. Pike mentions, 52

Herring, Francis P.: S. Dickinson marries, 76

Hiawatha (mail packet): 148

Hidalgo y Costilla, Father Miguel: and Mexican Revolution, 54–55

Hill, Alexander Campbell: 114

Hill, Campbell: 119

Hill, Minerva Frances Vernon: essay about, 113–120; children of, 114, 115; and her slaves, 115–116; bout with robbers, 116–118

Hill, Sarah Brown: 114

Hill, William Hickman, Sr.: 114

Hill, William Hickman, Jr.: essay about wife of, 113–120

Hitzfeld, Elizabeth and Herman: 277

Hobby, Oveta Culp: ancestors of, 177

Hobby, William, Jr.: mother of, 177

Holman, Amanda Burnam: essay about, 121–127; photograph of, 122; children of, 126, 127

Holman, George Tandy: land of, 126

Holman, Jerome Alexander: wife of, 126

Holman, John Thompson: wife of, 126

Hood's Texas Brigade: M. Allis in, 20; W. Darden with, 62

Hornberger, Adam: 109

Hornberger, Christian: 110

Hornberger, Fred: 110

Hornberger, Jacob: 110

Hornsby's Bend (Travis County): Indian attack at, ment., 261

"Horse-pen Creek" (Tyler County): Alabama village on, 247

Houston, Antoinette: 132

Houston, Elinor R.: essay by, 223–227

Houston, Sam: and the Runaway Scrape, 15, 25, 40–41, 125; Santa Anna surrenders to, 26; F. Darden recalls, 60, 61; and the Texas Navy, ment., 67; and Texas Revolution, ment., 97, 104; attends theater party, 106–107; and Anna Raguet, 130, 131–132; daughter of, 132; E. Raven and, 204; and A. Sterne, 235; and the Greenwood family, 240–241; and Alabama-Coushattas, 247; settles land dispute, 251

Houston, Texas: immigrant travel
to, 60; 1849 revival in, 76
Houston Chronicle: article in, noted,
131
Houston Telegraph: F. Darden writes
for, 63
Howe, John: and Galveston
Artillery Co., 68
Hoyal Memorial Library and
Museum (Nacogdoches): 237
Huling, Thomas B.: and establish-
ment of Beaumont, 252
Hunt, Flournoy: 107
Hunter, F.: 137
Hurd, Daniel: 200
Hurth, Father (St. Edward's
University): and Sister M.
Josephine, 139
Huss, John: 155
Hutchinson, Mrs. Joseph. *See* Tevis,
Nancy

I

Incarnate Word College (San
Antonio): C. Sylestine teaches
at, 248
Indians: San Antonio plazas closed
against at night, 52; entranced
by immigrants' music, 61; as
menace to settlers, 81, 98, 103,
107, 145, 178, 255, 261, 299;
trade in Columbia area, 104; on
Grimes Prairie, friendly with
settlers, 240; trade at
Fredericksburg bakery, 280;
Fredericksburg hanging of, 282
Institute of Texan Cultures (San
Antonio): xix
International and Great Northern
Railroad: Austin stations of, 110
Ireland, Gov.: and the
Sanctificationists, 187
Ireland: immigrants to Texas from,
229–232

Irion, Anna Raguet: photograph of,
128; essay on, 129–133; ancestors of, 129–130; designs Texas
seal, 131–132; and S. Houston,
131–132; children of, 132
Irion, Philip: 132
Irion, Robert Anderson: marriage
of, 132; county named for, 133
Irion County: naming of, 133
Irwin, E. R.: home of, ment., 62
Italians in Texas: first millionaire,
48; arrive at Galveston, ment.,
151–152

J

Jackson, Lela: essay by, 289–293
James, Eleanor: essay by, 181–190
James Lawrence (schooner): immi-
grants to Galveston via, 15
Jean Key de Teau (ship): arrives at
Galveston, 85
Jefferson County: N. Tevis land
grant in, 250. *See also*
Beaumont, Texas
Jena, Texas: early immigrants in,
274–275
Jensen, M. T.: 266
Jessen, Adalbert C.: 226
Jews in Texas: in early Galveston,
157–161
Johann Dethardt (brig): German
immigrants to Texas via, 277
John, I. G.: Bastrop church of,
ment., 68
Johnson Institute (Austin): and
Friday Mountain, 261
Johnson Station, Texas: the J. Lays
at, 150
Jones, John Rice: and Live Oak
Female Seminary, 210
Jones, Mary McCrory (Mrs. Anson):
107
Jones, Nancy Baker: women's con-
ference organized by, ix

323

Mitchell (at the Alamo): killed, 194

Moczygemba, Rev. Leopold: and Panna Maria church, 216, 217

Monclova, Mexico: Veramendi home at, ment., 191, 193

Montell, Texas: immigrant community established near, 230

Montgomery, William: 239

Moody children (Galveston): education of, ment., 261

Moore, Carolyn F.: xvii, xix

Moore, George: 93–94

Moore, John M.: leads Gonzales battle, 125

Moral, Texas: Sister M. Josephine's church and school at, 138–139

Morehead, Col.: F. Darden remembers, 59–60

Morgan's Point: immigrants washed ashore at, 101

mosquitoes: in Brazos bottom, 47

Moulton, Texas: moves to accomodate railroad, 21. *See also* Old Moulton, Texas

Moulton Institute (Moulton): M. and T. Allis establish, 20–21, 22

Mudville, Texas: early settlers at, 45, 48

Mueller, Esther: essay from notes of, 277–283

music: early Texas, 171

Musquiz, Ramon: and S. Dickinson, 74, 75; takes in Alamo survivors, 195, 219, 221

N

Nacogdoches, Texas: becomes seat of eastern district, 56; H. Raguet family in, 130–133; Sister M. Josephine's school in, 135–139; post-Revolution, old Spanish families at, 137–138; as refuge during Texas Revolution, ment., 219; A.

Sterne home in, 233–237

Nacogdoches University: Sisters of the Holy Cross and, 136–137

Natchitoches, Louisiana: plantation near, 233; immigrants to Texas via, 263

National Council of Jewish Women: 160

Navarro, Gertrudis: survives the Alamo, 191–195, 221

Navarro, Jose Angel, II: daughter of, 191, 195

Navarro, Jose Antonio: niece of, 191

Navarro, Juana: survives the Alamo, 221

Neches River: N. Tevis land grant on, 250–253; ferries on, 252–253

Neff, Pat: and A. De Zavala, 307

Nelson, Arvid: 200

Nelson, Estelle: on E. Waerenskjold, 265–266

New Braunfels, Texas: T. Koesters in, 141–144; furniture craftsmen in, 143

New Orleans: immigrants to Texas via, 13, 15, 45, 59, 67, 73, 101, 109, 130, 233, 263; yellow fever epidemic in, 109; cholera travels down Mississippi to, 124; 1860 fashion in, 148–149; Alabama Indians at, 247

New Ulm, Texas: Swensons in, 198–199

New York: cholera from Europe to, 124

New York City: Belton Sanctificationists visit, 188; Lincoln's funeral in, 158

Nichols, Pansy: essay by, 201–206

Nitschke, Willard Griffith: essay by, 71–78

Nohl, Alice: Austin school of, 110; photograph of, 111

Nolan Creek (Bell County): McWhirter home on, 185

Nordmai, L. E.: and Galveston Artillery Co., 68

Norge og America (*Norway and America*): 263

Norwegians: immigrants to Texas, 263–269

Notre Dame, Indiana: Sisters of the Holy Cross in, 136

Nuevo Leon (Mexico): governor of, Z. Pike mentions, 52

O

Ocker, Texas: Czech church at, 155

oil: Panhandle discovery of, 297

Old Moulton, Texas: school at, 20–21, 22

"Old Three Hundred" Colony: settlers in, 15, 23

Old Waresville, Texas: historical marker at site of, 257

Orizimbo Plantation (Brazos River): Santa Anna hidden on, 26

outlaws: post-Civil War, 29, 116, 118, 218, 286

Ownes, Bill: song book by, ment., 171

P

Palestine, Texas: Nacogdoches Sister trades at, 138; early immigrants at, 273

Palm, Anders: wife of, 197–200

Palm, Anna Hurd: church established by, xii; photograph of, 196; children of, 197, 200; essay about, 197–200

Palm, August: as Austin merchant, 199; and Williamson County cotton, 200

Palm, Gustav: comes to Texas, 198

Palm, Rufus, Jr.: ms. of, quoted, 199–200

Palm, Swante: comes to Texas, 198

Palm Valley: naming of, 197, 199

Palm Valley Lutheran Church: established, xii; land for, 200

Panna Maria, Texas: Christ statue at church at, 214 (photograph), 216; founded, 215; post-Civil War, 217–218

Parker, Dickerson: wife of, 175–176

Parker, Rev. Daniel: church organized by, 175; son of, 176

Parker, Edith Olbrich: essay by, 49–57

Parker, Quanah: visits Childress, 299

Parker County: L. De Zavala land grant in, 304

Patrick, Dr. George M.: 303

Patrick Academy (Anderson): 241

Patten, Col.: and the Runaway Scrape, 41

Peach Creek (Gonzales County): B. McClures settle on, 39–41; Santa Anna camps on, 41

Peacock, Col. Wesley, Sr.: school of, 21

Peacock School for Boys (San Antonio): T. Allis with, 21

Pease, Rowena: 113

"pecan hunts": described, 123

pecan trees: roots of, and clearing of land, 152

Peebles, Robert: 195

Penterides, Erhard: score illustrated by, ment., 87

Perez, Alejo [Sr.]: 193

Perez, Alejo, Jr.: 193, 195

Perez, Antonia Rodriquez: 195

Perez, Clemencia Hernandez: 49, 55–56

Perez, Florencia Valdes: 195

Perez, Jose: marriage of, 52

Perez, Juan: 195

Perez, Juan Ignacio: daughter of, essay about, 49–57; homestead of, 49, 56; as acting governor, 55

Perez, Manuel: 195

Perez, Paula: 51–52

Perry, Capt. (the *Ebro*): brings French immigrants to Texas, 85

Pike, Zebulon: in San Antonio, his impressions, 52

Pilgrim Predestinarian Baptist Church: comes to Texas, 175

pioneers, Texas: washing, 45; cooking, 45, 242–243; clothes, 46, 256, 259; entertainment, 47; dugout homes, 297

Plantersville, Texas: J. Stoneham home near, 241–244

Pocahontos: descendants of, ment., 37

Polish in Texas: Panna Maria settlement of, 214–218; and the Civil War, 217–218

Polk, James K.: and Mexican War, ment., 79

Polk County: Alabama-Coushattas in, 247–248

Pond, J. J.: 182

Port Lavaca: H. Castro's colonists arrive at, 85

Potard, Ernestine. *See* Sister M. Josephine (Ernestine Potard)

Potthoff, Carl Friedrich: 223

Presbyterian Church: Gay Hill seminary of, 209–213

Presbyterians: as missionaries to Alabama-Coushattas, 248

Presbyterian Synod of Texas: and Stuart Female Seminary, 212–213

Presslar's Gardens (Austin): concerts at, ment., 78

Price, Laurette F.: 20

Price, Willie Mae Smith: essay by, 79–82

Pulsifer, Joseph P.: 252

Purcell, Mabelle Umland: essay by, 207–213

Q

Quarterly of the Texas State Historical Association: D. Rose Harris reminiscences in, 107

quilts: slave, post-Emancipation patterns of, 292

R

Raguet, Henry and Marcia Ann: daughter of, essay about, 129–133

railroads: Moulton moves to accommodate, 21; shipment of rails for, ment., 198

Ranch de las Cabras (San Antonio de Bexar): maverick Spanish woman runs, 54

ranching: sheep, near Lampasas, ment., 34; in Uvalde County, ment., 230, 231

Raney's Creek: D. McCallister home on, 177

Rau, Laura Ann Dick: essay by, 13–17

Raven, Auguste Mentzel: essay about, 201–206; photograph of, 202; grandchildren of, 202, 204; children of, 203

Raven, Ernst: background of, 201; book-binding business of, 204, 206; as Consul for Texas, 205

Raworth, George: 295

Raworth, Mary Barker: 295

Raymond, Ida: on F. Darden, 63

Reagan, John H.: names Bastrop postmaster, 69

Reconstruction: in Bastrop area, blacks and, 28–29; Nuns keep Nacogdoches University open during, 136

Red, Dr. George Clark: marriage of, 209; as teacher, 210, 212

Red, George P.: home of, 212

church, 216; in the Civil War, 217; challenges thieves, 218

Rzeppa, Tecla: essay about, 215–218

S

Sabinal Canyon (Bexar County): early settlers in, 255–257

St. Edward's University (Austin): Sisters of the Holy Cross buried at, 139

St. Mary's College (San Antonio): T. Gentilz at, 87–88

St. Mary's Convent (Hallettsville): 99

Salado Creek: Mexican army defeated at, 126

Salado Creek: homesteaders on, 181

Salado River: immigrants on, 272

Salem Primitive Baptist Church: 179

Saltillo, Mexico: Canary Islanders travel via, 51; Veramendi home at, ment., 191

San Antonio, Texas: Peacock School in, 21; U.S. settlers pour into, 51; Spanish Governors' Palace at, city purchases, 52; H. Castro's land grant near, 83, 85; T. Gentilz in, 86–88; Gen. Woll captures, 126; Veramendi home at, 191, 193; Santa Anna at, 194; Incarnate Word community in, 222; Menger Hotel in, immigrants stay at, 230; Fredericksburg settlers find work in, 279; A. De Zavala family in, 304–305; Bicentennial celebration of, 307

San Antonio and Aransas Pass Railroad: Moulton, Tex., moves to accommodate, 21

San Antonio Conservation Society: A. De Zavala and, 307

San Antonio de Bexar: Spanish set-

tlers in, 49–57; Canary Islanders at, 50–52; plazas of, method of closing off at night, 52; Military Plaza in, military review in, 53; and Mexican Revolution, 54–55; 1819 flood at, 55

San Antonio Express: Alamo survivor interviewed by, 219, 221

San Augustine Tribune: article in, noted, 131

Sanctificationists, the (Belton): M. McWhirter and, ment., xii; essay about, 181–190; beliefs of, 183; Central Hotel of, 187, 189, 180 (photograph); economic motive for, 184, 188; men as, 186, 188; move to Washington, D.C., 189–190; photograph of, 180; naming of, 183; work of, 184, 187; travels of, 188, 189; worth of, 189–190

Sanders, Lee: 255

San Felipe de Austin: as capital of Austin's colony, ment., 121; 1835 Consultation at, 125

San Fernando Cathedral (San Antonio de Bexar): baptism in, ment., 49; position and form of, described, 51; weddings at, 53, 56, 87, 195; cemetery at, ment., 221

San Fernando de Bexar: plan of, Canary Islanders homesites shown, 50

San Francisco, California: Belton Sanctificationists visit, 189

San Gabriel River: slaves on, life after freedom, 289–293

Sanger, Texas: early settlers at, 285–287

San Jacinto, Battle of: M. Baker at, 59; W. Head's Co. at, ment., 97; victory at, ends Runaway Scrape, 125, 240, 251

San Jacinto battlefield: graves at, 60,

105; L. De Zavala home near, 303

San Jacinto County: Alabama-Coushattas in, 247

San Jacinto Day: Nacogdoches celebrations of, 236

San Saba Expedition (J. Bowie): B. McClures provision, 41

Santa Anna, Antonio López de: captured at San Jacinto, ment., 26, 240; and Texas Revolution, Peach Creek camp of, 41; and buildup to Texas Revolution, 73, 194; S. Dickinson and, 74–75; marches into Texas, 104, 193; capture of, and the Texas seal, 131; and Alamo survivors, 219, 221; and L. De Zavala, 301

Savannah, Georgia: yellow fever epidemic in, ment., 89

Sayle, William: settles Charleston, ment., 65

Schmidt, Mrs. Victor (Maria): 212

Schumann, Bruno Willibald: comes to Texas, 223

Schumann, Emilie Ploeger: essay about, 223–227; silhouette of, 224; children of, 225, 226

Scott, Anne Firor: on challenges of women's history, ix

Scott, Emma Holman: essay by, 121–126

Scott, Glenn: essay by, 191–195, 219–222

Scott, Winfield: in Mexican War, ment., 79

Seguin, Juan M.: and assault on Bexar, ment., 219

Shanks, William: 30

Shepherd, Texas: Alabama-Coushattas near, 247

Sherman: Texas settler remembers rampage of, 34

Sherwood, James Powell: outfits Texas Navy, ment., 67; during Civil War, ment., 69

Shipley, R. S.: Austin home of, 69

Shipman, Mike: 104

Sibley's Brigade: I. Webb with, ment., 275

Sims Bayou (Harris Co.): settlers return from Runaway Scrape via, 105

Singleton, L. L.: 147

Sister Claud: community founded by, 222

Sister M. Bernadetta: at Nacogdoches, 136

Sister M. Euphrosine Sister M.: comes to Texas, 136

Sister M. Joseph (Catherine Dunn): at Nacogdoches, 136

Sister M. Josephine (Ernestine Potard): photograph of, 134; essay about, 135–139; at Moral, 138–139

Sister M. Paula: at Nacogdoches, 136

Sisters of the Holy Cross: organized, 135; in Nacogdoches, 136–139; buried at St. Edward's University, 139

Sisters of the Incarnate Word: in Corpus Christi, 136

slavery: E. Waerenskjold on, 266, 268

slaves: immigrants bring to Texas, 13; the hire of, ment., 62; emancipation of, announced in Galveston, 69; brought to Smith plantation (Brazos), 103; Travis County, during Civil War, 115–116; M. Littlefield's, freed, 166; J. Bowie's, 195; for Tinnin plantation, 259–262; on San Gabriel River, life after freedom, 289–293; passes required by, 290; food of freed, 291; quilt patterns of, 292. *See also* blacks

Small, Ben Fort: slaves of, 103

Sweden: Palm family from, immigrates to Texas, 197–200
Sweetwater, Texas: cattle range at, 33
Swenson, Swante Magnus: East Texas plantation of, 197, 198; Austin mercantile establishment of, 199; donates land for Palm Valley church, 200
Sylestine, Bronson C. (Alabama-Coushatta Chief): 248
Sylestine, Colebe (Alabama Chief): 247, 248
Sylestine, Mozanna Thompson: 248–249
Sylestine, Sissie Thompson: essay about, 245–249; photograph of, 246; children and grandchildren of, 248–249
Sylestine, Washington: 248–249

T

Taylor, Virginia H.: essay by, 301–308
temperance movement: in Norway, E. Waerenskjold and, 265; in Texas Norwegian settlement, ment., 267
Terrell, Texas: Adina De Zavala teaches at, 305
Terry's Texas Rangers: W. Whitehead with, 286
Tevis, George Washington: 251
Tevis, Nancy: essay about, 250–253; children of, 251
Tevis, Noah: 250
Tevis, Reid W.: essay by, 250–253
Tevis Bluff. *See* Beaumont, Texas
Texas: immigrant route to, 73; capital of, moved to Austin, 107; as cure for tuberculosis, 114; path of cholera to, 124; seal of, design of, 131–132; Sisters of the Holy Cross in, 136; first

Protestant church in, 175; communal societies in, 181; German Consul for, 205; education in early, 209–213; child welfare in, first director of, 232; Alabama Indians migrate to, 247; southern and northern routes to, ment., 258. *See also* Republic of Texas
———, East: Spanish missions in, ment., 137; Alabama-Coushatta reservation in, 245–249
———, Mexican: Catholic prerequisite of, 235; divided into two districts, 56; religion in, 175
———, Panhandle: discovery of oil in, 297; early settlers of, 296–300
———, Spanish: San Antonio government of, 52–57; military uniforms of, 53; M. Austin petitions to settle, 55; 1820 population of, 55
———, West: early cattle raising in, 33
Texas Bicentennial: xvii, xx
Texas Convention, 1833: B. McClure in, 41
Texas Foundation for Women's Resources: history project of, viii–ix
Texas General Land Office: land grants on file at, 73, 121
Texas Heroes Day: first observance of, 305
Texas Historical and Landmarks Society: 307
Texas Historical Commission: and Stuart Female Seminary, 213
Texas legislature: and Alabama-Coushatta reservation, 247; A. Sterne in, ment., 233; and Live Oak Female Seminary, 210; and purchase of Alamo grounds, 306

333

Weimer, Texas: Holman brothers' land at, 126
Weisiger, Katherine: xvii, xix; essay by, 229–232
Wells, James: 103
West Texas Historical Association: *Year Book* of, article in, noted, 131
whaling: harpoon for, invention of, 265
Wheeler, Royall T.: and Live Oak Female Seminary, 210
White, John Henry: 163
Whitehead, Mary Burleson: photograph of, 284; essay about, 285–287
Whitehead, William F.: photograph of, 284; settles in Denton County, 285–287
Whitfield, Adelaide Coleman: 291
Whitfield, Allen: 291
Whitfield, Demmie: 292
Whitfield, Jim: 289
Whitfield, Rachel: xii; essay about, 289–293
Williams, Dan: photograph of, 294
Williams, Jean Lockwood: essay by, 31–36, 169–172, 295–300
Williamson, R. M.: district court of, 16
Williams, Rebecca Raworth: photograph of, 294; essay about, 295–300; children of, 296, 297, 298; medical knowledge of, 297, 298
Williams, Thomas A. B.: photograph of, 294; comes to Texas, 296; and early Childress, 298
Williamson County: cotton in, 200
Willis Creek: freed slaves on, 290–293
Wilson, Col. George: comes to Texas, 145; inventions of, 147
Wilson, Elizabeth McCoy: 145
Wilson, Joseph: inventions of, 147, 148
Wilson, William G.: 148
Winedale Inn: W. Townsend home in, 124
Woll, Gen.: captures San Antonio, 126
women: Belton commune for, 181–190; Alabama-Coushatta, 248
Women's Auxiliary Army Corps: O. C. Hobby and, 177
women's history: early non-critical works on, vii–viii; ethnic studies in, viii; challenges of, ix, x; development as field of scholarship, ix–x; historiographical works in, xiii; thematic studies in, xiii; work as boundary of analysis in, xiii–xiv; works on 19th-century experiences, xiv; political studies, xiv; biographical works, xv
W.P.A.: crews of, in Austin, 261

Y

Y'Barbo, Mrs. Carmel: 139
Yegua, the (Brazos River): Jourdan land grant on, 26–27
yellow fever: New Orleans epidemic of, 109; Savannah epidemic of, ment., 89; sickens immigrants on Red River, 233

Z

Zacatecas, the: Santa Anna has slaughtered, 73
Zavala, Lorenzo de: and N. Tevis land grant, 250
Zavala Point: L. De Zavala home at, 304
Zumwalt Settlement (Lavaca County): competes for county seat, 99